ROUTLEDGE LIBRARY EDITIONS:
THE MEDIEVAL WORLD

Volume 50

ENGLISH JUSTICE

ENGLISH JUSTICE

Between the Norman Conquest and the Great Charter, 1066–1215

DORIS STENTON

Routledge
Taylor & Francis Group
LONDON AND NEW YORK

First published in 1965 by George Allen & Unwin Ltd

This edition first published in 2020
by Routledge
4 Park Square, Milton Park, Abingdon, Oxon OX14 4RN

and by Routledge
605 Third Avenue, New York, NY 10017

Routledge is an imprint of the Taylor & Francis Group, an informa business

British Library Cataloguing in Publication Data
A catalogue record for this book is available from the British Library

ISBN: 978-0-367-22090-7 (Set)
ISBN: 978-0-429-27322-3 (Set) (ebk)
ISBN: 978-0-367-18003-4 (Volume 50) (hbk)
ISBN: 978-0-429-05904-9 (Volume 50) (ebk)

ENGLISH JUSTICE

BETWEEN

THE NORMAN CONQUEST

AND THE

GREAT CHARTER

1066—1215

DORIS M. STENTON

Jayne Lectures for 1963

PUBLISHED FOR
THE AMERICAN PHILOSOPHICAL SOCIETY
BY
GEORGE ALLEN & UNWIN LTD
LONDON

FIRST PUBLISHED IN GREAT BRITAIN
IN 1965

The Jayne Lectures of the American Philosophical Society honor the memory of Henry La Barre Jayne, 1857-1920, a distinguished citizen of Philadelphia and an honored member of the Society. They perpetuate in this respect the aims of the American Society for the Extension of University Teaching, in which Mr. Jayne was deeply interested. When in 1946 this organization was dissolved, having in large measure fulfilled its immediate purposes, its funds were transferred to the American Philosophical Society, which agreed to use them "for the promotion of university teaching, including *inter alia* lectures, publications and research in the fields of science, literature, and the arts."

Accepting this responsibility, the Society initiated in 1961 a series of lectures to be given annually or biennially by outstanding scholars, scientists, and artists, and to be published in book form by the Society. The lectures will be presented in successive years at the University of Pennsylvania, the Franklin Institute, the Free Library of Philadelphia, and the Philadelphia Museum of Art.

The third series, constituting the present volume, was delivered by Lady Stenton, on March 6, 13 and 20, 1963, in the Museum of the University of Pennsylvania, under the joint auspices of that institution and the American Philosophical Society.

PRINTED IN GREAT BRITAIN
BY OFFSET
UNWIN BROTHERS LTD
WOKING AND LONDON

FOREWORD

The historian is a phenomenon peculiar to the human race, since man is the only animal known to be curious about his past. His curiosity has led him to explore the interior of ancient tombs and burial mounds, whether of a Tut-ankh-amen or an East Anglian king at Sutton Hoo, to uncover buried temples and palaces, and to make the sea give up its secrets, guarded for more than three thousand years, and disclose the unhappy ship that foundered on a rocky reef off the coast of Asia Minor in the fourteenth or thirteenth century before Christ. He goes to infinite pains to penetrate the mystery of languages long dead, whether pressed in the cuneiform of Babylonia or scratched in the linear B of Mycenae and Knossos. He builds museums and galleries to exhibit the art and artifacts of his kind, libraries to house the books and manuscripts which chance has preserved, and establishes national repositories of the written documents and records which contain the evidence of man's more recent political, economic, and social evolution. For medieval and modern times it is these documents and records which are the historian's most important sources, and we who trace our political and cultural descent from this Anglo-Saxon (and, be it said, Danish and Norman) tradition may take pride in the fact that the medieval and early modern records of England are without equal in Europe in their richness and variety.

But these documents and records are not an open book to every one who might choose to consult them. They are in Old English, in Latin, in Norman French, and, as we approach modern times, occasionally in the English of the region and period. They are written in a variety of hands, which get worse rather than better as time goes on. To read them correctly requires preliminary training and considerable experience. What is more, scribes used many contractions and abbreviations, some of which are ambiguous. In extreme cases, as in the Controllment Rolls, they amount to a kind of shorthand which was sufficient to indicate an action or procedure that had become stereotyped and was familiar to all concerned, but it is doubtful that the clerk who did the writing could have expanded all

of the abbreviations if he had been called upon to do so. Finally, the very interpretation of the facts recorded requires a knowledge of administrative and legal history not easily or quickly acquired.

The century and a half following the Norman Conquest was a period of many changes. Much that was new in the legal and administrative system was only taking form, and tracing its emergence and later evolution is possible only to one who has lived for a long time with the records in which it is to be followed. No one better qualifies for this task than Lady Stenton, who has spent a lifetime editing and interpreting these records. One need only point to her edition of the Pipe Rolls for the reign of Richard I (eight volumes) and of King John (fourteen volumes), all published by the Pipe Roll Society; the two volumes of *Pleas before the King or His Justices, 1198-1202,* published by the Selden Society; her editions of the *Rolls of the Justices in Eyre,* covering certain years in the early thirteenth century for Lincolnshire, Worcestershire, and Shropshire, all of these likewise in the Selden Society's publications; and similar editions of the earliest assize rolls for Lincolnshire and Northamptonshire. The wide learning which she has acquired in the process, coupled with an unusual capacity to make the dry bones of the records come to life, makes her volume in the Pelican History of England (*English Society in the Early Middle Ages, 1066-1307*) not only authoritative but delightful to read.

The lectures which make up the present volume are on a subject of great importance to all of us today and one which Lady Stenton has made peculiarly her own. The first three were the Jayne Lectures of the American Philosophical Society for 1963, presented at the University of Pennsylvania. The fourth lecture, which rounds out her treatment of the subject, has been included in the volume at Lady Stenton's suggestion. It was originally delivered as the Raleigh Lecture before the British Academy in 1958, and is reprinted with the gracious consent of the British Academy.

ALBERT C. BAUGH

AUTHOR'S PREFACE

The invitation of the American Philosophical Society to give the Jayne Lectures for 1963 came to me at Christmas time in 1961. This most unexpected honour, for which I must express deep gratitude, has given my husband and myself very great pleasure. I owe particular gratitude to Dr. G. W. Corner, Executive Officer of the American Philosophical Society, and to Mrs. Corner, whose help, kindness, and hospitality during our visit to Philadelphia added so much to our enjoyment of the occasion. Throughout my historical studies, which began with charters and early eyre rolls, the building up of the common law through the twelfth century has been a major interest. The invitation to give these lectures has provided the opportunity to express some of the conclusions of this long preoccupation.

The bibliography which I have added to the lectures is not intended to be a comprehensive list of works dealing with this subject. It is a list of works to which I have made specific reference in the footnotes. While I was in America Mr. Henry Gerald Richardson and Professor George Osborn Sayles published *The Governance of England from the Conquest to Magna Carta* (Edinburgh University Press, 1963). I have not mentioned it in the bibliography as I had no opportunity of seeing it until my return to England, having left my lectures behind for publication.

My thanks are due to Professor Dorothy Whitelock for identifying in the Red Book of Thorney the charters of which I needed photostats and to Mr. Owen of the Cambridge University Library for obtaining the photostats for me; to Mr. C. A. F. Meekings, Assistant Keeper of the Public Records, for his interest in the project and for obtaining photostats of documents in the Public Record Office for me; to Sir Charles Clay, who, as always, responded at once to an enquiry; and to Dr. Patricia M. Barnes, Assistant Keeper of the Public Records, who made me new copies, at short notice of charters in the Duchy of Lancaster collections.

As a fourth chapter in this book the American Philosophical Society has been good enough to reprint my Raleigh Lecture

delivered before the British Academy in March, 1958. I owe thanks to the British Academy for permission to reprint the lecture here. Its subject, "King John and the Courts of Justice," is a necessary supplement to the three lectures delivered in Philadelphia. I have been able to make one or two corrections in the lecture, where errors had been pointed out to me by Mr. Meekings or since discovered by myself.

That the roots of the English common law lay far back in our Anglo-Saxon past I had realised long before I began work on the first of my Jayne lectures, but I should have hesitated to attempt any sort of summary of what the twelfth-century administrators owed to their Saxon predecessors had I realised how far the search would lead me into the intricacies of Anglo-Saxon pleas. Without the support of my husband, Sir Frank Stenton, I could not have approached the task. It was he who, many years ago, first introduced me to the then little-worked field of the rolls of itinerant justices. Through the years his readiness, at any moment, to discuss any problem has made of history a delight.

DORIS M. STENTON
Whitley Park Farm, Reading, England

CONTENTS

INTRODUCTION

THE HUNDRED and fifty years between the Norman Conquest and the Great Charter carried the English people from the blood feud and the ordeal to trial by jury, from the justice administered by peasant suitors in their immemorial local courts to trial before royal judges conscious of an omnipresent king. This is a period which has attracted the attention of many scholars on both sides of the Atlantic and, although this is not the time or place to estimate their individual contributions to our present state of knowledge, it is not possible to omit a word of gratitude to some of them. Felix Liebermann's devoted labour on the texts of our old laws has given twentieth-century scholars a new springboard for their studies. As Maitland said while the work was in progress, *"Lagam Eadwardi nobis reddit."* [1] He was working on individual texts through the 'eighties and 'nineties of the last century and his massive edition of the Anglo-Saxon laws appeared between 1903 and 1916. Before any of Liebermann's work had appeared, Melville Madison Bigelow, one of the founders of the Boston University Law School, had in 1879 and 1880 produced two pioneer works on Anglo-Norman law which are still of value today, a collection of cases which has not yet been superseded and a commentary on procedure based at every point on his study of individual pleas.[2] This was heroic work, done before Domesday Book had been adequately annotated and before modern work on the pipe rolls and the plea rolls of the Bench and Eyres had been begun, while twelfth-century charters and final concords were still merely material for the genealogist. But of all the eminent workers in this field the greatest and most sympathetic to the modern scholar is Frederic William Maitland whose classic *History of English Law,* done with the support of Sir Frederick Pollock and published in 1895 [3] is still the starting point for the enquirer. The modern scholar humbly plodding along in his footsteps often feels that he can merely add a footnote to

[1] *Hist. of Eng. Law* 1: p. 97, n. 3.
[2] *Placita Anglo-Normannica* (London, 1879). *History of Procedure in England* (London, 1880).
[3] 2nd ed., 1898.

that tremendous survey. Nevertheless, there still remains record evidence to be searched that even Maitland's omnivorous energy did not reach and the concentrated interest of two generations on the centuries immediately before and after 1066 has created a corpus of knowledge which has revolutionised the subject. The *History of English Law* is, moreover, more concerned with the thirteenth century than the twelfth. Bracton's Notebook and Bracton's Treatise and the growing volume of the English common law fascinated Maitland and drew him quickly over the earlier post-Conquest generations. His mind loved to play on "those few men who were gathered at Westminster round Pateshull and Raleigh and Bracton" and "were penning writs that would run in the names of kingless commonwealths on the other shore of the Atlantic Ocean." [4] Today, we turn to Ralf and Richard Basset in Henry I's reign; to Henry II and Rannulf Glanville; to Hubert Walter and Geoffrey fitz Peter at the end of the century; and even to King John and Simon of Pattishall in the years before the Great Charter.

This is a propitious moment to look again at the litigation of the twelfth century. The first half of the present century has seen a remarkable concentration of a few leading scholars on the problems of the centuries before and immediately after the Norman Conquest. In 1918 Professor Charles Homer Haskins of Harvard clarified many problems in early Norman history and demonstrated that some of Brunner's conclusions were based on a false premise.[5] It will be of great interest to learn what new evidence is at this moment being brought forward by Professor David Douglas in his Ford Lectures being delivered in the University of Oxford on William the Conqueror. Much work has been done on the charters issued by kings, magnates, individual freemen and sokemen, material of inestimable value for an age which has left no continuous records of the courts of justice.[6] Moreover, two long-promised books are at last available in print. The writs and charters of Henry I edited

[4] *Hist. of Eng. Law* **2**: p. 674.

[5] *Norman Institutions* (Cambridge, Harvard University Press, 1918). H. Brunner, *Die Entstehung der Schwurgerichte* (Berlin, 1871).

[6] J. H. Round led the way in the closing years of the last century by showing how much history can be extracted from a few charters, e.g., *Geoffrey de Mandeville* (London, 1892); and *Ancient Charters*, Pipe Roll Society **10** (1888). W. Farrer, *Honors and Knights' Fees* (3 v., London, 1923-1925); *Lancashire Pipe Rolls and Early Charters* (London, 1902); and *Early Yorkshire Charters* **1-3** (London,

by the late Charles Johnson and Professor Cronne[7] and the treatise known as *Brevia Placitata,* which that charming but impish scholar, the late G. J. Turner, projected as long ago as the 'nineties of the last century and kept for about half a century partially set up in print.[8] Professor Plucknett deserves the gratitude of all legal historians for securing its publication in 1951. A third book deserves mention as a courageous attempt to bridge the gap between 1066 and 1187. Professor van Caenegem's treatise on the judicial writs of this period provides a valuable collection of material and, even though not all of us may agree with all the conclusions he has drawn from it, his introduction has challenged contemporary opinion.[9] My criticisms of some of his statements should be regarded as an indication of the great stimulus his work has been to one who has been ploughing a parallel furrow for many years.

The pioneer work of Bigelow was soon followed by an attack on the unprinted records of the period conducted over a wide front. Maitland was responsible for the foundation of the Selden Society in 1884 to publish materials for the history of English law. The Pipe Roll Society had been founded in 1883, largely through the efforts of record agents, and one or two members of the staff of the Public Record Office. The interests of genealogists as well as historians were in the minds of the founders. Both societies now have long runs of volumes to their credit. Local record societies had already taken up the work. General Wrottesley supported by the Reverend R. W. Eyton had begun operations in Staffordshire in 1880, and it may seem invidious to single out certain societies for mention. But the influence of William Farrer in Yorkshire and Lancashire, of H. E. Salter in Oxfordshire and C. W. Foster in Lincolnshire was far reaching. The last of these men, in particular, did much to raise the general standard of editing by insisting on the accurate identification of places and the provision of good indexes. The Public Record Office under Sir Henry Maxwell-Lyte had begun many

1914-1916), continued by Sir Charles Clay and still in progress. F. M. Stenton, *Documents Illustrative of the Social and Economic History of the Danelaw* (British Academy, Oxford, 1920); and *Gilbertine Charters,* Lincoln Record Society, **18** (1922).

[7] *Regesta* **2** (Oxford, 1956).

[8] Selden Society **66** (London, 1951).

[9] *Royal Writs in England from the Conquest to Glanvill, Selden Society* **77** (1959).

valuable series of record volumes, although in the laudable desire to provide historians with their evidence quickly, sufficient care was not always exercised over the detail of editing and some documents which should have been printed in full were summarised. Nevertheless, the three volumes of the *Book of Fees* will always stand as a model of the way in which such work should be done.

Not until after the First World War could the Public Record Office turn its attention to the publication of the early rolls of the central court of justice. The Pipe Roll Society had with the help of Maitland already published one or two fragmentary rolls of Richard I's reign, taking up the task where for lack of funds the Record Commission had dropped it in the middle of the nineteenth century. The first volume of Sir Cyril Flower's *Curia Regis Rolls* appeared in 1922 and thereafter thirteen additional volumes have carried the publication of the bench rolls to 1232. Unfortunately, the same urge to get volumes in print as quickly as possible made the editor omit the essoins from his edition. Nor did the Public Record Office attempt to publish the rolls of itinerant justices. These were deliberately left aside in the hope that local record societies would print them. Hence the surprisingly full returns sent in by the judges who accompanied Simon of Pattishall and Eustace de Fauconberg on the eyre in 1202 through Lincolnshire, to Leicester, Coventry, Northampton, Bedford, and Dunstable and so back to Westminster could not be treated as a whole.[10] The Bedfordshire pleas were printed by the Bedfordshire Society which left out all pleas belonging to other counties. It cannot be stressed too strongly that the rolls of the justices in eyre are historical material every bit as important as the rolls of the justices at Westminster. Some of the most interesting and earliest cases involving proof of serfdom come from the eyre of 1202. Few passages in any early roll are more revealing than the remark of a certain Robert Drop, whose relatives had admitted their villeinage, that "if for reward or any other reason

[10] The Lincolnshire and Northamptonshire rolls from this eyre were edited in 1926 and 1930, respectively, by D. M. Stenton, *Lincoln Record Society* **22**; and *Northamptonshire Record Society* **5**. In the Lincolnshire volume are printed cases relating to that county heard at Bedford; and in the Northamptonshire volume all other cases omitted from the Bedfordshire roll by its editor, Dr. G. Herbert Fowler, in *Bedfordshire Historical Record Society* **1**: pp. 144-247.

they want to make villeins of themselves, he does not want to be a villein." In the end, his thirteen acres of land, and, by implication his freedom, were secured to him by a final concord with his lord.[11] In some ways the rolls of itinerant justices are more important historically than the rolls compiled at Westminster, for they contain cases between litigants who could never have afforded to initiate their pleas in the "court of luxury" [12] at Westminster. I hope that before long the Selden Society will be able to make good these omissions at least up to the end of John's reign. So much for the matter behind these lectures, which cannot cover the whole field of English justice between the Conquest and the Great Charter. I am for the most part confining my attention to those aspects of the subject on which I have particularly worked since I began my studies towards the end of the First World War, the procedure in civil pleas and the gradual creation of a bench of judges and a legal profession.

[11] *Earliest Lincolnshire Assize Rolls,* No. 423 and 279.
[12] *Brevia Placitata,* p. li.

I. THE ANGLO-SAXON INHERITANCE

A STRIKING FACT about the procedural development of the early twelfth century is its dependence on the Anglo-Saxon past. William I was not a voluminous legislator.[1] He willed that all should have "the law of King Edward in lands and in all things, having added thereto the things which I have appointed for the welfare of the people of the English." [2] To the city of London he promised that the citizens should "be worthy of all the laws they were worthy of in King Edward's days" and that "every child be his father's heir after his father's day." [3] He separated lay and ecclesiastical justice in conformity with continental practice [4] and substituted mutilation for the death penalty. He reshaped the murder fine for the protection of his followers,[5] but he added little to the procedure of the courts beyond trial by battle. Englishmen appealed of crime by Normans were allowed to choose either ordeal or the duel. A Frenchman appealed of crime by an Englishman who was unwilling to submit to proof "by judgment or the duel, must purge himself by an unbroken oath." [6] Maitland pointed out that this concession to Englishmen is confirmation of the fact that trial by battle was unknown to English law. It is impossible to follow him in his tentative conjecture that the absence of trial by battle is to be explained by the persistence of extra-judicial fighting.[7]

In any case the suggestion seems peculiarly incongruous in view of the government's anxiety to restrict the field within which recourse to violence might become inevitable. Its disapproval of self-help which is not sanctioned by immemorial custom is well known. Less familiar, but more obviously significant, is its civilised approach towards the problem of the violence endemic in the country that was afterwards to become known as the Marches of Wales. Far back in the tenth century,

1 *Gesetze* **1**: pp. 483-493.
2 *Ibid.*, p. 488.
3 *Ibid.*, p. 486.
4 *Ibid.*, p. 485.
5 *Ibid.*, p. 487.
6 *Loc. cit.*
7 *Hist. of Eng. Law* **1**: p. 50.

"the leading men of the English race and the counsellors of the Welsh people" attempted to provide a peaceful settlement of disputes between Welshmen and Englishmen in the border country on either side the river Wye below Hereford. Towards this end they appointed that twelve lawmen, six of them Welshmen and six of them Englishmen, should declare the rules to be applied in all cases when Welshmen and Englishmen were at law with one another.[8] The establishment of a composite bench of local judges for the settlement of disputes between men of different races reveals a habit of mind fully competent to undertake the experiments which were to issue in the Anglo-Norman jury.

It was a habit of mind prepared to take every opportunity of ending civil suits by compromise between the parties. An early code of Æthelræd II contains the elliptical clause: "Where a thegn has two choices, love or law"—that is, composition or judgment—"and he choses love, it shall be as binding as judgment."[9] The code was primarily drawn up for the Northern Danelaw, the phrase may well be a loan from Scandinavia, and it stands alone in pre-Conquest law. That it was a maxim of general applicability is shown by its re-appearance, in Latin, in the Anglo-Norman law-book called the *Leges Henrici Primi*, where it occurs as a principle to be observed when a partnership is to be dissolved. It is of wider importance because of the conception of law which it implies, which prefers peaceful settlements under the authority of a court to judicial decisions, likely to leave one party dissatisfied and in a mind to make trouble. It is fortunate that there still survives a considerable body of material, intractable, and sometimes impenetrably obscure, which has at least the merit of showing the Anglo-Saxon litigant in action.

The elaborate records of pleas, which had begun to appear already in the ninth century, are in no sense diplomatic documents, such as solemn charters put out in Latin by kings of this or a still earlier age. They are private memoranda, written in English for persons, lay or ecclesiastical, who are, or have

[8] *Gesetze* **1**: pp. 374-377. For Liebermann's commentary on this law, see *ibid.* **3**: pp. 214-219.
[9] *Ibid.*, **1**: p. 232.

recently been involved in pleas.[10] Being informal records, they cannot easily be brought under any general definition, but most of them can be described as unilateral narratives, setting out the grounds of a plea, the incidents which had occurred in its course, and the settlement, or at least the stage which it had reached at the time of writing. Most suits for land in this period seem to have opened with a detailed statement of the plaintiff's case—his *ontalu*—to which the opponent would immediately oppose his *oftalu* in reply. Some of these anomalous documents have every appearance of narratives produced in court, and most of them are obviously following the course of actual pleas. Some of them break off before the pleading has been brought to an end. Others carry on the history until the case has reached a solution that can be confirmed by the King in council. But it is remarkable how often a party who has been completely successful in the pleadings comes at last to a compromise leaving his opponent possessed for life of the land at issue. The conception of the *finalis concordia* made between individuals who have been disputing before a court of royal justice was certainly familiar to the *witan* of Edgar and Æthelræd II.

One outstanding plea of this period may be analysed here for the legal interest of the story which lies behind it. A wealthy Kentishwoman named Æscwyn gave the manor of Snodland, with its title-deeds, to the church of Rochester, but the priests (presumably of the cathedral) stole the deeds and sold them secretly to Ælfric her son. The Bishop demanded their return from Ælfric, and after his death from his widow, and at last brought the whole matter before King Edgar and a court basically composed of his ministers at London. Their decision was that the deeds should be restored to the Bishop and his church with compensation for the theft, and that the widow's own land at Bromley and Fawkham should be forfeited to the

10 The more important of these pleas are edited, with translations, by Dr. F. E. Harmer, *Select English Historical Documents of the Ninth and Tenth Centuries* (Cambridge, 1914), especially Nos. XIV, XV, XVIII, XXIII; and the late Miss A. J. Robertson, *Anglo-Saxon Charters* (Cambridge, 1939), especially Nos. IV, V, XXXVII, XLI, XLIV, LIX, LXIII, LXVI, LXIX, LXXIV, LXXVIII, LXXX, LXXXIII, XCI, CI, CV; of these, Nos. LIX and LXIX are discussed in the following paragraphs. See also Professor Dorothy Whitelock, *Anglo-Saxon Wills* (Cambridge, 1930), No. XVI (2). For comment on these documents see F. M. Stenton, *The Latin Charters of the Anglo-Saxon Period* (Oxford, 1955), pp. 43-45.

King. When Wulfstan the reeve was about to take it into the King's hand, the widow, after consulting with the Bishop, surrendered her own deeds to the King. Thereupon the Bishop, asserting a formal claim to the land, bought it, with its title-deeds, from the King for fifty mancuses of gold and fifteen pounds of silver, leaving the widow in occupation of the land for her life.

Then King Edgar died (975). A kinsman of the widow, himself an important Kentish landowner, took advantage of the anti-monastic reaction after Edgar's death and insisted that they should take violent possession of the land in which she had been reduced to the position of a life-tenant. The nature of their action, which may have been no more than a public demonstration of their rights, cannot now be recovered. What is plain is that they proceeded to an attack on the Bishop, which for a time at least was successful. Applying to the people whom the memorandum calls the enemies of God, that is the anti-monastic party in the state, they compelled the Bishop on pain of losing all his property, to surrender the long-contested title-deeds. The story ends at this point, but a final note complains that the Bishop in his defence was not allowed to use any of the three methods of meeting a plea for land made available by public authority to all the people; namely, the detailed statement of a case, voucher to warranty, and a solemn declaration of uncontested ownership.

After all this, Snodland drops out of history for some twenty years. When it comes to the surface again the widow and her aggressive kinsman are no longer in the picture and another bishop has come to Rochester. Finding that after all the litigation of the previous reign the Snodland title-deeds were still in the cathedral, he felt it his duty to re-open the claim of his church to the estate then in the possession of a certain Leofwine son of Ælfheah. When the Bishop's plaint became known to the King, he sent his writ and seal to Archbishop Ælfric of Canterbury, and ordered him and the King's thegns of East Kent and West Kent to decide the suit in accordance with the Bishop's case and Leofwine's reply. The plea was heard at Canterbury before the Archbishop, Leofric the Sheriff—still known by the vaguer title of "Sciresman"—the Abbot of St. Augustine's and all the chief men of the county. The court

plainly regarded the Bishop's newly recovered documents as conclusive evidence in his favour, but in the customary Old English fashion requested the Bishop to accept a compromise of the kind usual in such cases. Six members of the court—two abbots, the Sheriff, and three thegns—were deputed to arrange its terms, by which Leofwine remained in possession of Snodland for his lifetime on the understanding that it should return uncontested to the cathedral after his death, surrendering at once such documents relating to his possession of Snodland as were still in his hands, and giving to the Bishop a group of messuages in Rochester to the west of the church. The settlement was witnessed by a large company headed by the Archbishop of Canterbury and the Bishop of Rochester, which included the two monastic communities of Canterbury, the reeve and citizens of Canterbury, the Sheriff of Kent, and fifteen other laymen of position. It is rounded off by a solemn anathema against anyone who may try to break or alter its provisions.

It may be admitted at once that as a narrative, this record is unsatisfactory. It is written with a severe economy of words which ignores much relevant personal detail, familiar enough at the time but irrecoverable after all but a thousand years. Its onesidedness is only too apparent. None of all this affects its interest as a picture of a legal system in which ultimate authority resides with the King and a high court of unspecialised ministers, which can be influenced in its interpretation of the law by changes of policy within the state but has a toughness which comes from a firm grip upon technicalities, which is so sure of its ground that it can afford to bring suits to an end by the arrangement of a compromise. It is already developing an executive machinery which will secure its permanence. The Snodland case is the first recorded occasion on which the king's writ can be seen directing the course of proceedings in an English court of law.

The extant documents of this kind range from original texts in English to Latin translations of the twelfth, thirteenth, or even later centuries. Mainly for this reason, their evidence has often been undervalued by legal and constitutional historians. It is obvious that a twelfth-century translation cannot carry the authority of its tenth-century original, and that discretion is necessary before conclusions about Old English practice are

drawn from documents which are only known because an Anglo-Norman monk has felt that they ought to be made available for the immediate purposes of his house. What can now be said is that the editorial work spent on these documents in recent years has placed their general credibility beyond dispute. The identification of places and persons, often represented by initials in early editions, has explained the grounds of many pleas which were once obscure. Rules and principles known from the codes of Anglo-Saxon law can now be traced, more clearly than before, in local operation. Above all, the Anglo-Saxon instinct for narrative, which gives the English pleas of this series a place in the history of literature, repeatedly comes through the formalism of the Anglo-Norman translator in a way that disproves fabrication.

To give an adequate impression of these memoranda would involve the exploration of the family relationships of a vanished aristocracy and of various passages in national history which are still unexpectedly obscure. Many of the pleas, when closely followed, resolve themselves into hereditary claims upon estates which had been acquired by monasteries founded or re-founded by King Edgar (959-975). They were followed up with a pertinacity which nothing but a fundamental respect for law and pleasure in the details of its administration could have prevented from degenerating into violence. There seems to have been no significant change in the conduct of pleas under Edgar's weaker sons, Edward (975-978) and Æthelræd II (978-1016), and an often-quoted document from the reign of Cnut (1016-1035) reveals the system in full vitality.

Late in the reign of Æthelræd II a certain Leofric of Blackwell sold an estate at Inkberrow in Worcestershire to Bishop Æthelstan of Hereford with the leave of the King and his council "for ten pounds of red gold and white silver." The sale was completed without opposition from any quarter, and confirmed by a royal charter. After a peaceable possession of some twelve years the Bishop was impleaded for part of the estate in the shire court of Worcester, by a certain Wulfstan and Wulfric his son. The Bishop won his case, not by producing King Æthelræd's charter, but by showing that Leofric of Blackwell had sold him the land free from all possible counter-claims. By the appointment of the court, the Bishop, Wulfstan, and

his son, Leofric of Blackwell with the witnesses of his original sale of the land, and the local men who had then perambulated it, met on the estate and carried out a second perambulation which confirmed the Bishop in his boundaries. There remained matter for an interminable dispute between Wulfstan and his son, the defeated plaintiffs, and Leofric of Blackwell who had warranted the land to the Bishop. It was avoided by an agreement on which the document deserves to be followed as closely as possible:

Then both Leofric's friends and Wulfstan's said that it would be better for them to come to an agreement than to keep up any quarrel between them. Thereupon they made their agreement as follows, that Leofric should give Wulfstan and his son a pound and take an oath along with two thegns that he would have been satisfied with the same, if the case had turned out for him as it had for Wulfstan. This was the agreement made by all of us. Wulfstan and his son thereupon gave the estate without reservation to Leofric, and Leofric and Wulfstan and Wulfric gave it without reservation or controversy to the Bishop to be granted before or at his death to whomsoever he pleased. . . .

There are three of these documents; one is at St. Mary's in Worcester to which the estate belongs, and the second at St. Æthelbert's in Hereford, and the third shall remain with those in whose possession the estate is.

This is a remarkably elliptical document. It ignores the conquest of England by Cnut which occurred between the original sale by Leofric and the meeting of the shire court at Worcester, and may have made it possible for Wulfstan to bring his plea against the Bishop. It does not easily lend itself to translation. Its turns of phrase are characteristically Anglo-Saxon, and give the modern reader an impression of quaintness remote from the mentality of the hard-headed individuals among whom they arose. But from the standpoint of the common law it is much more remarkable as a foretaste of the future—a document recording a sale of land, a plea brought against the purchaser, voucher of warranty with the case proceeding against the warrantor and ending in a final concord recorded in triplicate. It is a tribute to the Anglo-Saxon regard

for record evidence that the top third of the document still survives.[11]

But the fact remains that most of the records of this type are only known from copies made after the Norman Conquest. Many of them were transcribed in English into one or other of the twelfth-century cartularies which begin with the *Textus Roffensis*,[12] still preserved in Rochester cathedral. They form part of the formidable mass of evidence for the long-continued viability of the Old English language. But by the middle of the century it was becoming clear that, if these documents were to be useful to their possessors, they must be translated into Latin. This was felt with especial force in the great fenland monasteries—Ely, Ramsey, Thorney, Peterborough, and Croyland—some of whose most important title-deeds took this form. The translations incorporated into the *Historia Eliensis* [13] and the *Chronicon* of Ramsey [14] are the largest collections of this material that we possess. The compiler of the Ramsey series, who was writing shortly after 1167, had the instincts of an archivist. His remarks about the condition of his ancient muniments [15] strengthen the belief in the accuracy of his account of a plea between the abbots of Ramsey and Thorney which has lately been taken to re-open the long-debated question of the origin of the English jury.

The dispute between the abbots turned on the question

which of them ought to have more lordship or right in the marsh about King's Delph, each claiming against the other the greater part. Strife went on between them for a long time; at last the neighbouring abbots and friends meeting together with them and, most diligently searching out the justice of the plea, brought the diverse desires of the disputants into the unity of peace, and, through

[11] British Museum, Cotton Charter, viii, 37. *Anglo-Saxon Charters*, No. LXXXIII. For the facsimile of this document see *Facsimiles of Ancient Charters in the British Museum* (London, 1878), Part IV, no. 14. Professor R. R. Darlington also refers to this document in his Creighton Lecture on *The Norman Conquest* (University of London, Athlone Press, 1963), which has reached me since my return from America.

[12] Ed. T. Hearne (Oxford, 1720), and in facsimile by Peter Sawyer (Copenhagen 1957 and 1962).

[13] Ed. E. O. Blake, Royal Historical Society (1962).

[14] *Chronicon Abbatiae Ramesiensis*, ed. W. D. Macray, Rolls Series (1886).

[15] *Ibid.*, p. 65.

faithful men of the neighbourhood, equally examined and sworn, they brought the strife to an end.[16]

The case is thus well summarised in the Latin Chronicle of Ramsey. But each house retained in its possession a memorandum written in Anglo-Saxon perhaps a generation after the agreement had been reached in about 1053. In this memorandum [17] the actual names of the five laymen, two of them fishermen, by whose sworn statement the agreement was reached, are recorded. Two of them were chosen by Thorney and three by Ramsey. They swore that two-thirds of the fen belonged to Ramsey and one-third to Thorney. The Ramsey Chronicle having recorded the settlement goes on to say that the Abbot, through his friendship with King Edward the Confessor, secured a confirmation of the agreement in the form of a royal writ. Unfortunately the text of the writ included in the chronicle cannot be accepted as genuine.[18]

Professor van Caenegem is the first historian seriously to consider the implication of this story. He sees it as an early example of what he describes as a "popular recognition." There is no hint that the "laymen" who swore were summoned by royal authority, nor is there any hint from either house that the parties met to settle their grievances in an established court of law. "The jurors," says van Caenegem, "were in no way oath-helpers, since the parties themselves did not swear; nor were they witnesses, since they adjudicate; nor were they arbiters, since they were not neutral strangers who reconciled the parties, but inhabitants who knew and spoke according to their knowledge." [19] Van Caenegem quotes several cases ranging in date from 1092 to 1175 in which rights were established through a sworn inquest of neighbours, brought together without the authority of a royal writ to swear to the facts they knew. Other examples could probably be added to this list. None of these cases falls into the category of any formal plea and the agreement reached could not have the authority of a decision in a royal

[16] *Ramsay Chron.*, p. 166.

[17] The Ramsey Memorandum is printed in the Ramsey Cartulary **1**: p. 188. The Thorney memorandum is unprinted, Red Book of Thorney, **2**: folio 372. Dr. F. E. Harmer, *Anglo-Saxon Writs,* pp. 254-255, after a careful discussion accepts the substantial accuracy of the memorandum and dates it 1053-1055.

[18] F. E. Harmer, *op. cit.*, p. 256.

[19] *Writs,* p. 71 n.

court of justice, but it provided a settlement acceptable to both parties in a dispute.

Dr. van Caenegem argues that the English jury has a double origin; what he describes as the popular recognition, of which this fenland case, Ramsey v. Thorney is the first clearly recorded example, and the inquest held on royal authority. He appears to accept without question, like Haskins before him, the doctrine so successfully taught by Brunner in 1871 that the inquest as it was used in England is directly derived through the Normans from the Frankish inquest by which royal rights were investigated. But he notices as others have noticed before him that there is no clear example of any inquest held by ducal authority in Normandy before 1066. Nor is there any hint pointing in this direction in the recently published edition of ducal charters issued between 911 and 1066.[20] The case quoted over and over again as evidence for the Norman employment of the jury comes from a memorandum printed in *Gallia Christiana* [21] from the cartulary of the abbey of Fontenay and composed about 1070-1079, recording that by the command of King William, to whose notice the depredations made upon abbey lands had come, four lawful men were chosen by common consent who set out on oath a list of the grants made to the abbey by its founders, the first and second Ralf Taxo. A long list of grants was sworn to by these four men, one of whom had been *prepositus* of both the founders, and incorporated in a solemn charter. Apart from the fact of the King's intervention instead of that of "neighbouring abbots and friends" the circumstances of the cases of Fontenay v. its neighbours and Ramsey v. Thorney seem strictly parallel. Is it not possible that King William was introducing to his duchy a procedure which he had found worked well in his new kingdom?

Seventy years before the Norman Conquest the twelve senior thegns of Æthelræd's Wantage code, who were to come forward in every wapentake and swear that they will not wrongly accuse any innocent man or conceal any guilty one, were taking the sworn inquest directly into the everyday life of the common

[20] Ed. Marie Fauroux, *Recueil des Actes des Ducs de Normandie* (911-1066), Mémoires de la Société des Antiquaires de Normandie, Caen, **26** (1961).

[21] Tom. XI. Instrumenta columns 61-65. The reference to the jury of four occurs near the end in column 65.

man. It is an arbitrary treatment of evidence to approach the origin of the English jury by disassociating the sworn presentments of the Wantage code from the inquests which within a lifetime were to appear in civil cases. Even if the code concerned only the district of the Five Boroughs it is worth noting that the fenland of Ramsey v. Thorney lay in those parts. Maitland accepted Brunner's conclusions about the origin of the English jury, but the way he writes of the twelve senior thegns suggests that he was not entirely happy about the unyielding decisiveness of the argument:

> No doubt there is here a field for research, but it seems unlikely that any new discovery will disturb the derivation of our English from the Frankish inquests. We cannot say *a priori* that there is only one possible origin for the jury. We cannot even say that England was unprepared for the introduction of this institution; but that the Norman duke brought it with him as one of his prerogatives can hardly be disputed.[22]

These are not the words in which a man who is fully convinced accepts an argument or embraces a new opinion.

Nowadays, there is no need to be so tentative. The strength of the Scandinavian influence in England is one of the great imponderables in Anglo-Saxon England. Nevertheless, during the sixty years since 1912 when Liebermann published his glossary to the *Gesetze*, traces of Scandinavian ideas and institutions have multiplied in Eastern England to an extent which has made the Danelaw a reality. To say the least, there is no longer any inherent improbability in the suggestion that the jury, common to the Scandinavian peoples on either side of the North Sea, rising to the surface for a moment under Æthelræd II, may have persisted in England to become incorporated into the fabric of the Anglo-Norman state.

Writing in 1908, Vinogradoff had been less ready than Maitland to follow Brunner's lead. He would not accept Brunner's dismissal of the twelve senior thegns as entirely unconnected with the indictment jury of the Assize of Clarendon, but even he came no nearer to claiming a native origin for the jury than saying: "The continuity of the Frankish and Norman inquest procedure . . . does not preclude that in preconquestual England itself there had existed legal customs which prepared the

[22] *Hist. of Eng. Law* 1: p. 143.

way for the indictment jury of the twelfth century." [23] Vinogradoff knew more than Maitland of the Scandinavian element in English law and was less ready than most of his contemporaries to write it off because there was little evidence about it coming from an early date. For my own part, I believe that the rich stream of English case-law flowing through the Anglo-Saxon period reflects the minds and spirits of a people responsive to reason, ready to welcome a generous settlement of a plea, with a clear understanding of the sacral virtue of an oath. It was in this atmosphere that the seeds of the English jury grew and flourished.

The establishment of the jury as an integral part of English civil procedure belongs to the Norman rather than to the Anglo-Saxon age. But it would have been impossible without the Anglo-Saxon invention of the sealed writ by which the king's commands could be carried in a stereotyped phraseology throughout the land. In time, the king's writ was to become the agent through which the Angevin transformation of English law was carried out. It was a continuation of the Conqueror's good fortune that there lay to his hand in England an instrument of government so effective in itself and so adaptable to so many purposes. These terse economically worded documents were ill suited for declarations of principle or policy, but an exceptional occasion might give rise to phrases which offer an insight into the king's mind. It is a writ in favour of the church of Ely which provides the clearest expression of the Conqueror's determination to maintain the processes of Old English law. It has often been printed, but its importance has not always been recognised:

William King of the English to Lanfranc the Archbishop and Geoffrey the Bishop and Robert Count of Mortain, Greeting. See that Remigius the Bishop does not demand new customs within the Isle of Ely. For I am unwilling that he shall have there anything except what his predecessor had in the time of King Edward, namely on that day the King died. And if Remigius shall wish to plead therein, let him plead therein as he would have done in the time of King Edward, and let that plea be in your presence. . . . Cause the plea touching the lands which William de Ou and Ralf son of Waleran and Robert Gernun are claiming to stand over if

[23] *English Society in the Eleventh Century* (Oxford, 1908), p. 7.

> they are unwilling to plead therein as they would have pleaded in the time of King Edward, and I will that as the abbey then had its customs, you cause it to have them completely as the abbot by his charters and by his witnesses shall be able to plead them—[24]

by his charters and by his witnesses—the civilised Anglo-Saxon legal process, which the Conqueror declares his determination to maintain even against the interest of his own barons.

The Old English tradition of the unilateral memorandum survived the Conquest, and many of the best-known of the *Placita Anglo-Normannica* take this form. T this is partly due their occasional obscurity, and their general failure to give any adequate account of pleadings, or even of judgments. Of the most important of them all, the great plea at which Archbishop Lanfranc deraigned the lands and privileges of his church before the shire court of Kent on Penenden Heath, Bigelow in 1879 could only observe "the record is not clear concerning the nature of the trial"—an opinion in which most modern students of the record would probably concur.[25] What the tenor of the document places beyond doubt is that the conditions of King Edward's day provide the norm by which all claims must be tested. Out of all the records of Anglo-Norman litigation the only incident that is commonly remembered is King William's order that Æthelric, the deposed Bishop of Selsey, a very old and learned man, should be brought to Penenden Heath in a cart to describe and expound the customary law of the Anglo-Saxons. A new edition of the Anglo-Norman pleas, taking into account the work that has been spent on them since 1879, would throw light on many dark passages in the early history of the common law. But its editor might in the end reflect that the art of reporting pleas had, if anything, deteriorated between the reigns of Edgar and Henry I.

It is unlikely that this edition will contain many new documents. The only important collection of Anglo-Norman pleas still unprinted seems to be the Red Book of Thorney in the

[24] *Liber Eliensis*, p. 206.

[25] *Bigelow, Placita*, p. 9, in a footnote to his edition of the plea. A bibliography of the modern literature relating to the plea is prefixed to the translation in *English Historical Documents*, ed. D. C. Douglas and G. W. Greenaway (London, 1953), 2: pp. 449-451. The date is fixed to 1075 by the presence of Ernost, Bishop of Rochester, who died in July 1075 after he had been bishop for only half a year.

Cambridge University Library. But there is material in long familiar sources on which the last word has not yet been said. In 1023, for example, King Cnut granted the port of Sandwich with its toll, customs, and all necessary appurtenances by land and water to the cathedral church of Canterbury. The gift was naturally resented by many interested persons and, in particular, by the ancient monastery now called St. Augustine's at Canterbury, the principal landowner in Thanet. A quarrel which began soon after Cnut's death threatened to arouse so much violence in 1127 that King Henry I intervened for its settlement. The plea which followed has long been known through an abstract preserved in Canterbury cathedral.[26] But a full record of the proceedings was copied into a custumal of Sandwich, now lost, which was printed in 1792 by William Boys in his vast volume of *Collections for an History of Sandwich*, where it has escaped the notice of most historians.[27] It is a poor copy, in which, for example, the Old English names of the jurors are often distorted. But its errors do not seriously affect the value of a record which preserves an otherwise unknown writ of Henry I, and gives a Latin translation of the actual wording of the jurors' oath.

The dispute arose over the growth of a new town on St. Augustine's land at Stonar on the side of the river opposite to Sandwich where vessels could lie up in good weather. This led to violent disputes about the tolls to be taken from ships entering the harbour and about the secret use by the Abbot's men of the ferryboat belonging to the Archbishop and monks which had been accustomed to ply between Sandwich and Stonar. Without pre-judging the case, the King caused an assembly of "wise men living near the sea" to meet at Sandwich, where the respective rights of the Abbot and the Archbishop could be discussed and settled on oath. The proceedings began with an address in which the Archbishop adjured the assembly to consider the matter in hand without fear or favour, adding that this was the King's command. After "nearly all" the assembly had said that to the best of their knowledge, "the profits of the port of Sandwich" had always belonged to the cathedral church of Canterbury, it asked that it might hear what the King had

26 Printed in *Regesta* 2, No. CXCVII, p. 358.

27 Printed at Canterbury. For the plea and translation, see pp. 551-555.

actually ordered. The following writ was then produced in court:

Henry, King of the English, to the Archbishop of Canterbury and the Abbot of St. Augustine and the Sheriff of Kent, Greeting. By the oath of twelve lawful men of Dover and twelve lawful men of the province of Sandwich, who are not men of the Archbishop nor men of the Abbot, cause the truth touching the claim of customs which is between them to be declared as they were in the time of my father and in the time of Lanfranc the Archbishop and of Anselm the Archbishop, and let the Archbishop have such customs and the Abbot have such customs as it shall be declared that their predecessors had at that time, so that each church shall fully have its right. Witnesses, the Bishop of Lincoln, and Robert de Sigillo, and Geoffrey of Glympton at London.

After the writ had been read and explained to the assembly, it chose twenty-four aged men, half from Dover and half from the country round Sandwich, whose testimony would cover many years. Their names, which are set out at length, show that twenty-one of them at least were of native Anglo-Saxon descent.[28] They were asked what of their certain knowledge they were prepared to prove by oath. They all declared that the port, the toll and the "maritime customs" of Sandwich on each side of the water "from Burgegate to Merkesflete" belonged to the monks of Canterbury cathedral. The whole assembly declared the same. Then a copy of the gospels was produced, and the twelve men of Dover followed by the twelve men from the parts of Sandwich, took, as individuals, an identical oath to this effect:

The first of them, Wulfwine son of Beornwine, standing in the midst of the multitude and holding in his hands the sacred book of the gospels, spoke thus: "I swear, the toll of the port of Sandwich, all the maritime customs on either side of the river from Burgegate as far as Merkesfliete, and the ferryboat, belong only to the Archbishop and the monks of Christchurch, Canterbury, nor has anyone else any right there save them and their servants, as I have learned from my ancestors and seen and heard from my youth up to now, so help me God and these holy gospels." His companions without delay declared the same.

[28] One of the oath-swearers who bore a continental name was "Odo," an otherwise unknown moneyer of Dover.

The record ends with a list of those who witnessed the proceedings beginning with William Sheriff of Kent "who held the place of judge."

There are few records of this type which suggest so strongly the hand of an eyewitness, describe the actual course of a plea so clearly, or bring out so emphatically the care taken that the oath shall not be a mere formality. There are no records revealing more plainly the extent to which the Anglo-Norman judicial administration depended for its efficiency on the cooperation of English free men of repute, capable of giving good testimony. The closest parallel to this Sandwich plea seems to be the inquest held by the King's command in 1122 into the encroachment made by his men of Bridport on the manor of Burton Bradstock belonging to St. Stephen of Caen. The complaints of the monks to King Henry I caused him to instruct the Sheriff to hear the plea, which was settled in favour of the monks by an inquest heard in a court of the seven hundreds around Burton and Bridport. Thirteen out of the sixteen named jurors were Englishmen by birth.[29] Great changes in the law were on the way. The impact of Norman energy on Saxon traditionalism had already broken the ground for the foundation of a new legal system. Many influences were to combine in the making of the English common law as it is known to us through Glanville and Bracton and the early records of the king's court at Westminster or on eyre through the shires. Beneath them all lies the basis of the Anglo-Saxon past.

[29] *The Collected Works of Sir Francis Palgrave,* ed. Sir R. H. Inglis Palgrave (Cambridge, 1921), 7: pp. 249-251.

II. THE ANGEVIN LEAP FORWARD

THE PROTECTION of his subjects in the quiet enjoyment of their land and goods was a main problem of a medieval king. Every war, every rebellion, even minor disturbances which hardly affect the steady course of history meant for many contemporaries eviction from their homes and lands. The petty local tyrant, even more than the over-mighty subject increased the volume of complaint rising to the ears of a weak king. Of the four Norman kings of England, 1066-1154, only the last was weak. Even he tried to cope with the dispossessions, disseisins, the civil war encouraged. The writs of all these kings show their preoccupation with this problem. Feudal courts of justice could not entertain pleas between men who held of different lords and justice was slow. Both parties must be present in court for the hearing of the plea, but no workable rules had been devised to govern the excuses, the essoins, which the tenant of the land might make to delay his appearance in court to answer a plea. If there had been, their enforcement might well have been beyond the competence of a feudal court. The man in possession had the land and its profits and could delay his appearance in court to answer claims against him. A plea between men who held of different lords met in the shire court the same delaying tactics. To many men disseised of their freehold self-help seemed the only answer. The temptation to self-help had been as great in the ancient as in the medieval world; it was as great in other European countries as it was in England.

Roman law in the third century had countered this primitive instinct with the rule that a man despoiled of his land should be restored to possession before being called upon to prove his title. In this way the conception of a preliminary restorative action began to make its appearance. The determination of the ninth-century forger—the pseudo Isidore—to protect the lands of the church, particularly episcopal lands, against violent usurpation led him to draft letters in the names of early popes setting out in the most definite terms that restitution must be made to an ecclesiastical person ejected from his land by violence before his ejector could bring any legal action to obtain the

land which he had tried to acquire in an extra-judicial manner. These false decretals were received into the body of canon law so that the possibility of a preliminary restorative action which should not touch the right was foreshadowed in both the law of empire and papacy.[1] The forged decretals reached England in the wake of the Normans and strongly influenced the author of the *Leges Henrici Primi,* himself a judge in the king's service. Several of his statements are based on the belief that no one should have to play the difficult part of plaintiff for land from which he has been evicted by the tenant.[2] But there is no sign of any formal preliminary action developing in England before the reign of Henry II.

The necessity of enabling a man to preserve the continuity of his own seisin of land so that he could enjoy the easier position of tenant rather than plaintiff in a plea was long recognised. Even in the thirteenth century law and custom allowed a man who had been violently ejected from his land or tenement four days in which to collect his friends to help him eject his disseisor and thus preserve the continuity of his own tenure. If he were away from home and at a considerable distance, or even abroad, he was allowed a longer time to recover his seisin with his friends' help. This right of immediate reprisal to a disseisor, which, as Maitland said, "has all the appearance of being very ancient," lasted long after a simple legal means of achieving the same end had been provided by Henry II.[3] In fact it seems to have acquired a new life with the necessity of establishing a rule about the length of seisin an ejector must enjoy to secure for himself the protection of the assize of novel disseisin. But under the strong rule of the first three Norman kings self-help

[1] F. Joüon des Longrais "La portée politique des réformes d'Henry II en matière de saisine," *Revue historique de droit français et étranger,* 4 sér., **15**: 547ff.

[2] *Gesetze* **1**: p. 574. Nullus a domino suo inplegiatus uel inlegiatus uel iniuste dissaisiatus ab eodem implacitetur ante legittimam restitutionem, 53.3. Et nemo dissaisiatus placitet, nisi in ipsa dissaisiacione agatur, 53.5. Et postquam aliquis dissaisitus legem uel rectum domino suo uadiauerit et plegios, si opus est addiderit, saisitus esse debet, 53.6.

[3] F. W. Maitland, "The Beatitude of Seisin," *Collected Papers,* **1**: pp. 415-423. An assize of novel disseisin, brought by a man against tenants who had ejected him from his free tenement within eight days of his recovering it against them by writ of right in the lord's court, failed because the jurors said that he was not disseised of his free tenement, *Rolls of the Justices in Eyre for Gloucestershire . . .,* Selden Society, **59**, case 293.

was clearly felt to be less effective than royal help and the kings proved very willing to sell their help and issue writs directing a royal officer to reseise a man who has been disseised of his land. A simple order commanding the Sheriff to restore a man or a bishop or an abbot to seisin without making any provision for examining the circumstances of the case seems almost as elementary a remedy as self-help within four days. Professor van Caenegem argues that the formulas used in these writs show a progressive attempt to guard against the danger of a simple order of reseisin issued to a complainant without proof shown that he has been unjustly disseised. But this is difficult to prove since writs of reseisin are not dated.[4] When the King ordered the Sheriff to reseise a man justly, or "if he has been disseised" it might appear to authorise him to make a preliminary investigation. The only way he could do it would be through the shire, or perhaps the hundred court. But a royal writ of reseisin might well be only the first of several writs sought from the king by both parties and the beginning of long and inconclusive litigation, often only ended as in Anglo-Saxon days by compromise.[5]

No fewer than six documents entered in the Red Book of Thorney were necessary to record the recovery by Abbot Robert of two hides at Sibson given, with land at Yaxley, by Abbot Gunter to his nephew, Robert of Yaxley without the consent of the chapter.[6] Gunter had ruled the abbey from 1075 to 1112 and his successor, Robert became abbot in 1113. He began the long plea by refusing to take Robert of Yaxley's homage and demanding the return of the land at Sibson. When Robert "proudly refused" the Abbot disseised him, broke his houses and stubbed up his holt, and went over seas to acquire a royal writ directing the justices to reseise the abbey with the land. By this violent action the Abbot was trying to avoid initiating a long and solemn plea of right. But it is clear from the second document in the Red Book that Robert himself

[4] Dr. van Caenegem's selected list of writs of reseisin hardly bear out his suggestion of progressive care and precision, e.g., No. 55 William II in favour of Ramsey abbey commands the sheriff to reseise "justly." No. 57 Henry I in favour of Ramsey abbey omits the word "justly," *Writs*, pp. 274, 440, 441, 414.

[5] E.g., suits between successive abbots of Abingdon and Simon, the dispenser of Henry I, and his son Thurstan, touching Marcham and Tadmarton, *Abingdon Chron.* **2**: pp. 166-168, 184-187, 223, 226.

[6] The documents are printed below, Appendix No. IV.

obtained a writ to the Sheriff instructing him to hear the case in the shire court of Huntingdon. The second document is a solemn statement by Fulk the Sheriff dated 1127 reporting the final hearing in the full shire court at Huntingdon. It records that on the Sheriff's advice Robert abandoned his claim and in the sight of the shire surrendered his writ to Fulk. The Abbot allowed him to retain his three and a half virgates of land at Yaxley and Robert swore fealty to him before the whole shire "as Hervey Lemoyne best knew how to set it out." This done, the Abbot gave Robert two marks of silver in four separate sums and by four separate individuals, the Abbot himself, the Sheriff, the Abbot of Ramsey, and Hervey Lemoyne. It had taken the Abbot some fourteen years to win this settlement which left bitter feelings behind it, for in each of the four remaining documents extorted from Robert, his son William and, finally, from William's nephew and heir, Ralf, the grantor, in abjuring his claims, includes the phrase "whether they were just or unjust." The issue of this long plea was given the utmost publicity in the villages where the defeated plaintiffs spent their lives. The Abbot left nothing to chance; a solemn abjuration on the altar at Thorney and on the gospels and the relics there, a ceremony "in the grange at Water Newton," and in "the court at Yaxley," and finally, a quit claim made by Ralf at Stanground. A hundred years later the Abbot would have acquired from the chancery a writ of entry *sine consensu capituli* so that the question could be quickly settled by a verdict of neighbours.

There is ample evidence in the surviving rolls of royal courts of justice, in Exchequer and Chancery documents to illustrate the development of judicial procedure between the modest treatise known by the name of Henry II's Justiciar, Rannulf de Glanville, and the majestic work produced by Henry III's judge, Bracton. But the years when the great leap forward was taken remain, despite the work of many scholars, mysterious. Professor van Caenegem has attempted in his comprehensive study of the judicial writs between 1066 and 1189 to trace a steady development in formula and practice from the Anglo-Saxon writs to the clear-cut common-law writs set out in Glanville, from which vast families of actions were to spring in the generations which followed. Although certain simple writs,

such as the writ of naifty,[7] show little change in wording between the early years of Henry I and the time of Glanville, Professor van Caenegem's work has only made it more plain, to me at least, that there is no gradual evolution between the writs of Henry I and those of his grandson's later years, or, indeed, between the *Leges Henrici Primi* and Glanville. Genius was at work. It worked on ancient material—the recognition, the sworn inquest, the formal oath, the writ. It may well have drawn inspiration from the civil law of Rome and the canon law of the church. Both these great systems of law were matter of eager contemporary study. The clauses in the *Leges* already quoted lend colour to this belief. It was supported by as able a group of ministers as ever served an English king, and in its determination to secure a well-governed land it produced a new and highly individualistic legal system.

It is probable that the early stages by which the momentous results of Henry II's reign were achieved will never be adequately recalled. The collapse of the machinery of government in Stephen's reign had been almost complete, although there are signs of recovery in his last years.[8] Chronicle accounts of the first years of Henry II's reign are meagre. The Becket quarrel and martyrdom diverted literary effort towards matters more dramatic than the development of the king's courts of justice. Details of decisions taken early in the reign may well have been forgotten as the King's plans moved majestically forward after 1166. It cannot now be determined when the fundamental rule that no one need answer for his freehold unless his opponent produced a royal writ was introduced. The extreme care and precision of Glanville's *Treatise* has made historians reluctant to doubt his statement that the rule was customary, but they have made no serious effort to consider what he meant by customary. In his brilliant introductory chapter to the *Legislation of Edward I* Professor Plucknett recalled that the civilian Azo regarded ten or twenty years' usage as a "long" custom, thirty years as a "very long" custom and

[7] *Brevia Placitata*, p. lxv.

[8] Notably in the last type of coin issued by Stephen, the so-called Awbridge type *see* the article by F. Elmore Jones, *British Numismatic Journal* **28**: pp. 537-554.

forty years as an "age-old" custom.[9] To the author of the *Treatise,* writing after 1187, the beginning of Henry II's reign must have seemed like another world.

Maitland's suggestion that the writ of right was the subject of a lost ordinance, possibly dating from 1166 and including also provision for the assize of novel disseisin,[10] can find no supporters today since contemporary record evidence is in print to refute it. G. J. Turner's conjectures so long turned over in his subtle mind deserve careful consideration. He held that all ordinary pleas of land were at the time of the Norman conquest initiated in the lord's court by plaint and that they could be removed by "the demandant into the county court by the ancient process of tolt," [11] and all pleas could be removed from the shire to the royal court by the writ of *recordari,* ordering the Sheriff to send a record of the plea to the royal court by the mouths of members of the court present when it was heard. Turner pointed out that Henry I's writs by which he intervened to expedite justice, although "resembling in some respects writs of right" were not "in settled form and there is little reason for thinking that they were necessary for the recovery of land." Apart from the fact that the process of tolt cannot be more ancient than the feudal courts themselves his argument seems so far unimpeachable. Turner further suggested that "early in the reign of Henry II, perhaps even in the closing years of Henry I, a royal ordinance issued declaring that no man should be impleaded of his freehold without a royal writ." Turner conceived this ordinance, or a subsidiary one, as declaring that all pleas that touched the freehold and all personal pleas in which the property involved exceeded 40 shillings must be initiated in the county court by writ and not by plaint: further that the ordinance provided that all pleas in the county court could be removed to the king's court at

[9] *Legislation of Edward I* (Oxford, 1949), pp. 6-7. Even the careful Richard Fitz Nigel in writing of his own department said "positively that Domesday makes absolutely no mention" of payment in the Treasury in blanched pennies. *See,* R. L. Poole, *The Exchequer in the Twelfth Century* (Oxford, 1912), pp. 30-31. Charles Johnson suggests, however, that this passage may be "an interpolation, not necessarily by Richard," *Dialogus de Scaccario,* Nelson's *Medieval Classics* (1950), p. 14 and n.

[10] *Select Pleas in Manorial Courts* 1; Selden Society, 2 (1898): pp. liv-lv.

[11] See Appendix No. III for an early reference to this process.

the request of the plaintiff by writ of *pone*.[12] But all this involves moving the conceptions of the thirteenth century back more than a hundred years.

While finding it impossible to go all the way with Turner, I find it equally impossible to agree with Professor van Caenegem, who apparently sees no need for any ordinance at all, or with Professor Plucknett who adheres to Glanville's statement that the rule is customary.[13] That the writ of right was in use by that name in the early years of Henry II is proved by two charters, one of them a cartulary copy and the other a sealed original charter, neither of which can be later than 1157-1158. Both of these charters have been used, in the long years before a collection of Henry I's writs was available in print, to support the tentative suggestion that the writ of right might perhaps be assigned to his reign. The cartulary copy records the acquisition from the King by two Lincolnshire peasants of Scandinavian descent, heirs of a man called Thowi son of Siwat, who had sold land to the prior of Spalding, of "a certain writ of right." They brought it to the prior, who, evidently anxious that no charge of a failure in justice could be brought against him, summoned the Sheriff to his court when the plea was heard. The court "justly judged" that the plaintiffs had lost their suit and before all the court they gave up to the prior the writ which they had brought. The fact that a record of this transaction was entered in the cartulary of Spalding priory and the fact that the defeated plaintiffs gave up their writ suggests that the court was not fully familiar as yet with the procedure on the writ of right.[14] The original charter which contains a reference to a writ of right is a grant of privilege to Kirkstead abbey, Lincolnshire, by Conan Duke of Brittany and Earl of Richmond, who promises that "neither he nor his heirs nor

[12] *Brevia Placitata*, p. lxviii. Turner is certainly too ready to assume that no private jurisdiction can be postulated for the late Anglo-Saxon age. But since that period in no wise concerns him in *Brevia Placitata* it is not fair to raise the point.

[13] *Legislation of Edward I*, pp. 26-28. Plucknett rejects the conclusions of G. B. Adams, *Origin of the English Constitution*, who, regarding this rule as "The most extraordinary and the most sweeping of all the regulations by which Henry II attacked the feudal system" (pp. 97-98) was inclined to regard Glanville's statement as merely his private opinion. Plucknett feels this to be "quite inadmissible."

[14] F. M. Stenton, "The Danes in England," *Proceedings of the British Academy* **13** (1927): 221-222.

their bailiffs will hold courts or pleas within the boundaries of the abbey's land, nor cite nor cause to be cited the Abbot, his free tenants or his serfs to their courts or pleas for any earthly service, neither for a *breue de recto* or any other writ." [15] Neither I nor Professor van Caenegem have been able to find any other record of the writ of right so called at this early date.

The civil war of Stephen's reign left far more work of restoration to be done than the barons' war at the end of the reign of John. Then a special writ was devised for the use of men or women disseised by reason of the war of land which they had held when the war began. It authorised the appointment of a jury of neighbours to settle the truth of claims.[16] By 1217 a long period had passed in which writs of diverse formulae had been drafted to get quick if, theoretically at least, temporary settlements in matters of seisin. In 1154 the forms of action were yet unborn. The King had not yet provided any writs of settled form to enable his free subjects to get automatic entry to his courts of justice. What more likely than that, faced with all the clamour of bishops and religious houses, barons and freemen seeking to recover land which they had lost during the fifteen years of what the Saxons would have called "unpeace," the King should lay down the general rule that his writ must be sought before the lord's court could entertain actions of right and that if the lord's court failed to do justice the Sheriff should do it? There is little point in the question whether this rule was promulgated by a general ordinance or a series of instructions to individual ministers. Henry II had appointed local justices at the beginning of his reign. All that was needed was that they and the Sheriffs should be acquainted with the provisions of the new rule as occasions arose for its application. That the writ of right met serious opposition in any quarter is unlikely. It was carefully devised so as to avoid even the appearance of an attack upon the seignorial courts. At the moment of its launching, it could be regarded as a spur stimu-

[15] Printed in full with facsimile by C. T. Clay, *Early Yorkshire Charters*, **4**, Honour of Richmond, Part i, pp. 37-38, plate VI. See also, *Cambridge Medieval History* **5**: p. 585, where I argued from this charter that the writ of right might well go back to the reign of Henry I.

[16] *Rolls of the Justices for Eyre in Lincolnshire and Worcestershire*, ed. D. M. Stenton, Selden Society, **53** (1934): pp. lix-lx.

lating them to the work which on feudal principles they claimed as theirs.

The pipe rolls of Henry's II's early years are singularly uninformative about the reasons for which money was paid to the King. It is not until 1176 that a pipe roll clerk records payment for a *breve de recto* in these words, although previous payments *pro recto* may well imply the purchase of a writ of right. In Henry III's day the writ of right was issued *of course,* that is free, save for a small payment to the clerk for writing it.[17] To have charged a fee for a writ of right would have contravened the Great Charter which promised that justice should not be sold. How soon in the history of the Angevin judicial writs the conception of the writ of course was established is not evident. The phrase is not mentioned in Glanville and the earliest reference to a writ of course which I have found comes from an essoin roll of the Hilary term, 1200.[18] It is highly probable that from the first the writ of right was issued "of course," that is free, if the land at issue was of small value. In the register of writs sent to Ireland in 1227 [19] for the use of the chancery there it appears that the writ was issued "of course" if it were for the recovery of half a knight's fee or less, services not exceeding a hundred shillings or a burgage tenement of a rent not exceeding forty shillings. By offering this writ free to his free subjects seeking to recover modest amounts of land or rents Henry II could soon persuade them to realise its efficiency. That men of substance should pay considerable sums to secure the benefit which would follow the issue of a writ of right was in line with current political thought.

The legal reforms of Henry II are so well documented at important points that it is easy to forget the unofficial, indeed almost casual nature of the record. Glanville's Treatise contains a number of references to assizes of which no text is

[17] The meaning of the phrase *de cursu,* of course, was first convincingly explained by G. J. Turner, *Brevia Placitata,* pp. xlviii-lviii. His demonstration that writs can be "of course"—free in the eyre, but "of grace"—at a price—at Westminster helps to explain matters which were confusing in the past; e.g., why the pipe rolls record so few payments for the popular writs beginning actions of novel disseisin or mort d'ancestor.

[18] *Pleas before the King or his Justices* 1, cases 2729, p. 254.

[19] This Register will soon be published by the Selden Society, edited by Elsa de Haas, T. F. T. Plucknett, and G. D. G. Hall.

known.[20] An example of the way in which important general orders can be ignored by chroniclers is the absence of any reference in a literary source to what Henry II in a writ issued early in the reign on behalf of the prior and monks of St. Swithin's, Winchester, calls my statute, *statutum meum*. The King forbade that the prior and monks should be impleaded "contrary to my statute" by any Englishman unless his ancestors had been seised of the land he claimed "on the day King Henry my grandfather was alive and dead or afterwards." [21] The King issued similar writs in favour of the prior and monks of St. Martin's Dover and the prior and monks of Worcester, although the phrase *contra statutum meum* is not included in them.[22] Henry I, the only one of the Conqueror's sons born in England after his father had been crowned as king, had gone far towards amalgamating the conquered and conquering into one race. He had taken an English wife himself, employed individual Englishmen, used English soldiers in his continental wars and encouraged the use of the traditional English courts of justice, the hundred and the shire.[23] This must have encouraged the descendants of dispossessed Englishmen, whose memories were

[20] Book viii, pp. 121, 122; Book xiii, pp. 163, 177: see also, Sir George Hill, *Treasure Trove*, pp. 190-191.

[21] Galbraith, V. H., "Royal Charters to Winchester," *Eng. Hist. Rev.*, **35** (1920): 398-399.

[22] These writs are discussed by van Caenegem, *Writs*, pp. 216-217 and notes.

[23] Van Caenegem states that the word *Anglicus* means "one of the ordinary non-knightly, non-ecclesiastical tenants, who made up the majority of any great land-owner's tenants," but there can be no doubt that *Anglicus* indicates a man of specifically English descent. These writs support the views expressed by F. M. Stenton, "English Families and the Norman Conquest," *Transactions of the Royal Historical Society*, 4th ser., **26** (1944): "There is some reason to think that the king regarded his English subjects as a counter-balance to the Norman lords who had come to power in the time of his father and brother" (pp. 8ff.). The writ issued by Henry II in favour of Abbot Gilbert of Colchester, commanding that he should hold all the lands and tenures of his predecessor, Abbot Hugh, contains the prohibition that the abbot shall be impleaded by any rustic who may claim an inheritance. This writ implies that in Essex and Hertfordshire, where the Colchester properties lay, men of "rustic" status in the twelfth century could look back to ancestors who in preconquest days had been landowners in their own right. *Cartularium monasterii Sancti Johannis Baptiste de Colecestra*, ed. Stuart A. Moore (London, 1897), **1**: p. 40. This writ is also quoted by van Caenegem, who equates Englishmen generally with villeins or rustics and regards Henry II's *statutum* as "an important step" towards "the exclusion from the common law protection of unfree tenures altogether," a conclusion entirely without warrant. (Writs, pp. 218-219.) The unfree had never, so far as evidence shows, enjoyed "common law protection" for the land they tilled.

long, to try in the opening years of a new reign to recover ancestral lands lost in the years of conquest. Confirmation of this suggestion that Henry II found it necessary to make just such a general order—a *statutum*—touching the seisin of Englishmen as the Winchester charter implies comes from the pipe roll of 31 Henry II, 1185. William of Leathley, Yorks, offered 15 marks for a recognition touching the land of Baildon in the same county which John son of Essulf was claiming against him, if the predecessor of the said John, who was an Englishman and through whom John claimed the land, was seised thereof on the day and year when King Henry the grandfather of the lord King was alive and dead.[24]

The real leap forward came when the King and his advisers devised the formula of the returnable writ. Those final sentences in a writ which initiates an action in the king's court are generally cut short in any formulary or register of writs by the words *et cetera,* but they are of fundamental importance. "Summon by good summoners the aforesaid R. to be there then and have there the summoners and this writ." The writ has instructed the Sheriff to choose—usually he will cause his hundredal bailiff to choose—good men to summon the tenant or defendant to appear in court on the day named in the writ and on that day the Sheriff must be in court himself with the summoners, the summoned and the writ. The returnable writ depended for its viability on the presence of the King or his justices on the day and at the place appointed for the hearing of the plea. The writ of right was not returnable. It was a patent and was obtained from the chancery by the plaintiff who took it to his lord to whom it was addressed and could receive it back from him after the plea had been heard.[25] None of the old executive or *justicies* writs of Henry I's days or the early years of Henry II were returnable. They remained with the recipients and sometimes were copied with title deeds into

[24] *Pipe Roll 31 Henry II,* p. 66. This debt first appeared on the Pipe Roll of 28 Henry II, 1182, p. 45, among the new pleas of Godfrey de Luci, Alan de Furnell', and Hugh de Morewich. In this and each successive roll until 1185 the debt is merely noted with the statement added, "but he has not yet had right."

[25] *Brevia Placitata,* p. lxiii, "There is no return to this writ which in every event remains with the demandant"; and Professor Plucknett's footnote, on p. xlvii, which corrects the erroneous statement in the text that "in the seignourial court the writ remained with the lord."

cartularies. The new common law writs of Henry II's day were returnable in his court and began a new era.

The first writ in Glanville's *Treatise* is the writ *Precipe:*

> When anyone complains to the King or his Justices concerning his fee or his free tenement, if the complaint be such that it ought, or the lord King wills, that it be dealt with in his court, then he who sues shall have such writ of summons:—The King to the Sheriff greeting, Command N. that justly and without delay he restore to R. one hide of land in that village whence R. complains that he has disseised him. And unless he does, summon him by good summoners to be before me or my justices on the morrow of the close of Easter at that place to show wherefore he has not done it, and have there the summoners and this writ. Witness, R. de Glanville at Clarendon.

Writs *precipe,* being returnable, did not survive in the sheriffs' archives. They were never directed to religious houses and so were never copied into monastic cartularies and never filtered through into the great houses of those who obtained monastic property and title deeds. The earliest returned writs surviving in the Public Record Office are a burst file from the Michaelmas term 1199, with one or two strays from the earlier years of Richard I.[26] The writs in Glanville must date from about 1187. There is no evidence when the writ *precipe* was first drafted. It may well be as old as the writ of right. If so, by drafting the formula of the returnable writ, the King had already in the early years of his reign taken a long step towards the more elaborate formulas needed for the writ which initiated the assize of novel disseisin.

Professor van Caenegem has recently argued strongly that the history of this most famous action begins with the writs by which William I and William II ordered that individual religious houses or, indeed, individuals, who have complained to the King of disseisin shall be reseised of their land.[27] He includes in his list of writs of novel disseisin examples of such writs of reseisin issued by all the Norman kings. But he is not able to produce one which appoints a day for the hearing of the action, indicates the way it shall be dealt with, or instructs the recipient of

[26] *Pleas before the King . . .,* 1. These writs are discussed in the Introduction, pp. 5-33. They are printed in full, dated and fully annotated, pp. 350-418, with photographs of twelve writs.

[27] *Writs,* pp. 444-464.

the writ to send men to view the land at issue and to appear when the case is heard with the summoners and the writ. Not one of these early writs is, in fact, returnable. The problem that faced the Norman kings was the same as that which faced Henry II—the restoration of seisin to one unjustly disseised, but by 1170 the method of dealing with the problem has been revolutionised. There is no continuity between the Norman writs of reseisin and the writ of novel disseisin taken from Glanville with which van Caenegem ends his list.

The earliest writs of Henry II styled writs of novel disseisin by van Caenegem show no advance on those of his Norman predecessors. But there is evidence that the King's mind was moving towards a preliminary action concerning merely the seisin and not the right, and also towards a greater use of local recognitors, just as it was moving towards the returnable writ. The overriding necessity of securing peace and order was the spur. A notification by Archbishop Theobald of Canterbury (1154-1161) of the way in which a controversy between a certain Peter and the canons of St. Paul's had been ended "by judgment of our court by the king's command" is revealing. Peter had been claiming land at Wimbledon and Barnes on the grounds that his father had possessed it at the time of Henry I's death and that his mother had held it afterwards until she was violently ejected. But Peter made "no mention of inheritance or fee" nor "produced either documents or witnesses nor offered any present, nor promised any future proof." Therefore

> the court judged that he ought no longer to seek seisin. And since Peter had wearied the canons now for three years and always failed in proof, they are absolved from the petition of seisin which he would have had if he had abounded in proof, reserving nevertheless the question of right if Peter should think fit to plead it.[28]

This is a difficult document, but it is sufficient proof that at least six years before the critical date 1166 the King has commanded that a preliminary action which shall not bar a subsequent plea of right shall be heard in a lord's court.

One of the many writs of Henry II in favour of the church of Lincoln is in point here. Indeed, van Caenegem prints it as

[28] Avrom Saltman, *Theobald, Archbishop of Canterbury* (London, 1956), p. 390.

a writ of novel disseisin.[29] The King commanded the Sheriff to cause "a recognition to be made by the oath of lawful citizens of Lincoln if the canons were seised" of certain land "in the year and day King Henry my grandfather was alive and dead, and afterwards were unjustly and without judgment disseised." In this case without delay "they shall be justly and honourably reseised thereof and shall hold well and in peace, and justly and freely, quietly and honourably, and they shall not be impleaded therein until I return to England unless I command." Here, in a writ which was probably issued between March and May, 1165,[30] the King clearly envisages the possibility of future litigation even after local men have given their verdict. The writ is not returnable, nor is the plea to be dealt with by royal justices, but it is a little nearer what Glanville called the *beneficium* of novel disseisin.[31]

The first indication of this new action appears in the pipe roll of 1166 which contains the first returns sent in by the judges who enforced the Assize of Clarendon. The Assize as we have it [32] contains no suggestion that the King has instructed the judges to make any enquiries about disseisins, and pipe rolls are dangerous material from which to make far-reaching deductions about matters which were no concern of pipe roll

29 *Writs*, p. 462, no. 96.

30 *Registrum Antiquissimum* 1: p. 100. Canon Foster dated this writ 1155-1166. Delisle. *Recueil* 1: p. 513, who printed it from a photograph taken by H. E. Salter, dated it 1156-1172/3. The writ is dated at Tinchebrai. Eyton *Itin.* records no other writs dated there in the first half of the reign. It must have been issued during the King's visit to Normandy, August, 1158-January, 1163, or his visit, March-May, 1165, the latter being more likely. Manasser Biset, who witnessed the writ, does not seem to have witnessed documents issued later than 1166, but he did not die until ten years later. He received £40 annually from Rockbourne, Hants; but in the Pipe Roll of 1177, his son is receiving it. *Pipe Roll 23 Henry II, p.* 165.

31 One Pipe Roll debt should be mentioned, although its background and circumstances are unknown. On the Shropshire account in 4 *Henry II*, 1158, p. 170, ed. J. Hunter for the Record Commission (1844), there first occurs the entry "Richard de Bealmes owes 10 marks for a plea of seisin." The debt was recorded in the previous year merely as "pro loquela" *Pipe Roll 3 Henry II*, p. 89. It was pardoned in 1160. *Pipe Roll 6 Henry II*, p. 26.

32 The Royal manuscript of Howden's chronicle, which Stubbs judged to have been written in the early thirteenth century at the latest, and probably in the last decade of the twelfth, and Bodleian Library, Rawlinson MS C 641, which Stubbs thought was a twelfth-century hand. I do not, myself, think that it should be dated earlier than about 1220. See, *Pleas before the King* . . . 1: pp. 151-153. See p. 42 below.

clerks intent only on recording the amount of money collected for, or due to the King. In 1166 none of these clerks, whether they worked in the exchequer on the pipe rolls or followed the justices round the country recording the pleas which came before them, had any store of experience to guide them. The main point of their work was financial. It was only gradually that they acquired the skill which enabled their successors to indicate in a few revealing words the precise reason for a judicial debt.

Nevertheless, the hints the pipe rolls give about the origin of the momentous action of novel disseisin must be scrutinised, for they are all that remains. Among the debts resulting from the work of the judges who enforced the assize are payments for "disseisin," [33] for "disseisin upon the king's writ," [34] "disseisin upon the king's assize," [35] "unjust disseisin," [36] "for disseising a girl of her land unjustly," [37] and "because he broke a house upon the assize." [38] An offer of 50 marks on the Yorkshire account by Gerold the canon "that he may keep his seisin until judgment is made therein" [39] may possibly relate to the same order. Were it not that itinerant justices imposed collective amercements on Lifton hundred, Devon, for concealing disseisin,[40] and on "Gara Hugonis de Mara," Wilts, for "disseisin concealed and afterwards acknowledged" [41] historians would have had little hesitation in saying that the writ of novel disseisin and the action itself dated from 1166. As it is they generally pass lightly over this problem. When nearly forty years ago I wrote the chapter on Henry II in the *Cambridge Medieval History* I suggested that Henry II at first made his benefits compulsory before he offered his writs for sale,[42] but now I do not feel so sure. Pro-

[33] *Pipe Roll 12 Henry II*, p. 14.

[34] *Ibid.*, pp. 7, 10.

[35] *Ibid.*, p. 65.

[36] *Ibid.*, p. 4.

[37] *Ibid.*, p. 98.

[38] *Ibid.*, p. 8.

[39] *Ibid.*, p. 41.

[40] *Pipe Roll 14 Henry II*, p. 133.

[41] *Ibid.*, p. 164. The men of Tixover who refused to swear the King's assize, *Pipe Roll 12 Henry II*, p. 65, presumably refused to make the full presentments required of them by the Assize of Clarendon touching pleas of the crown.

[42] 5: pp. 586-587. This was before G. J. Turner had explained the meaning of writs, of course, of grace, and of light grace. Forty years ago, historians assumed that payments were made for judicial writs, although not all of them were entered in the Pipe Rolls.

fessor van Caenegem takes the same view and follows it to the logical conclusion that disseisin had been made a matter of presentment by hundred-jurors and therefore a plea of the crown. But thus casually to create a new crown plea and equally casually to allow it to become a civil action does not seem to me consonant with the general course of development of royal justice under Henry II.

There is one collective debt first recorded in the Pipe Roll of 14 Henry II, 1168, which may give a hint about the way in which the writ of novel disseisin was introduced to the knowledge of the freemen who assembled before the king's judges. The Sheriff of Sussex accounted in 1168 for 20 shillings from the hundred of *Ristona* for a plea concealed, paying 10 shillings.[43] In the pipe roll of the next year the debt is still recorded as "10 shillings for a plea concealed." [44] In 1170, that is, the Pipe Roll of 16 Henry II the debt, still owed, with no attempt to reduce it further, is described as "10 shillings for disseisin concealed." [45] It may be possible that the judges who enforced the Assize of Clarendon asked of those assembled before them what pleas of disseisin were before the local courts at that moment so that the plaintiffs could be given the opportunity of enjoying the new action available on the King's new writ. If this procedure were adopted it can only have been used as a means of promulgating information about the new civil action, not as a means of initiating a new crown plea.

In 1176 the Assize of Clarendon was reissued in stronger terms at Northampton. It included the carefully drawn directions which lie behind the assize of mort d'ancestor and also instructed the judges to enquire into "disseisins made upon the assize from the time when the lord King came into England after peace had been made between him and the King his son.[46] Professor van Caenegem, having examined the pipe rolls with meticulous care and made graphs [47] of the debts incurred for disseisins and other identifiable actions, concludes that the two

[43] *Pipe Roll 14 Henry II*, p. 196.

[44] *Pipe Roll 15 Henry II*, p. 58.

[45] *Pipe Roll 16 Henry II*, p. 138.

[46] Stubbs, *Charters*, p. 180.

[47] In justice to van Caenegem, I should add that he, again and again, stresses the inevitable limitations of these graphs. The large number of debts in the early pipe rolls for which no reason is assigned makes the rolls unsatisfactory evidence about the problems of judicial development.

great assizes of the reign, Clarendon in 1166 and Northampton in 1176 mark "two great repressions of unjust disseisins,"[48] which he frequently describes as "criminalistic."[49] He makes no clear suggestion as to the date when anyone disseised of his free tenement could automatically obtain a writ of novel disseisin to bring a civil action for its recovery beyond assigning it to the last decade of Henry II's reign and saying that "in all probability the wording of the writ as it stands in Glanville was very recent."[50] According to him the same process was followed in setting up the assize of mort d'ancestor, the origins of which have "a criminalistic tinge." "What," he says, "was probably intended as a single police drive against lords of ill-will, became under the pressure of the public a civil action open to litigants."[51]

He assumes that the enquiry into disseisins authorised in 1166 was over by 1171 and that the second enquiry "swept over the country" between 1175 and 1178 and that thereafter "repression of disseisins by royal justices ceased to be spasmodic and became a regular technique."[52] His explanation of how this was achieved seems far from convincing. He also fails to explain why the second drive against disseisins, which he associates with the Assize of Northampton of January, 1176, was already showing results in the Pipe Roll of 1175. In 1167 a full-scale forest eyre meant that other judicial visitations were in abeyance so that only one belated new payment for disseisin is

[48] *Writs*, p. 288.

[49] *Ibid.*, pp. 285, 289, 292, 303. Van Caenegem argues that "the last criminal tinge which *novel disseisin* kept" was the fact that "final concords in an action of novel disseisin were very rare, although in ordinary civil actions and even in the younger petty assizes they were common enough." This overlooks the fact that final concords which ended genuine litigation were made in order to bring a more speedy end to a plea. The assize of novel disseisin was in the twelfth and early thirteenth centuries so rapid as to make a final concord unnecessary. Canon Foster suggested *Final Concords* **2**, Lincoln Record Society, vol. **17** (1920): p. xxi, that, "Since a plea of novel disseisin presupposed a breach of the king's peace, no one whose aim was to obtain a final concord would begin his action by suing out a writ of novel disseisin." Mrs. Walker has shown that a genuine action of novel disseisin was occasionally followed by a final concord without the issue of a new writ. *Feet of Fines, Lincolnshire, 1199-1216*, ed. M. S. Walker, Pipe Roll Society, n.s. **29** (1954): pp. xvii, xviii.

[50] *Ibid.*, p. 301.

[51] *Ibid.*, p. 319.

[52] *Ibid.*, p. 288.

recorded.[53] Similarly during the four years 1171-1174 political events prevented justices from going out on eyre. The Becket murder and its aftermath, the Irish expedition of 1172 with the need to raise money for it by general taxation, followed by the rebellion of the King's sons, made it impossible to maintain steady judicial eyres throughout the land. But the Assize of Clarendon remained in force as the eyre of 1175 shows. The clause about disseisins in the Assize of Northampton was necessary to change the time-limit within which the action was available, to exclude, that is, disseisins done in time of war from the scope of the enquiry.

To the question "when was the writ of novel disseisin drafted and made generally available to litigants?" Dr van Caenegem would answer "Not long before Glanville's *Treatise* was written," [54] but I see no reason why the writ should not have been drafted before the Assize of Clarendon was promulgated. To find the precise wording of difficult new writs with centuries of history before them was no new task for Henry II and his advisers in 1166. The writ of right and the writ *precipe* had been launched. The writ *utrum* had been available since the Constitutions of Clarendon were issued in 1164. The Assize of Clarendon itself cannot have been produced without long and even anxious consultations between the King and his advisers, particularly with his chief justiciar, Richard de Luci. Bracton has preserved the office tradition of the sleepless nights passed in formulating the writ of novel disseisin. The excitement of launching a new form of action, and, indeed, a new policy towards an old problem, implicit in this tradition makes it unlikely that the King would have been content to leave the problem touched upon, but not settled, by making disseisin a matter of presentment in February, 1166, before crossing the Channel for a four-years stay in March. Dr. van Caenegem suggests that the absence of any mention of the action in the Assize of Clarendon may be explained by regarding the enquiry into disseisins as a last minute decision taken as the justices were about to set out on their eyre.[55] But a last-minute decision

[53] The sheriff of Wiltshire paid part of the debt of 20 marks imposed on Edulf of Winterbourne for disseisin contrary to the assize, *Pipe Roll 13 Henry II*, p. 134.

[54] *Writs*, p. 301. "In all probability, its wording, as it stands in Glanville, was very recent."

[55] *Ibid.*, p. 284.

The earliest returned writ of novel disseisin surviving in The Public Record Office, KB 136/1/1 No. 58. Printed with the permission of the Controller of Her Majesty's Stationery Office. This writ is printed in *Pleas before the King* 1: pp. 400–401. At that time four vertical and one nearly horizontal marks made by folding up the writ for delivery were clearly visible. The hole presumably made in court when the document was filed can still be seen near the left margin.

This plea should have been dealt with at Westminster in the Michaelmas term 1199, but nothing about it can be found on the rolls of the Michaelmas term or the following Hilary term 1200. In the Easter term 1200 Bridmar, described as Brichmer the miller, came and withdrew himself from the writ of novel disseisin which he had brought against Walter Guntard touching a mill and 23 acres in Welton and quitclaimed them for ever to the same Walter for 5 marks of silver and put himself in mercy (*Rot. Cur. Reg.* 2: p. 187). Bridmar had evidently combined the trades of smith, miller and small-holder. The delay in the settlement of the plea is undoubtedly due to the protracted negotiations between the parties which ended in the agreement recorded in the roll of the Easter term. Bridmar had, in effect, sold out to Walter Guntard, for his amercement due to the king would not amount to more than half a mark. There is no evidence that the parties made a final concord, but they probably ratified their agreement by a document made by a local clerk.

G. filius Petri, comes Essex' vicecomiti Norf' Salutem. Questus est nobis Bridmar' faber quod Walterus Guntard, iniuste et sine judicio dissaisiuit eum de libero tenemento suo in Walton' post festum sancti Michaelis proximo ante coronationem domini Regis. Et ideo tibi precipimus quod si idem Bridmar' fecerit te securum de clamore suo prosequendo tunc facias tenementum illud resaisiri de catallis que in eo capta fuerunt . et ipsum tenementum cum catallis esse in pace usque ad festum sancti Michaelis in j mensem et interim facias xii liberos et legales homines de visneto illo uidere tenementum illud et nomina illorum inbreuiari. Et summone eos per bonos summonitores quod sint coram nobis apud Westmonasterium ad predictum terminum parati facere inde recognitionem . et pone per vadium et saluos plegios predictum Walterum uel balliuum suum si ipse inuentus non fuerit quod tunc sit ibi auditurus illam recognitionem . et habeas ibi summonitores et hoc breue et nomina plegiorum. Teste . G. de Bocland' apud Westmonasterium iiij die Augusti per magistrum Radulfum.

Geoffrey fitz Peter Earl of Essex to the Sheriff of Norfolk Greeting. Bridmar the smith has complained to us that Walter Guntard has disseised him unjustly and without judgment of his free tenement in Welton after the Michaelmas next before the coronation of the lord King. And therefore we command you that if the same Bridmar shall give you security of following up his plaint that you then cause that tenement to be reseised of the chattels which were taken in it, and that tenement, with the chattels, to be in peace until a month from Michaelmas, and meanwhile cause twelve free and lawful men of that neighbourhood to view that tenement, and their names to be enrolled. And summon them by good summoners to be before us at Westminister at the aforesaid term ready to make recognition therein, and put the aforesaid Walter, or his bailiff if he shall not be found, by gage and safe pledges to be there then to hear that recognition, and have there the summoners and this writ and the names of the pledges. Witness, Geoffrey of Buckland, at Westminster on 4 August, by master Ralf.

seems a violent and unnecessary explanation of what may well be a clerical error.[56] When the earlier of the two surviving copies of the Assize was written about 1200 the origins of the action of novel disseisin had long passed into history. Even if in 1166 disseisin, like serious crime, had been made a matter for presentment, nevertheless, it also remained, as it always had been, a matter for plaint. The elaborate writ of novel disseisin recognises this in its opening words *Questus est nobis.* The strong dislike shown in judicial circles in the early eyres after the abolition of the ordeal for using the presenting jury as a trial jury supports the argument that judges were unlikely to have followed this practice in regard to disseisins in 1166 and subsequent years.[57] In the course of the eyres enforcing the Assize of Clarendon (1166-1175) the availability of the new writ must have become known to all the King's free subjects.

It is worth while to scrutinize the pipe rolls of the early years after the Assize of Clarendon to see whether they provide any evidence either of a developing action of novel disseisin [58] or of the initiation of the action by the man disseised. In 1168 there are four debts which suggest that nuisance,[59] not full disseisin; was the offence—one for a ditch made upon the assize,[60] one for a ditch unjustly made,[61] and two for a boundary broken upon the assize.[62] In the Devon account on the same roll Richard son of William the dispenser owed 5 marks "for having the assize touching the land which Roger Martel holds." [63] More-

[56] *Pleas before the King* . . . 1: pp. 151-153.

[57] See, *Pleas of the Crown for the county of Gloucester,* ed. F. W. Maitland (1884), pp. xxxvii ff. *Rolls of the Justices in eyre for Gloucestershire. . . ., 1221-1222,* ed. D. M. Stenton, Selden Society, **59** (1940): pp. lviii ff.

[58] The conservatism of the Pipe Roll clerks meant that they were slow to use the names, now familiarly given to writs or actions (see *Pipe Roll 6 John,* pp. xxiii-xxiv. They do not use the phrase "pro nova disseisina" before 1181, *Pipe Roll 27 Henry II,* pp. 26, 44. Ten years later they at last record two payments for a "writ of novel disseisin," *Pipe Roll 3 Richard I,* pp. 103, 122. See also *Writs,* p. 294.

[59] G. J. Turner suggests that the writ of nuisance was framed at the same time as the writ of novel disseisin or soon afterwards, *Brevia Placitata,* p. cxix. Already in 1166 Earl Geoffrey and Richard de Luci had imposed an amercement of a mark for "a pool broken upon the assize" in Essex, *Pipe Roll 12 Henry II,* p. 128.

[60] *Pipe Roll 14 Henry II,* p. 38.

[61] *Ibid.,* p. 219.

[62] *Ibid.,* p. 107.

[63] *Ibid.,* p. 137.

over, every eyre roll of John's reign shows many cases of novel disseisin which were unsuccessful and result in an amercement "for a false claim." It is extremely likely that some at least of the increasing number of debts for a false claim which appear on the pipe rolls from 1166 onwards are owed by men who have failed in an action of novel disseisin. Certainly, the emphasis in the pipe rolls is passing to the plaintiff. Since a successful action of novel disseisin secured damages from the defeated party, many men in later years seem to have brought an action of novel disseisin when they should properly have brought some other form of plea. It may be acknowledged that in these early years some of the debts for a false claim may be due for an appeal of crime which has been unsuccessful. But that some of the steadily increasing number of debts for failure to prosecute an undefined claim were charged on men who had failed to follow up a plea of novel disseisin is certain. Herbert the smith who owed a mark for a false claim which he made as a freeman although he was a rustic [64] and the Abbot of Peterborough's men of Quadring, who, in the same year, 1170, owed a mark for seeking an assize as freemen when they were rustics [65] are examples in point. Similarly, Alan Malet's amercement before the same justices for "failure of a claim touching the assize" [66] indicates an assize of novel disseisin brought by him in vain. The roll for 1175 contains a number of amercements for "a recognition," one "for having an assize," one "that he may have a recognition and seisin of land . . . and he has seisin." It is hard to believe that the action of novel disseisin was still inchoate in 1170.

The history of the assize of mort d'ancestor begins with the Assize of Northampton of 1176. A long clause sets out the heir's right to hold as his father had held on the day of his death and to have his father's chattels to carry out the terms of his will. If the lord refuses to allow this, the judges are instructed to cause a recognition about the dead man's seisin to be made by twelve lawful men and to make restitution to the heir in accordance with the verdict.

[64] *Pipe Roll 16 Henry II*, p. 150.
[65] *Ibid.*, p. 149.
[66] *Ibid.*, p. 148.

The clause runs:

Also if any free tenant shall die his heirs shall remain in such seisin as his father had on the day he was alive and dead of his fee, and they shall have his chattels whence they shall make the will of the dead; and they shall afterwards seek his lord and do to him in regard to relief and other things what they owe touching his fee. And if the heir is under age, the lord of the fee shall take his homage and hold him in wardship as long as he ought. The other lords, if there are several shall receive his homage and he shall do to them what he ought. And the wife of the dead man shall have her dower and the share of the chattels which belong to her. And if the lord of the fee denies to the heirs of the dead man the seisin of the dead man which they ask, the justices of the lord king shall cause recognition to be made by twelve lawful men what seisin the dead man had on the day he was alive and dead, and as it shall have been recognised, so it shall be restored to the heirs. And if anyone acts contrary to this and is convicted thereof, let him remain in the king's mercy.[67]

Curiously enough the pipe rolls provide no evidence about any action before the justices on this clause in 1176 or the two following years. It is not until 1179 that any hint of the assize appears. Then Henry de Manerio accounted for 80 marks for seisin of the land of his wife's father [68] and Hugh de Stanton paid 6 marks for the same reason.[69] In the next year more fines appear on the roll; three concern an uncle's land,[70] one a grandmother's,[71] two a father's,[72] and one a wife's father's.[73] All these are payments made or promised to the King for having the plea. None are amercements imposed on the lord for refusing seisin to an heir of one of his tenants. This slow beginning is the natural response to a new action to be begun by writ acquired from the Chancery and dealing specifically with the feudal relationship between lord and man. There can be no doubt that writs of mort d'ancestor had already been drafted for the use of litigants when the judges went out on eyre in 1176 to enforce the Assize of Northampton. It needed a little time for indi-

[67] Stubbs, *Charters*, pp. 179-180.
[68] *Pipe Roll 25 Henry II*, p. 28.
[69] *Ibid.*, p. 82.
[70] *Pipe Roll 26 Henry II*, pp. 6, 80.
[71] *Ibid.*, p. 41.
[72] *Ibid.*, pp. 14, 57.
[73] *Ibid.*, p. 73.

viduals who could not get their inheritances from their lords to realise the benefits of the new action. Both these new and momentous actions, novel disseisin and mort d'ancestor, had still to gather round them through daily practice in the courts the body of rules which can be seen in operation in the eyre rolls of the reign of John.

Curiously enough, Glanville discussed the assize of novel disseisin last of all the actions touching seisin only which "from a beneficial constitution of the kingdom called an assize are generally settled by recognition."[74] He discussed first of all the assize of mort d'ancestor round which many regulations had already been established in practice during the eleven years in which it had been available. Glanville sets out the rules with beautiful concision and supplies examples of the writs of slightly varying formula which had been drafted to suit the different circumstances of litigants. The ancestor might have died "his own death," or on Crusade, or he may have died to the world by entering religion. The heir might be a minor or the tenant of the land might be a minor. If the plaintiff were a minor the plea could proceed, but if the tenant were a minor the plea awaited his age. The ancestor must have died within the assize, that is, since the King's first coronation, and he must have held the land "as of fee" for the assize to be successful. All the writs in Glanville assume that the ancestor from whom the land should descend is a father. In practice, he could be either father, mother, brother, sister, but no more distant kin. No longer as in 1180 was it possible to purchase a recognition touching the death of a grandmother.[75]

From mort d'ancestor Glanville proceeds to the assize of darrein presentment, the last of the four great possessory actions of Henry II's reign to be made available. The Lateran Council of 1179 authorised the diocesan bishop to intervene if, after six months, a patron had not appointed a successor to a vacant benefice. It is possible that the writ was more hastily drafted than the writs which initiated the two more famous actions. It certainly worked less well. The writ which Glanville preserves orders the sheriff to summon twelve free and lawful men to be before the King or his justices to declare on oath which patron

[74] *Glanvill,* Book xiii, pp. 157-158.
[75] See above, p. 44.

presented the last parson, who is dead, to the said church. On the jurors' verdict he or his heir presented again and the parson so presented and properly instituted by the bishop retained the benefice even if the opposing party thereafter won a plea of right. As the action appears in the earliest surviving writs and plea rolls the question put to the jurors was "which patron in time of peace presented the last parson." As well as omitting the words "in time of peace" Glanville's writ also omits the instruction to the sheriff that he shall cause the recognitors to view the church.[76] It is possible that both these omissions were due to copyists, although the clerks who transcribed registers of writs and made copies of such works as Glanville were working for clients who needed precision in just such points as these. Glanville considers what shall be done if the plaintiff's ancestor made the last presentation but afterwards gave the fee to which the advowson belonged to the tenant or his ancestor by a good title. He says that either party can have a recognition on this point. Complications often arose in this action because since the parson had been presented the patron had given the advowson to a religious house. Many of these gifts were made in the last twenty years of the twelfth century, sometimes on the deathbed of the giver. Hence the rule was introduced into the 1217 Great Charter that the assize of darrein presentment shall always be taken before justices of the bench and there terminated.

He deals next, even more briefly, with the recognition *utrum*, whether land is free alms or lay fee. This was in point of date the first of all the assizes, for it was set out in the Constitutions of Clarendon which purported to state the relations between church and state which had been observed in Henry I's reign. The clause in the Constitutions was carefully drafted to allow the plaintiff in such a suit to be either a clerk or a layman, but in the case begun by Glanville's only writ *utrum* the plaintiff was a clerk. He notes that if by the recognition a tenement was proved to be an ecclesiastical fee it can never afterwards be treated as a lay fee. Although almost every parish church had its glebe, acquired by gifts of land in free alms, the number of these assizes was never at this period high either in the eyres or at Westminster. This may be why individual judges, who had

[76] *Pleas before the King or his Justices* I, p. 23.

few means of finding out save by talk between themselves, how tricky problems were dealt with in their absence by their fellows, tended to be inconsistent in their treatment of assizes *utrum*. The heads of religious houses generally preferred to use the layman's forms of action, although in the middle of John's reign the Abbot of Westminster sued by the Prior of Bicester for a virgate of land as the free alms of Launton church, Oxfordshire, chose to plead that the land had been given in free alms to Westminster by King Edward the Confessor, and the plea went to court Christian.[77] Despite the writs of prohibition, of which Glanville provides examples, there is little evidence of rivalry between lay and ecclesiastical courts in the twelfth century. Joslen Bud was amerced 10 marks by justices in eyre in Lincolnshire in 1188 because he drew a plea belonging to the church court into lay fee.[78] By Bracton's day the assize *utrum* had developed into a proprietary action in the royal court available to the parish priest deprived of his glebe. It had become the parson's writ of right.

The pipe rolls of Henry II's later years, beginning with 1175, reflect the ever-increasing volume of work before the royal courts of justice, but since no rolls of pleas survive nor any writs which initiated the actions the picture the pipe rolls give cannot be complete and may be wildly inaccurate.[79] One fact is certain. The King and his little group of learned judges were bending all their skill and experience towards shortening the slow process of cases through the courts. Slowness encouraged self-help, which might lead to serious disorder. The preliminary actions were certainly introduced with this end in view, as they doubtless were in ancient Rome. They were welcomed by all classes of free society, but by themselves they could not solve the whole problem. They could not take the place of the action for right. Dower gave rise to innumerable quarrels, which did not admit of preliminary actions. The general feeling that a man engaged in litigation should be present in court to conduct

[77] C.R.R. 4. p. 291, quoted in *Hist. of Eng. Law* 1: p. 248, n. 2, from *Placitorum Abbreviatio*, Record Commission (1811).

[78] *Pipe Roll 34 Henry II*, p. 74.

[79] The surviving fragment of the roll of pleas of the crown heard before justices itinerant in East Anglia in 1198 contains 76 cases, but only 25 of them produced debts entered on the Pipe Roll of 1199. See *Pleas before the King* . . . 1: p. 40.

his own suit had always meant that litigants were allowed much latitude in making excuses for non-attendance. To appoint an attorney was a privilege which only the court, originally only the King could grant. To the end of John's reign it was necessary for the principal to be present in court to make the appointment or to be visited by four knights specially ordered by the court to hear him make it. Only serious illness or absence on important business or crusade were considered to justify the appointment of an attorney who could win or lose on a litigant's behalf.

The rules governing essoins, or excuses for non-attendance in court, are generally brushed aside by modern writers as tedious medieval irrelevancies, but to contemporaries they were of vital importance, for by a judicious use of his essoins a tenant might drag out a plea of right for months or even years. The only publicly expressed rule about essoins of which the text has been preserved was part of the Inquest of Sheriffs of 1170 and is described in the only manuscript which preserves it as "the assize touching essoiners." [80] By this assize rules for royal, shire, and baronial courts were set out to ensure that only proper essoiners, prepared to give gage and pledge to have their principals at the day set for them, should be appointed. It is noteworthy that the King in 1170 showed no hesitation in establishing rules to improve the working of shire and baronial courts as well as his own royal courts. That this matter was dealt with in 1170, soon after the frequent eyres necessitated by the Assize of Clarendon had begun, suggests that the itinerant justices responsible for enforcing the assize had found confusion over essoins and essoiners a considerable handicap in their work. There is no evidence when other rules about essoins, clearly ennunciated by Glanville, were established, but the work had been done in time for the Treatise on the Laws and customs of the realm of England to be written by 1187.

One fact is clear; no new form of action could be introduced before the King and his advisers had determined the number of essoins it should carry. In his thirteenth book Glanville deals with matters "where seisin alone is in question" and voices a general rule that "in no recognition where seisin alone is in

[80] *Pleas before the King* . . . 1: pp. 150-170, with a frontispiece illustrating the only manuscript containing the assize of essoiners.

question are more than two essoins allowed." This rule governs not only the new forms of action but also inquests made by the consent of the parties on some question of seisin which might arise in a plea of right. The rule was of fundamental importance as a means of shortening what would otherwise be a long-drawn-out plea. The rule that "in a recognition of novel disseisin no essoin is permitted" must have been established before any writ of novel disseisin was issued. It is a fair assumption that the acceptance of this rule by the King and his advisers was one of the matters dealt with in those night watches of which Bracton preserves the memory. The fact that the law of essoins formed an integral part of the legal programme of Henry II is conclusive evidence that the two fundamental actions of novel disseisin and mort d'ancestor were from the first *beneficia* proceeding from the King through the chancery to the individual litigant. They were not matters for presentment by hundredal jurors, but civil actions to be brought by plaintiffs against tenants of the land sought.

Having provided the two preliminary actions of novel disseisin and mort d'ancestor for the protection of seisin and its safe transit to a dead man's heir the King could proceed to the next step of easing the burden of an action of right, without in any way lessening its solemnity. In 1179 by the Assize of Windsor he introduced the Grand Assize by which he made available at the choice of the tenant the use of a jury of knights instead of the duel as the proof of right to land.[81] It is doubtful whether the procedure by grand assize was ever as popular as the King and his judges expected. "A royal benefit granted to the people by the clemency of the prince," [82] it might seem from the angle of the bench, but it still took many sessions before a well-contested writ of right could wind its way through the jungle of essoins to a judicial sentence passed on the jurors' verdict. The tenant's position, already unduly favourable, was made even easier since he, and he alone, could choose a jury rather than a duel. Further developments in two directions were made during the 1180's. On the one hand judges encouraged the development of the final concord as a means of ending a plea

[81] J. H. Round, "The Date of the Grand Assize," *Eng. Hist. Rev.* **31** (1916): pp. 268-269.

[82] *Glanvill*, Book II, cap. 7, pp. 62-63.

of land by a solemn agreement under the authority of the court. On the other hand they could seek to isolate some point of seisin vital to the plaintiff's claim and obtain the agreement of both parties to put it to a jury. This would hasten matters since "in no recognition where seisin alone is in question are more than two essoins allowed."

Occasional payments noted in the pipe rolls illustrate the beginnings of this practice. Already in 1179 Warin of Pilsdon, Dorset, owed 40 shillings for an enquiry whether Burstock was a pledge of Warin de Halla.[83] In 1186 Gilbert de Wandeville offered 40 shillings for a recognition touching 16 virgates of land whether they were gage or fee,[84] and in 1188 William of Sevenhampton offered 100 shillings for a recognition whether the same William or Nicholas de Meduana were seised in demesne of the land of Knighton on the day of the duel between William and Robert Malherbe.[85] Only two essoins and a decision made on a point of seisin meant a far more rapid, if less conclusive, decision than a judgment in a fully pleaded action of right or a final concord. Such questions prepared the way for the great family of writs of entry which multiplied rapidly in the early years of Henry III. Glanville actually provides the formula of a writ instructing the Sheriff to command a man to whom land was pledged at a term which has expired to return the land and receive the money lent. This was the first approach to the writs of entry.[86] Through the reign of John the writ of entry *ad terminum qui preteriit* was brought in increasing numbers instead of a writ of right when a plaintiff wished to recover land which he himself or an ancestor of his had pledged for a term of years which had expired. Many other questions of seisin frequently arising in the courts could be cast into common form writs to suit the varying needs of litigants, but the date when any particular form of writ of entry became a writ of course is not easy to establish. In the eyre of Simon of Pattishall in 1202 a widow, Avice de Normanville, sought to recover land of her inheritance which she alleged had been alienated by her hus-

[83] *Pipe Roll 25 Henry II*, p. 71. The entry appears to be unfinished.
[84] *Pipe Roll 32 Henry II*, p. 9.
[85] *Pipe Roll 34 Henry II*, p. 163.
[86] Book x, cap. 9, p. 140. George E. Woodbine, "Cases in the New Curia Regis Rolls Affecting Old Rules in English Legal History," *Yale Law Journal* **39**: pp. 509-513.

band, whom in his life she could not gainsay. Against one tenant Avice offered to deraign by the duel performed by a free man of hers, but the case was settled by final concord. Against another tenant Avice offered deraignment by the duel, or, alternatively one mark to the King for a jury of lawful men to declare whether the tenant had entry through Avice's husband who had no right save through her.[87] The writ *cui in vita* was not yet a *breve de cursu.* The only date that can be set as marking the time when a particular writ of entry became a writ of course within this period comes from a note on the Close roll of 1205 that henceforward the writ of entry *sur disseisin* shall be a writ of course.[88]

Maitland noticed that the year 1175 seemed to mark the time when final concords in their traditional formulas begin to appear, but Mr. Salzman as long ago as 1910 pointed out that isolated documents of considerably earlier date showed that the traditional formulas found in final concords were by no means new in 1175.[89] That year is notable simply because it marks the beginning of more frequent judicial eyres which made it possible for men who could not afford to prosecute pleas far from home to enjoy the benefit of making a final concord before royal justices visiting their own shires. Since Maitland wrote, it has been possible to collect, largely from manuscript sources, over a hundred examples of final concords made during Henry II's reign. More will certainly be noticed as unprinted monastic cartularies are published and the archives of old families are systematically examined in their new homes, the County Record Offices. From 1181 onwards the pipe rolls show a rapid increase in the number of payments made for licence of being brought into agreement—*pro licencia concordandi.* In 1185 some counties produced so many offerings for the privilege that the pipe roll clerks collected the payments up together and even inserted a special heading touching gifts made to the lord King through the same justices for licence of being brought into agreement concerning a plea of land.[90] The sums paid for the privilege were rarely large, often half a mark from each party;

[87] *Earliest Lincolnshire Assize Rolls,* pp. lxxi-lxxii. *Pipe Roll 6 John,* pp. xxx-xxxi.

[88] *Rot. Lit. Claus.* **1**: p. 32.

[89] "Early Fines," *Eng. Hist. Rev.* **25** (1910): 708-710.

[90] *Pipe Roll 31 Henry II,* pp. 152 (Northumberland), 187 (Cumberland).

sometimes one mark or twenty shillings. The convenience of being able so cheaply and so quickly to reach a final settlement of a family quarrel or a longstanding dispute between neighbours soon led to the use of the final concord as a means of selling land or making a family settlement. The fine was found to be an extremely versatile instrument. When on that momentous Sunday, 16 July, 1195, Hubert Walter Archbishop of Canterbury and the other barons sitting with him at Westminster determined that in future final concords should be recorded in a triple chirograph so that a record of the agreement—the foot of the fine—could be handed to the Treasurer for preservation in the Treasury, the long history of the Feet of Fines was begun.

The demand for royal justice grew far more rapidly than the King or his judges can ever have expected. The contrast between the way which Chroniclers, even such a man as Roger of Howden, speak of judicial eyres as intolerable burdens and the way litigants flock to the chancery for writs is fantastic. "By these and other vexations, whether just or unjust," writes Howden, having entered into his chronicle the articles of the 1198 eyre, "the whole of England was reduced to poverty from sea to sea." [91] But during this eyre over 200 final concords were made by Norfolk litigants alone.[92] Howden may well have had no pleas which he wished to prosecute and like other folk he probably suffered financially from the taxation placed upon the shires by the judges during their eyre.[93] The volume of judicial business which faced groups of itinerant justices continued to increase. In 1202 the general eyre which began in June should have been over in time for the Michaelmas term at Westminster to open in the octave of Michaelmas, but it dragged on in the north until 3 December with no apparent pause for rest. The judges whose circuit was Lincoln, Leicester, Coventry, Northampton, Bedford, and Dunstable were not back at the bench until the middle of November. Those who visited East Anglia, Essex and Hertfordshire, Cambridgeshire and Huntingdonshire were recalled to Westminster when the Michaelmas term began

91 *Howden* **4**: p. 62.

92 *Feet of Fines, Norfolk, 1199-1202*, ed. Barbara Dodwell, Pipe Roll Society, n.s. **27** (1952).

93 *Pipe Roll 10 Richard I*, pp. xxv ff.

to man the bench and finish their eyre at Westminster.[94] That the vast mass of eyre rolls made up in the last years of Henry II have been destroyed and that pitifully few survive from the reigns of his sons is disastrous. But even as it is, sufficient evidence from the twelfth and early thirteenth centuries survives to show that it was Henry II with his returnable writs and his carefully built up bench of judges, through his own versatility and that of his great Justiciar, Rannulf de Glanville, who had started the wheel in perpetual motion which generated the English common law.

[94] *Pleas before the King* . . . 1, Section vi, pp. 140-149.

III. COURTS OF JUSTICE AND THE BEGINNING OF THE LEGAL PROFESSION

In 1066 William Duke of Normandy had conquered an ancient kingdom in which the foundations of the English common law were already firmly laid. Despite the diversity stressed by twelfth-century legal writers in the laws by which the men of Wessex, Mercia, and the Danelaw lived, there were strong influences making for unity. During the last centuries of the old English state, local courts of justice throughout the country had administered a law handed down through the knowledge and practice not only of the suitors who attended the courts but also the ealdormen and reeves appointed by the crown to preside over them. Throughout Anglo-Saxon history kings, whether in Kent, Mercia, or Wessex, had been legislators. They had studied the laws of their predecessors. King Alfred knew the lost laws of King Offa of Mercia and, even though these kings had their own laws written in their own tongue, they felt that they were legislating, as Bede said of Æthelbert of Kent "in the Roman fashion." Cnut's code was made for all his subjects, Danes as well as Englishmen, though he recognised that local customs might vary. Changes in the law were made known to local courts through the ealdormen and their deputies who presided over them. The shire courts, the riding courts, the hundred and wapentake courts provided a remarkably complete coverage for the judicial needs of the people and the administrative needs of the crown. For the day-to-day quarrels of neighbours their lord's hall moot sufficed. The more serious crimes, at least in theory, were preserved for the King's judgment or that of great magnates whom he had allowed to hear his pleas. They formed the basis on which a national criminal law would in later centuries be built.

In 1066 there was no legal profession although there were many men learned in the law administered in the local courts of justice,[1] and there was no judicial centre to supplement the activities of the migratory court and household of the King comparable to Westminster at the end of the twelfth century.

[1] E.g., The *causidici* at Abingdon were probably matched by others in every ancient religious house. *Abingdon Chron.* 2: p. 2.

But the technical responsibility of those who administered the law was fully recognised throughout the later Anglo-Saxon period. Edward the Elder's command to his reeves to "judge as just judgments as you most justly can and as the lawbooks," that is the code of his father King Alfred, "direct" does not stand alone. It confirms Asser's use of the word "judges" to describe the ealdormen and reeves who were set over local courts.[2] The fact that it is generally assumed that the suitors in these Anglo-Saxon courts were responsible for applying the law in individual cases does not mean that the courts lacked the guidance and control of an officer of the law, a judge, appointed by, and responsible to, the king. When William I separated secular and ecclesiastical justice so that the Bishop had his own court and no longer sat in the shire court with the Earl, the Sheriff came to inherit the presidency of the court, a position which only the constant oversight of the King and the traditional vigilance of the suitors could prevent its holder from magnifying into a judicial dignity.

Most of the officials who were administering the law in the shires before the rise of the sheriff have almost vanished from legal memory. Neither the rolls nor the law-books of the twelfth century take any account of them; and it is largely a matter of chance whether the private documents which mention them have attracted notice. Nevertheless, it is hard to avoid the impression that at least in the remoter parts of England their successors were playing a more important part than is generally allowed them, far into the thirteenth century. In the age of Bracton, for example, it was clearly an important question how far private courts of high justice could be entered by the official called the "sacrabar" when carrying out his pre-feudal duties as a public prosecutor in a shire or hundred.[3] At the date of the Great Charter, even Earl Rannulf of Chester, the greatest feudal lord in England, when defining the limits within which a lord can protect his man accused of crime, reserves the

[2] See Professor D. Whitelock's article on "Recent Work on Asser's Life of Alfred" in *Asser's Life of King Alfred*, ed. W. H. Stevenson (Oxford, 1959), pp. cxlv-cxlvi.

[3] Ff. 150*b* and 154*b*. The meaning of the word sacrabar has caused much discussion because of the different forms in which it appears. Its derivation from an O. Scand. sakaráberi (bearer of a suit) was demonstrated by Johannes C. H. R. Steenstrup, *Normannerne* (Copenhagen, 1882), part iv: pp. 330 ff.

right of the sacrabar to pursue him.[4] In Yorkshire a few years earlier Peter de Brus places the process begun by the "sacrabord" beside the judgment of the wapentake among the reasons which may bring his knights and free tenants into his court of Langbargh wapentake.[5] In Lincolnshire: a lord of no more than local consequence includes the sacrabar in an otherwise commonplace list of general exemptions from suits of court, customs and demands; [6] more positively, another minor lord, in three separate charters stipulates that a tenant must make a special appearance in his court if the sacrabar demands his presence; [7] a priory releases a tenant from the burden of attending all inquests in its own court except those held at the instance of the sacrabar, in cases to which the tenant or his heirs are parties, or under the king's writ.[8] It is more remarkable that a thirteenth-century custumal declares that no one shall engage in pleading in the port of Wainfleet "save through the sacrabar and by gage and pledge." [9] But despite these signs of life, when Bracton laid down his pen, which faltered somewhat as he approached the sacrabar,[10] itinerant justices were steadily turning him into a fading memory rather than an active participant in the administration of the law.

How much litigation the new feudal courts immediately drew from the old courts of shire and hundred can only be a matter of speculation. Much of the work of the new honorial courts was itself new litigation between new men and it was at their peril that these new men, who had acquired the lands and rights of their predecessors, could ignore the old courts, the custodians of legal and tenurial memory. It was with good reason that William I ordered all men to seek "the hundred and shire courts as our ancestors commanded" [11] and Henry I willed that all men should go to the shires and hundreds as they had in the

[4] *Chartulary of St. Werburgh, Chester,* ed. James Tait (Chetham Society, 1920), vol. **79**, New Series, part 1: p. 103.

[5] Quoted by Professor J. C. Holt from the *Guisborough Chartulary,* **1**: pp. 92-94, in his article "The Barons and the Great Charter," *Eng. Hist. Rev.* **70** (1955): 21.

[6] B. M. Stixwould Cartulary, f. 134. See Appendix II, 1.

[7] Quoted by F. M. Stenton, "The Danes in England," *Proceedings of the British Academy* **13** (1927): p. 235. See Appendix II, 2, 3 and 4.

[8] F. M. Stenton, *op. cit.*, p. 236.

[9] See Appendix II, 5.

[10] Ff. 150*b* and 154*b*.

[11] *Gesetze* **1**: p. 488.

time of King Edward.[12] The feudal courts could only hear pleas for land and deal with the petty quarrels between their own men. They could not, even the greatest of them, pronounce the sentence of outlawry or conduct ordeals. Their work could be inspected, at the request of a dissatisfied litigant who had obtained a royal writ, by the sheriff or an officer of his with four knights sent from the shire court to hear the conduct of a plea.[13] The fortunate survival of Henry I's famous writ to Bishop Samson, Urse d'Abitot and all the King's barons French and English of Worcestershire provides an authoritative definition of the relation between feudal and shire courts in civil pleas: a plea "touching the partition or seizure of lands"—*de divisione terrarum vel de preoccupatione*—"if between my demesne barons," that is, tenants in chief, "shall be treated in my court. If between the men of any baron of my honour, the plea shall be treated in the court of their lord, and if between the men of two lords it shall be treated in the shire court, and let this be done by the duel unless it stand over between them," [14] that is, unless the sentence falls to be delivered by default or unless the parties come to an agreement by licence of the court. This writ authorises the traditional English court to make use of the traditional Norman procedure already authorised by William I for dealing with pleas of land.

Within the traditional English courts of shire and hundred, men of modest estate held a responsible position in the interpretation of the law. The *justiciarii hundredi* who decreed that Gamel the miller of Culham should pay the Abbot of Abingdon five mancuses of pennies for his secret depredations on the Abbot's turves [15] were obviously drawn from the suitors of the hundred court. Justices of this type appear in several shires in the Pipe Roll of 1130 as *iudicatores* or *judices.* In Yorkshire the Sheriff accounted for 31 marks from nine *judicatores comitatus,* and for 336 marks and 5 shillings from

[12] Stubbs, *Charters,* p. 122.

[13] The process of tolt described by Glanville, book xii, cap. 7, was already established in the time of Abbot Gunter of Thorney (1075-1112). The writ initiating the process in this case was witnessed by Bishop Roger of Salisbury, and is dated by its editor 1107-1111. See Appendix III.

[14] Stubbs, *Charters,* p. 122.

[15] *Abingdon* 2: p. 118. This happened in the time of Abbot Faritius who died in 1117.

the "little judges and jurors." [16] In Suffolk the Sheriff accounted for £25 :15:0 from the "judges of the shire and hundreds." [17] In Lincolnshire "four judges of the Island," that is the Isle of Axholme, were charged with 8 marks.[18] The Sheriff of Buckingham paid 40 shillings on behalf of the judges of the borough of Buckingham.[19] The experiences of the "judges and jurors of Yorkshire" had been so unhappy that they offered £100 that "they might no more be judges nor jurors." [20] The only qualification of such "judges" [21] in the local courts was the possession of means sufficient to pay from their own substance any fines they might incur *si iusticiam sine iudicio dimittunt.*[22] Private charters prove the existence of large numbers of such men in twelfth-century England.

No regular and therefore adequate supervision of the local courts of justice could be carried out in early post-Conquest days. William I of necessity used his barons and household officers as his counsellors, his judges, and his sheriffs. Although he was able to employ the Old English royal secretariat, he was bound to increase it, largely with Norman clerks, into what was soon being described as his Chancery. In the reigns of the first two Norman kings there is no sign of any central court of justice more highly organised than a fluctuating and mobile *curia regis.* From time to time the kings charged trusted members of their council, both bishops and barons, to make specific investigations or hear important pleas, as their Saxon predecessors had done. Before the Conqueror died, his clerical staff had been sufficiently expanded to reduce the findings of the commissioners of baronial rank who conducted the Domesday Inquest into the two volumes of Domesday Book. In the second Anglo-Norman generation, this clerical staff produced in Rannulf Flambard a man whom contemporaries regarded as the King's chief financial and judicial minister—*Summus regiarum*

16 *Pipe Roll 31 Henry I,* pp. 27, 28.
17 *Ibid.,* p. 97.
18 *Ibid.,* p. 118.
19 *Ibid.,* p. 101.
20 *Ibid.,* p. 34.
21 There is no indication whether the little judges refer to the judges of wapentakes or suggest that in Yorkshire there existed an upper bench of suitors in the shire court.
22 *Gesetze* 1: 563.

procurator opum et justiciarius factus est [23] active, according to the Peterborough Chronicler, in stimulating the courts of justice throughout the land.[24] On two occasions under William II Rannulf is associated with two barons of the King's court, Hamon the dapifer and Urse d'Abitot, in a capacity implying that the three men were accustomed to act together in the King's executive business. On the first occasion, with the Bishop of Chichester, they are ordered by the King, as *justiciarios suos,* to put the abbey of Fécamp in the possession of the church of Steyning.[25] On the second occasion, with the Bishop of Lincoln, they are ordered, without any official description, to reassess the abbey of Thorney to public taxation.[26] On each occasion, the Bishop is brought into the group because the business concerns his diocese—leaving Rannulf and his two lay companions functioning as the King's agents in a way which contemporaries would think appropriately covered by the title *justiciarius.* Groups of men on whom the King will increasingly rely are beginning to form. But they cannot yet be seen engaged in missions which in the range or variety of their business anticipate the general eyres of the late twelfth century.

The accession of Henry I was soon followed by signs that intelligence of another order than administrative capacity was at work in the central government. Before 1108 the Exchequer was in being. The integration of this permanent financial bureau into the fluctuating group of ministers, through whom the King governed England is the outstanding achievement of Henry's reign. Long before its close, the barons of the exchequer were acting as a court of justice and their rolls were providing the King with a yearly record of the state of his finances. The visits of the sheriffs to render their accounts twice a year, and the intermittent visits of exchequer officials to sit as judges in the shire courts gave the King a new means of controlling the local administration of justice. No one has ever doubted that the principal agent in this momentous innovation was Roger the priest of Avranches cathedral [27] who had entered Henry's

23 *Orderic,* vol. iv, p. 107.

24 Ed. Cecily Clark, Oxford (1958), *sub anno* 1099, p. 27.

25 *Regesta* 1: p. 137, LXXIV.

26 *Ibid.,* p. 136, no. LXXII.

27 N. R. Ker, *English Manuscripts in the Century after the Norman Conquest* (Oxford, 1960), plate 9*a*.

service before his accession and received the bishopric of Salisbury from him in 1102. Although he was regent of England while the King was abroad after 1118, and at the centre of affairs until his dramatic fall in 1139, Roger of Salisbury is constitutionally an elusive figure. Contemporaries give him titles such as *provisor* or *procurator* which stress the financial side of his work. He himself generally uses his episcopal style in the writs which he issued on the King's behalf.[28] In fact, he was the King's *alter ego* in an age when the techniques of government were still experimental, and there was as yet no constitutional scheme into which he could be neatly fitted.

Nevertheless, an officer whom contemporaries could regard as the King's chief justiciar of England makes a fitful appearance in records coming from the central years of Henry's reign. Modern work on the justiciarship has left no serious room for doubt that this position was held by Ralf Basset until his death some years before 1130 and afterwards by Richard Basset his son.[29] Ralf Basset is thus described in records going back to the year 1116, and also in an account of his death, written in the monastery of Abingdon by one who was living there at the time. Richard Basset's far-reaching activity as a judge is proved by the Pipe Roll of 1130. By that date he had acquired by marriage the important midland honour of Robert de Buci, which raised him to baronial rank, and on which it is interesting to note that he had enfeoffed a tenant by the service "of finding for the justiciar a messenger to go through the whole of England." [30] It is more remarkable that even on his private business

[28] *Ancient Charters*, Pipe Roll Society, **10** (1888): p. 38, no. 22. R. episcopus Sar' Sibille que fuit uxor Pagani filii Johannis' Salutem. Precipimus tibi ex parte regis et mea quod . . . Date, 1135-1138. The late Mr. Charles Johnson expressed doubts as to the authenticity of the Reading charter issued by Bishop Roger as *regni Angliae procurator;* see D. M. Stenton, "Roger of Salisbury Regni Angliae Procurator," *Eng. Hist. Rev.* **39** (1924): 79-80, but he admitted that it and other charters under discussion "probably replace originals not materially different in substance." *Essays presented to James Tait* (Manchester, 1933), pp. 141-142.

[29] Ralf Basset died at Northampton while Vincent (died 1130) was abbot, *Abingdon* **2**: p. 170. It seems probable that he died in 1127. That this part of the Abingdon Chronicle was written by a contemporary was shown by F. M. Stenton, *The Early History of the Abbey of Abingdon* (Oxford, 1913), pp. 4-6. W. Farrer, *An Outline Itinerary of Henry I* (reprinted from *Eng. Hist. Rev.*, 1919), note to no. 541, states that Ralf Basset does not attest documents issued in England after the King's passage to Normandy in 1127. Richard Basset "does not usually attest" documents issued before 1127, *Regesta,* **2**, no. 1479.

[30] *The Leicestershire Survey c. A.D. 1130,* ed. C. F. Slade (Leicester, 1956), p. 15.

he used a seal which to all appearance symbolises his sense of his duty as a judge. It bore the device of a knight in full armour striking with his sword a rampant monster which grasps in its mouth a helpless, naked, figure. This interpretation has at least a respectable antiquity. It comes from Sir Simonds Dewes, an eminent member of the band of scholar-collectors who illuminate the seventeenth century, who acquired the seal and described it enthusiastically in his autobiography.[31] The *Leges Henrici Primi* show that judges of the period were capable of reflection upon the morality of the duties to which they were committed.[32] But no other of them is so far known to have advertised his conception of his office upon his seal.

The Pipe Roll of 1130 shows that Ralf Basset had been as active in holding pleas in the shires as his successors were in the days of Henry II and his sons. In Surrey,[33] Berkshire,[34] and Buckinghamshire[35] debts incurred in "old pleas" held before him are still entered on the roll. He had presided over forest pleas in Surrey[36] and pleas which are not yet "old pleas," but are certainly not new pleas, are recorded under Nottinghamshire and Derbyshire,[37] Lincolnshire,[38] Norfolk and Suffolk,[39] Berkshire,[40] Wiltshire,[41] London, and Middlesex.[42] Debts resulting from his work in Huntingdonshire have been discharged, but chronicle evidence shows that he had presided in the shire court there when an Englishman, Bricstan, was charged by a minor royal official, Robert Malarteis,[43] with concealing treasure trove, letting it out at interest and trying to enter Ely abbey

31 *Book of Seals*, pp. xvi-xvii, plate III.

32 F. M. Stenton, *The First Century of English Feudalism* (2nd ed. Oxford, 1961), pp. 220-221.

33 *Pipe Roll 31 Henry I*, p. 49.

34 *Ibid.*, p. 123.

35 *Ibid.*, p. 101. Richard, son of Alfred the butler, still owed 15 marks of his fine for sitting with Ralf Basset at crown pleas.

36 *Ibid.*, p. 49.

37 *Ibid.*, p. 9.

38 *Ibid.*, p. 114.

39 *Ibid.*, pp. 92, 96.

40 *Ibid.*, p. 124.

41 *Ibid.*, p. 19.

42 *Ibid.*, p. 145.

43 As "Malarteis" he was pardoned 5 shillings of Danegeld in Huntingdonshire and 3 shillings in Bedfordshire. *Pipe Roll 31 Henry I*, pp. 49, 104. A later generation of the same family was holding land at Washingley, Hunts, in 1167, *Pipe Roll 13 Henry II*, p. 166.

as a monk to avoid prosecution.[44] The Peterborough chronicler is the authority for the session held in Leicestershire late in 1124 before Ralf Basset "and the king's thegns" when forty thieves were hanged and six mutilated.[45] Between these pleas in which he was the trial judge, he might return to the king's court and join with its other members in deciding suits which the King had ordered to be heard there. In 1116, for example, he was sitting at Brampton near Huntingdon when the *curia regis* dismissed the claim of a certain Azo Wardeden to a rent of forty shillings against the Abbot of Peterborough.[46]

Not until Henry II has been more than ten years on the throne can a single pipe roll again display so much judicial activity as the Roll for 1130. It is not easy to extract accurate information about the eyres it displays because unlike later rolls the clerk did not, in the case of any eyre save the Yorkshire visitation of Walter Espec and Eustace fitz John, record judicial debts under a heading indicating the names of the judges who imposed them. The only subheading in every other county account in the earliest surviving pipe roll is that which indicates the *Nova Placita et Nove conventiones* for the year. Visitations which have left little mark on the roll, like William of Houghton's pleas in Suffolk[47] or those of Henry de Port and his fellows in Kent,[48] may well have taken place some years before. But the amercements imposed by Walkelin Wolf face and his fellows for assarts are only recorded in Berkshire and Surrey and in each county appear under the "new pleas" heading.[49] Similarly Walter of Gloucester appears as a forest judge only in Warwickshire with one debt recorded above and others below the "new pleas" heading.[50] Apart from these anomalous

[44] *Orderic* 3: pp. 123-133.

[45] Ed., Cecily Clark, *sub anno* 1124.

[46] Peterborough Cathedral, Henry of Pytchley's Book of Charters, f. v d. "Cuius quidem iudicii testes fuerunt atque iudices episcopus Saresberiensis atque episcopus Lincolniensis atque Hugo et Gillebertus uicecomites et Walterus de Gleoucestre et Radulfus Basset." I owe my knowledge of this manuscript to the late Mr. W. T. Mellows of Peterborough.

[47] *Pipe Roll 31 Henry I*, p. 96.

[48] *Ibid.*, p. 65. The editors of the *Regesta*, vol. ii, p. xix, suggest that William of Houghton and Henry de Port may have been acting as local justices (see p. 65, below), but considering that Henry de Port was acting with other justices this seems, at least in his case, unlikely.

[49] *Pipe Roll 31 Henry I*, pp. 124, 50.

[50] *Ibid.*, p. 107.

references to pleas the roll reveals at least five major visitations in addition to the work of Ralf Basset which had presumably taken place some years before. It must also be borne in mind that the pipe roll itself is incomplete.

In the far southwest Devon and Cornwall had been visited by Robert Arundel and his fellows, who appear to have heard both ordinary and forest pleas.[51] The membrane is much damaged, but it is apparent that in both shires a considerable number of judicial debts had been incurred. Since in later times the peninsula tended to have fewer visitations than nearer shires, it is highly probable that most if not all these debts may be attributed to Robert Arundel's eyre. In the west of England, Miles of Gloucester and Pain fitz John heard both ordinary pleas and pleas of the forest in Staffordshire,[52] Gloucestershire [53] and Pembroke.[54] It is impossible to attribute a date to these visits. The debts are not recorded under the "new pleas." Geoffrey of Glympton (de Clinton') and his fellows heard pleas in Yorkshire,[55] Nottinghamshire and Derbyshire,[56] Staffordshire,[57] Warwickshire,[58] Lincolnshire,[59] Norfolk and Suffolk,[60] Northamptonshire,[61] Huntingdonshire,[62] Buckinghamshire and Bedfordshire,[63] Berkshire and Wiltshire,[64] Essex,[65] Kent and Surrey,[66] and Sussex.[67] In some counties debts imposed by him for forest offences are also recorded. Such widespread

[51] *Ibid.*, pp. 154, 155, 159.

[52] *Ibid.*, pp. 73, 74.

[53] *Ibid.*, p. 78.

[54] *Ibid.*, p. 136.

[55] *Ibid.*, p. 26.

[56] *Ibid.*, pp. 8-10. These debts appear some above and some below the "new pleas" heading. This may indicate more than one visit or that the session overlapped from the previous to the current financial year.

[57] *Ibid.*, p. 74.

[58] *Ibid.*, p. 107. The two entries "de eisdem placitis" occur below the "new pleas" heading, but they probably belong to the forest pleas before W. of Gloucester from which one debt is entered on the same page above the "new pleas" heading.

[59] *Ibid.*, p. 112.

[60] *Ibid.*, pp. 93, 98.

[61] *Ibid.*, p. 83.

[62] *Ibid.*, p. 47.

[63] *Ibid.*, pp. 101, 103.

[64] *Ibid.*, pp. 123, 124, 17.

[65] *Ibid.*, pp. 55, 59.

[66] *Ibid.*, pp. 50, 65.

[67] *Ibid.*, p. 69.

visitations must represent more than one year's activities for an important royal servant with other responsibilities. Some of the debts imposed by Geoffrey in Essex and in Nottinghamshire and Derbyshire appear under the "new pleas" heading, but in all other shires they are entered above that heading and by later rules should represent debts incurred in previous years. Nevertheless, the position of all these debts on the roll and their volume seems, to me at any rate, to imply that they have not been owing for many years. Most of them probably go back no further than two or three years. In the Berkshire account, for example, Abbot Vincent of Abingdon's amercement of 60 marks is pardoned because he is dead.[68] He died in 1130, the year the pipe roll was made up after ten years as abbot. The impression the entry gives is that the debt first entered the roll in, say, 1128 or, more probably, 1129. Walter Espec and Eustace fitz John had recently toured the north, Yorkshire, where "the pleas of W. Espec and Eustace fitz John" [69] have a separate heading, Northumberland,[70] Durham,[71] Carlisle,[72] and Westmorland.[73] All the debts resulting from their work appear under the "new pleas" heading, but there seems no doubt that they began their eyre in 1128.[74] Richard Basset and William d'Albini Brito visited Lincolnshire,[75] Nor-

68 *Ibid.*, p. 123.
69 *Ibid.*, pp. 33, 34.
70 *Ibid.*, p. 35.
71 *Ibid.*, p. 132.
72 *Ibid.*, p. 142.
73 *Ibid.*, p. 143.
74 *Regesta* 2, no. 1561, p. 220, *Notitia* of a sworn inquest concerning the fishery of the Tyre made in the time of King Henry I and Bishop Rannulf (died September 5, 1128) in the presence of Walter Espec and Eustace fitz John, justices.
75 *Pipe Roll 31 Henry I*, pp. 114-121. A writ of Henry I addressed to William d'Albini, Richard Basset, and Aubrey de Vere and the Sheriff and all the King's ministers of Nottinghamshire must refer to this eyre, and shows that Aubrey de Vere, the Chamberlain, was one of the judges. The King orders that if the Bishop of Lincoln's wapentake of Newark defends itself as half a wapentake, they shall summon therefrom to the King's pleas and to the shire no more than two men as in the time of Bishop Robert, the Bishop's predecessor. *Registrum Antiquissimum* 1: p. 21, dated by the editor 1123-1135. That Aubrey de Vere was also an itinerant judge in East Anglia during this eyre is shown by the King's writ addressed to his justices, Richard Basset and Aubrey de Vere and his burgesses of Norwich, informing them that the livery formerly paid from the farm to Odlent shall in future be paid to the hospital of St. Paul in Norwich, *Regesta:* 2, no. 1608. These writs provide contemporary record confirmation of the claim made by Aubrey de Ver's son, William, that his father had acted as a royal judge, but they do not justify his statement that Aubrey was *totius Angliae justiciarius*. *The Itinerary of John Leland*, ed. T. Hearne (3rd ed. Oxford, 1769), 8: p. 47.

folk and Suffolk,[76] Leicestershire,[77] and Sussex,[78] probably in the summers of 1129 and 1130. William d'Albini seems to have been the leader in the sessions held in Lincolnshire and Richard Basset in Leicestershire and East Anglia. Richard Basset may well have visited Sussex without his fellow judges. All this shows that before 1130 the conception of a general eyre has been translated into fact and that during the middle years of the reign Ralf Basset had done most to prepare the way for its establishment.

But already by the year 1100 the increasing complexity of public business in the shires was creating problems which could not be settled by the intermittent dispatch of royal agents. In particular, it was becoming vital for the efficiency of local government to find some means of breaking down the concentration of functions—executive, judicial, financial, and military—which was turning the shire reeve of King Æthelræd's time into an officer of state more powerful than any but the greatest of Æthelræd's earls. A partial solution, which lasted for more than fifty years, was the removal of the pleas of the crown from the jurisdiction of the Sheriff, and the creation of a local justiciar in each shire or recognised group of shires with the specific duty of hearing them. This step had certainly been taken by the earliest years of Henry I. There is good evidence that William II had anticipated him in the statement of a memorandum from Ramsey abbey, that at a date which must fall between 1091 and 1095, Abbot Aldwin in a plea at Thetford had proved his right to a fat fish cast ashore in Norfolk against Ralf de Bellofago the sheriff and Ralf Passelew "justiciar of that province." [79] Ralf Passelew is the first known member of a family afterwards much employed in the king's service, which became important territorially by the acquistition of subtenancies in eastern England. But he, himself was in no sense a magnate, and, like the early Bassets, whom in position he much resembles, plainly rose to power because the kings of his time found him useful.

On the other hand, the work of the local justiciar could not

[76] *Ibid.*, pp. 94, 98.

[77] *Ibid.*, p. 88.

[78] *Ibid.*, p. 70.

[79] For a full account of contemporary references to the office of local justiciar, see Professor Cronne's excellent article, "The Office of Local Justiciar under the Norman Kings," *University of Birmingham Hist. Jour.* **6** (1937): 18-38.

be confined to pleas of the crown in the strict sense of the phrase. Once established, the importance of the office inevitably grew, and it became an object of baronial ambition. Geoffrey de Mandeville, for example, the first Norman earl of Essex, combined the justiciarships with the sheriffdoms of London and Middlesex, Essex and Hertfordshire when he was consolidating his power in this region. But the county justiciarships survived the feudal reaction of which Geoffrey de Mandeville was a symbol. The only official definition of the office which is on record comes from a writ of King Stephen's issued at the siege of Drax in 1154 in favour of Robert de Cheney, Bishop of Lincoln. Its precise wording deserves consideration:

> Stephen King of the English to the earls, barons, abbots, sheriffs, ministers and citizens of Lincoln and to all his faithful people of Lincoln and Lincolnshire, Greeting. Know that I have granted to Robert Bishop of Lincoln my justice—iustitiam meam—of Lincoln and Lincolnshire. Wherefore I will and firmly command that the same Robert shall hold my justice as well and in peace and honourably and fully as Robert Bloet or Alexander, Bishops of Lincoln, best had it. And I command you that by the summons of his ministers you come to hold my pleas and make my judgments as you did best and most fully in the time of King Henry my uncle. And if you do not do this, he (the Bishop) will do justice on you through your chattels that you do it. Witness, Hugh the Bishop of Durham, Richard de Luci and Richard de Canvill' at Drax.[80]

Robert Bloet was Bishop of Lincoln from 1094 to 1123, so that in Lincolnshire the office may have been in episcopal hands at its beginning.[81] Although King Stephen's charter comes from the last phase of the local justiciarships, it can be taken as an accurate statement of the duties of the office throughout its history.

Its implications are wide: the removal of the pleas of the crown from the Sheriff's control to that of a judge deriving his

80 *Registrum Antiquissimun* 1: pp. 63-64, from the *Calendar of Charter Rolls* 4: p. 139 (13).

81 It is possible that in the gap between the death of Bishop Alexander on 20 February, 1148, and the grant of the office to bishop Robert, Earl William de Roumara may have been the local justiciar of Lincoln and Lincolnshire. King Stephen, in a writ in favour of the church of St. Mary of Lincoln addressed to the reeves and burgesses of the city, threatens that if they do not carry out his order, "my justice Earl William will do it, lest I hear any further plaint for lack of full right or justice." *Registrum Antiquissimum* 1: p. 60.

authority from a direct royal grant and commanding a staff of ministers to summon suitors to the court, to collect amercements from defaulters and carry out the judgments of the court. It proves that, although the court of the local justiciar may have met where the shire court met, it was not the shire court. It was a royal court transacting the king's business and needing a special summons to call it together. The charter also proves that the clause in the Great Charter which states that no sheriff, constable, coroner, or other bailiff shall hold our pleas of the crown is enunciating a rule which had already been the law of the land for at least a century. The appointment of local justiciars could only be a temporary expedient, for, like the sheriffs themselves, local justices were often men with powerful local connections, many other preoccupations, and no particular training for the position. Nevertheless, for at least fifty years they and their servants provided a valuable check on the sheriffs and their servants until later generations had grown up to provide the King with a genuine official class.

Of the detailed work done by the local justices in their shires and by the early itinerant justices in their eyres all too little can be said. The Pipe Roll of 1130 affords glimpses of judicial movements on circuit. Judges who visited Yorkshire sat at Blythe in Nottinghamshire [82] as well as at York, and those who visited the eastern shires sat at Boston [83] as well as Lincoln and at Thetford [84] as well as at Norwich and Ipswich. The entries on the pipe roll are always brief and too often uninformative, for example, "the same sheriff renders account of 55 shillings for the little pleas of Walter Espec and Eustace fitz John. And the same sheriff renders account of 4 marks of silver for the other pleas of W. Espec and Eustace fitz John." [85] In all these eyres individual debtors are charged one after another with debts of varying amounts *de eisdem placitis.* Debts for murder fines, treasure trove, breaking the peace, default of a duel, wreck and false judgment are interspersed among these noncommittal entries. The fines offered for special privileges, such as peace for homicide,[86] or permission not to plead against certain indi-

82 *Pipe Roll 31 Henry I,* pp. 25-7.
83 *Ibid.,* p. 120.
84 *Ibid.,* p. 93.
85 *Ibid.,* p. 142.
86 *Ibid.,* p. 156.

viduals,[87] or even not to plead at all,[88] or that neither the debtor nor his heir shall have to plead for their land,[89] or that the debtor shall not have to plead for his land during his life [90] supply a little more information, but not about the pleas which are being avoided or postponed. The fines offered for having right touching land or an inheritance, for having the king's help to collect a debt, for a relief, for a marriage portion, for having a widow with her dower do not greatly differ in wording from such entries in later rolls, but they cannot be regarded as peculiar to the work of the king's itinerant judges.

Local justiciars finally disappeared when Henry II felt free to make his first grand gesture towards a more centralised and efficient judicial administration. But since he rarely names his local justices in his writs it is not possible to set out a list of them and the shires which they controlled. The Bishop of Lincoln may still have been in office in Lincoln and Lincolnshire for in 1156 the Sheriff accounted for 10 marks from the Bishop's pleas in Holland.[91] Even in the early years of the reign when he was distracted by the necessity of repressing a rebellion, of reducing the many still existing unlicenced castles in England and the castles of his younger brother in France, Henry II did his best to maintain the practice of his grandfather's later years and to send justices out on eyre. In 1156 Gregory of London, who had previously held office as sheriff in the city,[92] heard pleas in Buckinghamshire [93] and probably in Surrey [94] also while he was assisting the Bishop of Chichester and Ralf Picot in assessing a scutage. In the same year one of the King's constables, Henry de Pomerai, sat in Cambridgeshire and another constable, Henry of Essex, sat with the chancellor in Kent and, apparently alone in Somerset, Dorset, Devon, Hampshire, Wiltshire, and Sussex. The pipe roll entries suggest that Henry was largely occupied with criminal pleas—"the pleas and murder fines of Henry of Essex" is a description of his work in several shires. One or both of Henry II's two chief justiciars, the Earl of Leicester and

[87] *Ibid.*, pp. 83, 154, 157.
[88] *Ibid.*, pp. 40, 113, 118.
[89] *Ibid.*, p. 87.
[90] *Ibid.*, p. 14.
[91] *Pipe Roll 2 Henry II*, p. 26.
[92] *Red Book* 2: p. 658; *Pipe Roll 2 Henry II*, p. 5.
[93] *Pipe Roll 2 Henry II*, p. 22.
[94] *Ibid.*, p. 11.

Richard de Luci, heard pleas in Bedfordshire and Buckinghamshire and the Chancellor sat with the Earl in Lincolnshire. In 1156 or 1157 the Chancellor sat with the Earl in Shropshire.[95] But in these early years the King had few men to spare who could undertake the duties of a general eyre.

The pipe rolls of Henry II's early years contain few subheadings to indicate the official reason of the debts due to the King. The familiar *Nova placita et nove conventiones* which in the later rolls and in that of 31 Henry I marks the new fines in each account reappears tentatively in the Roll of 3 Henry II.[96] It is not until 12 Henry II, 1166, that clerks begin to enter judicial debts under the names of the judges responsible for the work. But incidental references in the Roll of 6 Henry II, 1160, show that a William fitz John has been hearing pleas in Devon and Somerset, Gloucestershire, and Herefordshire.[97] He must have sat also in Yorkshire in the previous year, for a debt which first appears in 1159 without any indication by whom it was imposed is described in a later roll as coming from the pleas of William fitz John.[98] He was hearing pleas in Somerset again, probably in 1165, and imposing so heavy an amercement on Samuel the priest of Pilton that four years later by a sworn inquest of his neighbours Samuel was pardoned £40 for his poverty. William fitz John is only recorded as the trial judge when Samuel's pardon was entered on the Roll of 14 Henry II.[99] There were several men in the royal service named William fitz John, but there seems no doubt that the judge of the early years was an usher of the royal household who was later employed in providing for the maintenance of individuals of the royal family.[100] He does not seem to have acted as a judge

[95] *Ibid.*, pp. 15 (Henry de Pomerai); 31, 32, 47, 54, 57, 60, 61 (Henry of Essex); 22 (Justiciar); 26 and *3 Henry II*, p. 89 (Chancellor and Earl of Leicester).

[96] *Pipe Roll 3 Henry II*, pp. 73, 78, 84, 87, 91, 95, 98, 99, 102.

[97] *Pipe Roll 6 Henry II*, pp. 51, 59, 28, 31.

[98] William Tisun's debt of 10 marks, *Pipe Roll 5 Henry II*, p. 31. William "was never found" according to *Pipe Roll 7 Henry II*, p. 36. In 1163 he was still "not found": and it is noted that the debt was "de placitis Willelmi filii Johannis." Among the neighbouring entries is a payment by the sheriff "from the old pleas of William fitz John," *Pipe Roll 9 Henry II*, p. 58.

[99] The debt first appears in 1165, *Pipe Roll 11 Henry II*, p. 64; and Samuel paid 72s. and 6d. in 1168 when he was pardoned £40 for poverty, *Pipe Roll 14 Henry II*, p. 141.

[100] Delisle, who warns readers that William, son of John, is a common name, has notes about a William fitz John employed in Normandy, *Recueil*, Intro-

in his later years. It is all the more interesting to find him being employed as a judge in the King's immediate circle early in the reign. The King "called together his justices, namely Gregory of London, William fitz John, and Nigel de Broc and other wise men of his court" to hear and determine the suit between the Abbot of Abingdon and Thurstan the despenser which had begun in Stephen's reign between the Abbot and Thurstan's father, Simon the despenser. The judges found in favour of the Abbot, but, not surprisingly, asked the King to confirm their judgment and deliver it from his own mouth.[101] William fitz John does not appear in the records after 1175.

That in 1157 a quarrel between a household officer of the crown and an ancient religious house was referred by the King for judgment to a former sheriff of London and two household officers, certainly of no higher status than Thurstan himself, shows that Henry II has not yet retained in his court men trained in the law to deal with such cases. All the men who served as justices in eyre in the early years were either officers of state or the holders of some domestic office in the royal household.[102] Two of them, the Earl of Leicester and Richard de Luci, were among the greatest magnates in the land. The Earl had been educated at Abingdon.[103] He could hold his own in talk about the purpose of kingship with John of Salisbury,[104]

duction, pp. 479-480. He seems to have been a Norman and can hardly be identified with the judge of Henry II's early years as king. The younger brother of Pain and Eustace fitz John was also named William, and seems to be the William fitz John of Harptree, who defended Harptree castle against the King in Stephen's reign, *Gesta Stephani*, p. 44. A William fitz John was holding ten knights' fees of the Earl of Gloucester in 1166, and is probably the brother of Pain and John, and is the same William who defended Harptree. The judge of early Henry II seems also to have been a Somerset man. He is probably the William fitz John who was pardoned Danegeld in that county, *Pipe Roll 8 Henry II*, p. 23, as William son of John and William son of John the usher. He was presumably the descendant of the John who in Domesday Book was holding land in Somerset by the serjeanty of serving as usher in the King's hall, Round, *King's Serjeants and Officers of State*, p. 110.

101 *Abingdon* 2: pp. 186-187.

102 Nigel de Broc was responsible for authorizing the payment for the King's maintenance at Peak castle in 1157, *Pipe Roll 3 Henry II*, ed. J. Hunter, p. 90. He does not appear on the rolls after 1158.

103 In a plea over which he presided as *justicia et judex*, the Earl bore witness that when he was a boy and was being brought up at Abingdon, he had seen the market in operation there in the time of King William. *Abingdon Chron.* 2: p. 229.

104 *Ioannis Saresberiensis episcopi Carnotensis Policratici*, ed. C. C. I. Webb (Oxford, 1909), 2: p. 74.

but there is no hint that Richard de Luci had any legal training other than that which any baron might acquire from the right to hold a court of his own. There is little evidence that between 1160 and 1166 the King made any attempt to maintain judicial eyres apart from a list of debts paid under Carlisle in 1163 "from the pleas of Richard de Luci." These may well have been imposed during a visit paid to the north by the justiciar for political motives while the King was abroad between August, 1158, and January, 1163. In most counties, although not every year, new debts were being entered in the pipe roll under the heading *Nova placita et nove conventiones,* but the reason for an individual debt is by no means always given. Even in 1165 there is no attempt to enter judicial fines and amercements separately from scutage payments. But the roll for that year contains a considerable number of new entries recording amercements, payments for right touching land or debt, for concords, for duels, for hastening right. Some of them may come from the work of local justices. Some may have resulted from application to one or other of the chief justiciars. Some were certainly the result of application to the King through some member of his household.

Every historian who has tackled the problems raised by Henry II's legal reforms has seen the year 1166 as the turning point of the reign. The Assize of Clarendon was promulgated at the council held there in February of that year and the King left England for Normandy in March. He was out of the land for four years. The country at large learned of the measure through "the pleas of Earl Geoffrey and Richard de Luci." Although the line of descent from the chief thegns of Æthelræd's Wantage code through the jurors of the Pipe Roll of 31 Henry I to the presenting jurors of the Assize of Clarendon proves that the presentment of crime was no innovation in 1166,[105] the stern uniformity of practice established by the Assize was undoubtedly new. The reflections of the work in the pipe roll—the building of county jails, the digging and blessing of ordeal pits and the lists of men who in most shires "perished in the judgment of water" all show that these visitations were of unprecedented severity. The King put in charge of the operation

105 N. D. Hurnard, "The Jury of Presentment and the Assize of Clarendon," *Eng. Hist. Rev.* **56** (1941), pp. 374-410.

two magnates whose authority no one could question, the Earl of Essex and the younger of the two justiciars, Richard de Luci. The Earl died in October, but before then he had visited a large part of England with Richard de Luci. The work was done remarkably quickly. Judges in later generations always found more work to do in the large and litigious counties of East Anglia, Lincoln, and York. When a general eyre went out the countries on the Welsh border and Cornwall were often left to be dealt with later. In 1166 Carlisle, Lancaster, Shropshire, Devon, Herefordshire, Cornwall and, possibly, Northamptonshire. seem, from the pipe roll evidence temporarily to have escaped visitation.[106]

It is sometimes said or at least implied by historians that the assize was a temporary measure which lapsed when the judges had done their work of enforcement.[107] But the King "wills that this assize shall be held in the realm as long as it pleases him" must mean what it would mean today. In Henry II's day and in regard to the Assize of Clarendon the words mean that it remained in force until it was reaffirmed and extended at Northampton in 1176. In 1166 the enquiries covered the years "since the king was king." In 1176 the King declared that "the assize shall be held from the time when the assize was made at Clarendon, continuously to the present time and from now as long as the lord King pleases." The only exceptions were in regard to minor thefts and robberies done in time of war and in the new limitation of the time within which disseisins covered by the assize must have been committed—"from the time when the lord King came into England after peace was

[106] The Sheriff accounted for the profits coming from the chattels of fugitives and those who perished in the judgment of the water separately from the individual debts entered under the heading "touching the pleas of earl Geoffrey and Richard de Luci." This heading appears in the following accounts of the Pipe Roll for 1166 only: Lincolnshire, Buckinghamshire and Bedfordshire, Yorkshire, Cambridgeshire and Huntingdonshire, Northumberland, Norfolk and Suffolk, Surrey, Nottinghamshire and Derbyshire, Kent, Essex, Hertfordshire, and Leicestershire. This alone does not prove that other shires were not visited during this eyre. The justiciar may well have been drawn from the eyre by other business and deputed his work to a substitute. In Rutland debts resulting from the assize are entered without any special heading, *Pipe Roll 12 Henry II*, p. 65, and in Staffordshire it is possible that Alan de Neville presided, *ibid.*, p. 62.

[107] N. D. Hurnard, *op. cit.*, p. 403. Miss Hurnard relies on the King's promise to the Bishop of Durham that the enquiry is for this occasion only, but that promise was peculiar to the Bishop. Similarly, Van Caenegem, *Writs*, p. 285.

made between him and the King his son." [108] The King and his advisers were adding to the machinery of the law.

The creation of a bench of judges was at once necessary. The pipe rolls, soon to be supplemented by final concords, show the King appointing additional judges almost every year. The enforcement of the Assize of Clarendon went on during 1168, 1169 and 1170. There had been a pause in 1167 while the chief justice of the forests, Alan de Neville, was conducting a full-scale forest eyre which he had begun in the previous year.[109] In 1168 the work of enforcing the Assize of Clarendon mainly fell on the chief justiciar, Richard de Luci, who again visited Yorkshire, and on Richard of Ilchester, Archdeacon of Poitou, Guy the dean of Waltham, and Reginald de Warenne, supported in Kent by Henry fitz Gerold, the Chamberlain, and elsewhere by William Basset, the third generation of his family to serve the King as judge. All these men were public figures, naturally fitting into one or other of the categories of Ralf de Diceto's famous description of Henry II's judges in 1179—"now abbots, now earls, now captains, now household servants, now his most familiar friends." Apart from the justiciar, they had never, so far as can be seen, gone on eyre before, but most of them were to be used again and again, as long as they had strength to ride a circuit. In 1169 a younger Alan de Neville, working with William Basset,[110] and Oger the dapifer working with Guy the Dean of Waltham joined in the work. In 1170 the names of John Cumin, younger brother of a Warwickshire landowner and later to be Archbishop of Dublin, and Gervase of Cornhill, who had been justiciar of London under Stephen,[111] were added to the company of judges in eyre, while in the north two barons

108 Disseisins committed in time of War were not a matter for enquiry. See, *Rolls of the Justices in Eyre . . . for Yorkshire 3 Henry III*, ed. D. M. Stenton, Selden Society, **56** (1937): p. liii; "Things done in time of war have no place." Case 979.

109 There are signs of its early stages in 1166, notably in Devon, *Pipe Roll 12 Henry II*, p. 95. There are hints of forest amercements in other shires also. in 1167 Alan de Neville's work as a forest Judge is the outstanding feature of every account.

110 A charter in the Kirkstead cartulary shows that Adam of Yarmouth was also with them as judge, sitting at Nottingham in September, *Mon. Ang.* **5**: p. 420.

111 J. H. Round, *The Commune of London* (London, 1899), pp. 107, 120. W. R. Powell, "The Administration of the Navy and the Stannaries, 1189-1216," *Eng. Hist. Rev.* **71** (1956): p. 177, and n. 3.

of those parts, William de Stuteville and Hugh de Moreville, were tried out. The large number of amercements for disseisin in these years shows that all over the country the King's free subjects were taking advantage of the new means of redress.

The work of these judges undoubtedly revealed to the King and justiciar abuses both in the shire and the feudal courts. Hence the pause in the purely judicial activities of royal emissaries in 1170 while the far-reaching Inquest of Sheriffs was carried out by companies of clergy and barons. In 1173 and 1174 the necessity of tallaging the royal demesne strained the resources of the government. It was not easy to find enough men qualified by character, position and training to do the work. Even Richard fitz Nigel, the King's Treasurer, who could rarely be spared from his work at the Exchequer table was obliged to help by visiting Kent and Sussex, Bedfordshire, Buckinghamshire, and Oxfordshire in company with Nicholas de Sigillo and Reginald de Warenne. Some of those who would naturally have been used on such an occasion were, like Rannulf de Glanville, in disgrace as a result of the Inquest of Sheriffs. Men new to the responsibility of acting as itinerant agents of the crown were pressed into service. Walter Map and Thurstan son of Simon the despenser were among the more important of such men and Leonard knight of Thomas Basset and Hamo Morgan "in place of the constable of Winchester" perhaps the least important. Nevertheless, during these difficult years there were younger men learning to play the part of judges both in the royal household and under the guidance of the chief justiciar. From the household of William the King's brother, who died in January, 1164, William fitz Ralf and Hugh de Cressi, passed into the King's service and were soon acting as judges. With Richard de Luci there sat at Oxford in September, 1172, Richard de Camville, Bertram de Verdun, Hugh de Morewich, Richard Barre, Richard Breton, William Torel and William fitz Ralf.[112] Of these Richard de Camville died in Italy in 1176 where he went as one of the barons who escorted the King's daughter to her Sicilian marriage.[113] The rest of Richard's company outlived the King.

[112] Sir Charles Clay, "Yorkshire Final Concords of the Reign of Henry II," *Yorkshire Archaeological Jour.* **40**: 82, no. 1.

[113] *Pipe Roll 3 and 4 Richard I*, pp. xxv-xxvi. Mr. H. G. Richardson's article on "Richard fitz Neal and the Dialogus de Scaccario," *Eng. Hist. Rev.* **43**:

The years immediately following the rebellion of 1173-1174 were crucial in the development of the royal courts of justice. When he returned to England in May, 1175, the King made the most momentous of all his appointments by commissioning Rannulf de Glanville to visit the counties north of the Thames with Hugh de Cressi. To the southern shires the King sent William de Lanvalei and Thomas Basset, both new appointments as itinerant justices. With the King himself as he moved about the land went William fitz Ralf, Bertram de Verdun, and William Basset acting as judges in the King's own itinerant court. The results of their work appear in the pipe roll as amercements imposed *in curia regis* or *in curia.* In these years the pipe roll clerks begin to distinguish between "pleas in the king's court" or "in the court" or "of the court," "pleas before the justices at the exchequer" and "pleas before justices *errantes.*" In 1177 *de placitis ad scaccarium* occurs as a heading to a list of amercements in several shires.[114] The debts imposed by the six companies, each of three judges, who enforced the Assize of Northampton of 1176 are entered under the names of the judges, who are described as *justic' errantes.* Although it is possible to distinguish three sets of judges at work, those with the King, those at the exchequer in Westminster hall, and those itinerant through the shires, there is no specialisation discernible in their work.

The commission under which the itinerant justices worked lasted two years. They sent returns to the Treasury both in 1176 and 1177. Their work, the enforcement of the Assize of Northampton, was done so effectively that it aroused resentments such as no medieval king could afford to ignore. When Henry II returned to England he found it necessary to appoint two clerks and three laymen of his privy household "to hear the complaints of the people and do right." He expressly ordered that they should remain in his court so that if any question should arise which they could not bring to an end themselves "it should be brought to the king's hearing and ended as pleased him and the wiser men of the kingdom." There was nothing

168-170 contains in footnotes the most recent listing of eyres in Henry II's reign. I hope to include a comprehensive study in a forthcoming volume of the Selden Society.

[114] Already in 1171 a litigant offered 5 marks for a plea to be heard "before the justices at the Exchequer." *Pipe Roll 17 Henry II*, p. 73.

revolutionary in this measure. The King was simply bringing a prolonged eyre to an end and at the same time making provision within his own court for the hearing of urgent pleas. In appointing five judges to move about the land with him in his own court and household Henry II was continuing the practice he had adopted in 1175 when he chose William fitz Ralf, Bertram de Verdun and William Basset to be the judges in the "curia Regis."

When the King cut short the work of his eighteen itinerant justices, the chief justiciar, Richard de Luci, was nearing the end of his long official career. After Easter, 1179, he retired to die in his Kentish abbey of Lesnes. In the Easter council at Windsor, in which the King introduced the Grand Assize, he made arrangements for another general eyre, employing even more judges than before—twenty-one in all. The country was divided into four circuits with the provision that the six judges who were to ride the northern circuit, like the special commission of clerks and laymen of the previous year, were required to be available in the king's court "to hear the complaints of the people." These complicated arrangements represent the fact that recent improvements in the administration of justice were steadily making the general eyre more important as a means of communication between the King and his subjects. The new forms of action, particularly the assizes of novel disseisin and mort d'ancestor, and the increasing readiness of the king's court to arrange final concords, were becoming better known and appreciated with every appearance of itinerant justices in the shires. The local courts also needed instruction in the new procedure of the Grand Assize. It was time that itinerant justices went round again. So long as the King, the mainspring of the whole judicial system, remained in England, it was unnecessary to appoint a successor to Richard de Luci. But when he was abroad neither the financial work of the Exchequer nor the judicial work of the barons of the exchequer could be adequately done without a single minister in supreme authority. Before he crossed the Channel in 1180, Henry appointed Rannulf de Glanville as his chief justiciar.

In the last ten years of Henry II's reign there was a rapid coming and going of itinerant justices to hear an ever increasing volume of pleas; to enforce the Assize of Arms in 1181 and

the Assize of the Forests in 1184; to make enquiries into the King's feudal rights in 1185. The justiciar himself, not bound by the terms of a commission as were his colleagues, was ready to hear pleas in whatever part of the country political circumstances caused him to visit. In this matter, as in others, he acted as the King would have done had he been in the land. The chief justiciars of Richard I and John can be seen behaving in like manner. The chroniclers give little information about the development of the courts in these years. Roger of Howden did not even notice the appointment of Glanville as chief justiciar in the first version of his chronicle, commonly known under the name of Benedict of Peterborough.[115] He made up for it in his longer history, when, having recorded the appointment, he added the ambiguous phrase "by whose wisdom the underwritten laws which we call English were compiled." [116] Among the miscellaneous matter collected at this point is a text of the Treatise on the Laws and Customs of the realm still known by Glanville's name.

The *Treatise* is both a guide-book for aspiring judges and a reflective discussion of the practice of the king's court, and sometimes of the ideas which lie behind it, as a hundred years of feudal rule and a generation of Angevin experiment have shaped it. Most of the writs in use at the end of the century are there, as a comparison with the surviving file of writs from 1199 shows.[117] The great family of writs of entry is already foreshadowed. Two specimen final concords provide an approximate date for the Treatise, one made on 2 November and the other on 29 November, 1187.[118] This last fine is remarkable. It is the record made in the king's court of a final concord made in the court of Geoffrey fitz Peter, later Earl of Essex and chief justiciar, ending a suit to which he himself was a party. No similar document seems to have survived from this period. It leads by way of the procedure when final concords are not kept by either party to a general discussion of the different kinds of "record" belonging to different courts. After considering the punishment which may fall upon the

[115] D. M. Stenton, "Roger of Howden and *Benedict*," *Eng. Hist. Rev.* **68** (1953): 574-582.

[116] *Howden* **2**: p. 215.

[117] *Pleas before the King* . . . **1**: p. 25.

[118] *Glanvill*, book viii, caps. 2 and 3, pp. 117-118.

lord of a private court which makes a wrong judgment Glanville considers how the king can help a lord faced with a case too difficult for his court to determine. This issues in a passage which for the relationship between royal and feudal justice is the most important in the whole Treatise:

> The lord himself can place his court into the court of the lord king, so that he may have the advice and agreement of the lord king's court touching the matter in doubt. And this the lord king owes to his barons as a matter of right for this reason, namely that he may cause his barons to have advice in his court from his learned men. But when a baron's doubts are resolved in the lord king's court he can return with his plea and determine it in his own court.[119]

This is not the language of an arrogant royal court, contemptuous of feudal justice and anxious only to draw suits to itself. It is a revealing passage which makes nonsense of any suggestion that Henry II and his advisers in introducing the new forms of action were trying to reduce the scope of feudal justice, though it proves that they intended that feudal justice should be good and the lords of feudal courts responsible.[120] The grievances which feudal barons felt against King John and his government were freely expressed in the Articles of the Barons and in the Great Charter, but it is in clause 34 only of the Charter that any criticism of the increase of royal justice seems to be voiced. The Charter seeks to correct the abuses not to limit the activities of the central and local courts; to provide more rather than fewer appearances of judges to take the popular assizes. The importance of clause 34—the writ called *Precipe* shall not henceforward be issued for anyone touching any tenement whereby a freeman may lose his court—can easily be overstressed. Like the majority of the clauses in the Charter it sets out the law of the time. The lord had always had the power of safeguarding his court in his own hands. He could claim his court when a plea which on feudal principles should have been heard in his own court was about to be heard in the royal court on a writ *precipe*. He could appoint a clerk to guard his interests in the royal court. There is no hint in any roll of

119 *Ibid.*, cap. ii, p. 123.

120 As is shown by the introduction of the process of "tolt" early in the history of the feudal courts, see above, p. 57 and *n*.

proceedings or essoins that such claims were being rejected in John's reign on any other than reasonable grounds. Clause 34 was never removed from the Charter nor its wording altered, but many lords had not the freeholders necessary to form a court and many had no wish to hear difficult pleas which might well in any case soon be removed to the royal court by grand assize. Hence the appearance in Henry III's reign of the writ of right which included the phrase "because the lord has released his court to the lord king."[121] It was inevitable that feudal justice should gradually wither away, but in 1215 the manner in which this would happen was part of the unforeseeable future.

That the increasing activities of the royal judges should draw business from all subordinate courts, both feudal and shire, was only to be expected. The disappearance of local records makes it hard to draw firm conclusions about the impact of the new royal justice upon the activities of the shire court. It is often implied that the impact was purely destructive. But the twelfth century was an age of expansion. Increasing international trade, increasing population, more land won from marsh and forest all brought more pleas to the local courts. Royal judges coming at irregular intervals could not take the place of a local court which as far as the memory of man went back had been available month in month out for men and women to have their complaints against enemies and oppressors heard. Small debts could be recovered in the shire court, boundary disputes, always numerous in unhedged open fields, could be heard. Offences which "broke the peace of the sheriff"[122] might well be more numerous than those which broke the peace of the king. It may reasonably be said that the prestige of the shire court was enhanced when the king's judges sat there to deal with cases brought by royal writ and to hear the pleas of the crown which had already been presented before the shire court sitting under the presidency of the sheriff. In asserting that no sheriff, constable, coroner, or any other royal bailiff shall hear the pleas of the crown the Great Charter

[121] *Cf.* N. D. Hurnard, "Magna Carta, Clause 34," pp. 174-179.

[122] "The county with the wapentake says that they were not appealed of the King's peace, but the Sheriff's peace, so that that plea was and is in the shire and therefore they were not attached to be before the justices." *The Earliest Lincolnshire Assize Rolls,* case 542, pp. 95-96.

was not making new, but re-affirming existing law which an over-mighty or over-anxious sheriff sometimes ignored.[123] Nevertheless, even if the Sheriff of Lincolnshire was exaggerating in 1226 when he claimed that owing to the unwillingness of suitors to sit for more than one day, seven score cases stood over,[124] there can be no doubt of the volume of ordinary business still left to the shire court of Lincoln in Henry III's reign.

To say, in the words of Professor van Caenegem, that the legal innovations of Henry II gave the sheriff "the air of the errand boy of the royal courts with few important or responsible tasks" is hardly fair to an office which John's great justiciar, Geoffrey fitz Peter, and his colleagues on the bench, Simon of Pattishall and James of Potterne,[125] were pleased to hold. The recurrent phrase in early eyre rolls "Precept to the sheriff to do this or that" and "To judgment touching the sheriff" for not doing what he ought to have done, or the reverse, may give colour to this view of the thirteenth-century sheriff. But it is surely an exaggeration to say that the sheriff "from being a great local lord was turned into a royal official who except for his office was a nonentity." The only period when the sheriff could truly be described as a great local lord was in the first generation of Norman rule before the sons of William the Conqueror had begun the reforms in local government carried forward by Henry II. No "nonentity" could have been a success as sheriff. The thirteenth-century sheriff was the head within his shire of a complex system of local government centred on the county town, often on the royal castle, and employing an undersheriff and a large staff of bailiffs or serjeants and clerks. Often much of the sheriff's work was done by his deputy, but the sheriff was responsible for his efficiency. Even the orthodox theory that in the shire court not the sheriff, but the suitors, were the judges requires considerable modification, at least for the period between the Norman Conquest and the mid-thirteenth century.

Many of the early writs collected and classified by Dr. van Caenegem as leading up to the action of novel disseisin are

123 See above, p. 67.

124 *Bracton's Note-Book* case 1730, pp. 565-567. C.R.R.: 12, pp. 434-435.

125 James of Potterne acted as Geoffrey fitz Peter's undersheriff 1198-1199. P.R.O., Lists and Indexes, No. IX, *List of Sheriffs*, p. 161; *Pipe Roll 1 John*, p. 38.

addressed to the sheriff ordering him to restore the complainant to seisin. Some are addressed to a magnate or to the person against whom the complaint has been made and threaten the king's justice or sheriff will take action. Those which are addressed to the sheriff are surely the direct predecessors not of the writs which initiate the forms of action but of the many *justicies* and viscontiel writs which continue to flow from the chancery after the new returnable writs have been devised. Glanville's Treatise contains many writs of this pattern, not all of them containing the *justicies* formula, but all authorising the sheriff to act on the king's behalf in a judicial or an executive capacity. They are not returnable writs. The last sentence before the witness clause generally contains the ancient formula "that I hear no more complaint for default of right," or "that the plaintiff need no more complain for default of right." The King in devising the writs which opened his court to all freemen suffering from some clearly defined wrongs still left a large field of litigation for his local representatives to deal with as they had done in the past.

Beside the traditional pleas which began by plaint in the shire, needing no writ from the chancery to initiate them, and judged in the traditional fashion by the suitors of the court there grew up during the twelfth century an undefined area of jurisdiction in the shire court derived from the increased power of the crown in the Anglo-Norman and Angevin state. The number and variety of the *justicies* and viscontiel writs directed to the sheriff increased with the increasing volume of business in the royal courts held before justices itinerant.[126] The very word

[126] On the "nature and extent" of the jurisdiction of the county court, see G. J. Turner, *Brevia Placitata*, pp. lxvi-lxix. Glanville's list of viscontiel writs should be compared with the list given by Turner as mentioned in *Brevia Placitata*, p. lvii.

customs and services, Book ix, cap. 9; Book xii, cap. 15.
niefty, Book xii, cap. 11.
replevin, Book xii, cap. 12.
purprestures, Book ix, cap. 12.
admeasurement of pasture, Book xii, cap. 13.
admeasurement of dower, Book vi, cap. 18.
dower of knights' widows, Book xii, cap. 20.
estovers (easements in wood and pasture), Book xii, cap. 14.
recognition touching boundaries, Book ix, cap. 14; Book xii, cap. 19, a writ necessitated by the fact that the sheriff had assigned others to act in his place despite the special instruction of the justices. This writ includes a reproof to the sheriff in question. Also caps. 16 and 17.

justicies implies that the sheriff in obeying such writs was acting through the shire court as a judge in the modern sense. In obeying many viscontiel writs he was certainly acting in an executive capacity only, but it must have been difficult for a hard-pressed sheriff to be mindful of the distinction. But whether the suitors of the shire court were giving judgment in a case brought by one of their number by plaint, or the Sheriff was acting on a *justicies* writ, or was leading the *posse comitatus* without writ to force a lord to replevy plough-beasts, all these pleas were part of the sheriff's work in the shire court. To quote Professor Plucknett: "the implication seems clearly that down to the middle of the thirteenth century a large part of the nation's litigation was in the shire court." [127]

In the last twenty years of Henry II's reign the number of highly educated men about his court steadily increased. Not all of them had the qualities which make good judges. Walter Map, for instance, had other virtues. The title of "master" given to many who acted as judges in the last years of the reign, implies the existence of an academic element in the English judiciary. All medieval kings were accustomed to reward their clerks with ecclesiastical preferment and to continue to employ them in their service. Archdeacons were, or should have been, the businessmen of the church, but under Henry II their ecclesiastical functions clearly had to take second place to the royal service. Some of the outstanding judges of the reign can be seen first as clerks, then as archdeacons, and then as bishops, but not all of them reached this eminence. Master Thomas of Hurstbourne, already a judge in Henry II's last years and next in importance to the Justiciar on the bench at the end of Richard I's reign, had no higher ecclesiastical preferment than a canonry of St. Paul's. Master Henry of Northampton, who served as an itinerant justice at the end of Henry II's reign, and was still active until the last eyre of John, was similarly rewarded. More is known of his origin and background than is usual at this date, for his father was Peter son of Adam of Northampton, the first of the forty burgesses of Northampton who had been responsible for recording in the twelfth century

[127] T. F. T. Plucknett, *A Concise History of the Common Law* (5th ed., London, 1956), p. 92.

the laws of the town.[128] An interesting example of hereditary ability among the judges at the end of the century is master Aristotle, for Sir Charles Clay has recently demonstrated that he was grandson of Henry Archdeacon of Huntingdon, the historian, who was brought up at Lincoln in the household of Bishop Robert Bloet and died in 1156-7.[129]

Of all the clerks who entered the king's service the most eminent and probably the ablest of that brilliant company was Hubert Walter, nephew of Rannulf de Glanville's wife. Brought up in his uncle's household, he probably learned his law at its source. As archbishop and justiciar he ruled both church and state in Richard's reign. His influence as chancellor is incalculable in John's. In Richard's absence and under Hubert Walter's guidance the court at Westminster assumed a new importance. The justiciar, bound to supply increasingly large sums of money to meet Richard's insatiable demands, imposed taxation through itinerant justices. Their eyres became highly organised political, financial and judicial instruments of government. The articles of the 1194 eyre were the prototype of the instructions issued to itinerant justices as long as the general eyre remained a feature of the English judicial order. Topical matters, like the enquiries into the payment of Richard's ransom or the fate of crusaders' chattels could be omitted and new articles added as the years went by. To Henry II the general eyre was of vital importance in making known new laws or reinforcing old ones. Hubert Walter used it in the same way. Through it he established the office of coroner throughout the land, forbade sheriffs to act as justices in their own shires or those which they had recently held, and set up the Exchequer of the Jews. A general eyre began again in 1198 under Geoffrey fitz Peter's direction. He had succeeded Hubert Walter as justiciar in that year. Judges went out again, apparently acting under the same directions in 1200-1201 and 1202-1203. The need for more frequent visits to take assizes and deliver gaols was met by sending smaller companies of judges between the general eyres. This was done in 1195-1196 and in 1206. But these smaller companies although commissioned to take assizes generally heard whatever cases awaited

128 *Leges Ville Norht*, ed. Councillor Frank Lee (Northampton, 1951), pp. 4-5.
129 "Master Aristotle," *Eng. Hist. Rev.* **76** (1961): 303-307.

settlement in the shires and final concords were made before them.[130] It is the feet of fines which provide historians with the most detailed information about the men who went on eyre together, the places where they sat and the dates at which the sessions were held.

In the reigns of Henry II's sons a powerful lay element can be observed among the judges. There are barons, like Earl Roger Bigot, William de Warenne of Wormgay, Robert fitz Roger of Clavering. William de Albini of Belvoir, lords of great estates with responsibilities and courts of their own, but such men, unless like Geoffrey fitz Peter they have risen through service to the crown, are rarely permanent members of the bench of judges. They serve the King in their own parts in many capacities and they sit as justices itinerant, generally returning to the bench to complete the business of their eyre. Without the help of what may be described as "unprofessional" judges it would have been impossible to send out a full eyre through the land. At the end of the century it took far longer to complete a general eyre than it had done in 1166 when the earl of Essex and Richard de Luci seem to have done their work in a matter of weeks. More interesting than the public spirited magnates are the laymen of undistinguished origin, coming from many parts of England who have made the law their profession and can be seen sitting at Westminster throughout the law terms and touring the country as itinerant justices. They are generally the first of their families to rise from rustic obscurity. Sometimes they are the younger sons of modestly landed families, like Geoffrey fitz Peter son of Peter the forester of Ludgershall or Roger Arundel who frequently served in Yorkshire. One eminent judge of the next generation was certainly of English descent. Stephen of Seagrave, chief justiciar under Henry III was the son of Gilbert son of Hereward who makes an undistinguished appearance as an itinerant justice in 1196 and was developing his father's modest inheritance into an estate which formed the nucleus of the great Seagrave barony.[131] But nothing is known of the origin of the Wiltshire James of Potterne, the Sussex John of Guestling, the Hampshire Richard

130 *The Earliest Lincolnshire Assize Rolls,* pp. xli-xlii.
131 *Complete Peerage* **11**: pp. 596-597.

of Herriard. Of them all the Northamptonshire Simon of Pattishall is the most interesting. That his home was at Pattishall in Northamptonshire is proved by his agreement by final concord to pay a mark every year to a widow or her certain messenger at Pattishall.[132] His rolls show him the master of procedure, sometimes declaring a rule of law for the benefit of his court.[133] The London legal miscellany of the thirteenth century preserved the opinion of both judges when he differed from Richard of Herriard on a point of procedure.[134] That John chose Simon of Pattishall to head the court *coram Rege* is a testimony to his contemporary reputation, a reputation which survived beyond the next generation.

The succession of King John brought to the throne a man as closely interested in legal development as his father. Chance has preserved some of the *coram rege* rolls of his reign. They are records of a rapidly moving court, working closely under the King's supervision. As soon as he succeeded to the throne John took command of the work of his courts of justice, ordering important cases to be transferred from the bench to his own court. In his brief visit to England between 28 February and mid-April, 1200, while he was waiting to secure a settlement with the kings of France and Scotland, John took his justices with him as far north as Yorkshire, leaving the barons of the exchequer in charge of the bench.[135] The roll of proceedings kept during this progress demonstrates that had political affairs gone well for John his reputation as a ruler might have stood high. The quarrel with Pope Innocent III which resulted in the interdict in 1208 meant a violent disturbance in the ordered administration of justice. When the sentence of excommunication passed on the King became known in 1209, he lost the services of many of his judges. I have discussed elsewhere the means by which he tried to maintain a skeleton service in the courts with the help of Simon of Pattishall, James of Potterne, and other laymen.[136] He was even able to appoint some new lay judges, Henry de Pont Audemer, Robert d'Au-

132 *Feet of Fines,* Northamptonshire, 171/11/177.

133 *Earliest Lincolnshire Assize Rolls,* p. xxiii.

134 M. Weinbaum, *London unter Eduard I und II* (Stuttgart, 1933), 2: p. 65.

135 *Pleas before the King . . .* 1: pp. 61, 294.

136 "King John and the Courts of Justice," *Proceedings of the British Academy* 1958: 103-127 and below, pp. 88-114.

mari, and Roger Huscarl, the last of whom had been acting at Westminster as an attorney throughout the reign. It is this disruption in the ordered procession of the judicial terms at Westminster and of eyres through the land after 1208 which makes it difficult to trace any legal development in the last years of the reign.

But the legal profession was advancing to maturity with a confidence which the interdict could not shake. The rolls reveal all too little of the men responsible for carrying out the business of the courts, but it is obvious that the judges are but the leading figures in what was becoming an elaborately organised profession. Immediately below the judges are those who will themselves be judges in the near future, men who sometimes themselves preside during an eyre when the pace of business grows hot or when one of the judges is for some reason unable to sit.[137] Each judge has in attendance his personal clerk or clerks. The diverse handwriting of the feet of fines is proof that several, if not many clerks were always in waiting, whether the judges were working at Westminster or on eyre. The curiously oldfashioned handwriting of some of the products of an eyre, both feet of fines and odd membranes of essoins and pleas, suggests that sometimes local men had to be employed to supplement the regular clerical staff. Some clerks were charged with particular duties, such as keeping account of monies due from litigants and taking charge of documents brought into court or notes of final concords made there. Some of the clerks, like Martin of Pattishall, the clerk of Simon of Pattishall, rose to judicial rank themselves. One was a humorist who alleviated with bad jokes the solemnity of the record he was keeping.[138] Professional attorneys are appearing alongside the personal representatives, kinsmen or servants of the past. John Bucuinte is a certain example of a man who acted both as an attorney and as a counsellor, speaking for his principal.[139] Even the

[137] Richard of Seething, who in the East Anglian eyre in 1198 sat "in place of Robert fitz Roger," does not appear as a judge in his own right before he went on eyre with Simon of Pattishall in 1203 and 1206. See *Earliest Lincolnshire Assize Rolls*, pp. xl, 242.

[138] *Curia Regis Rolls* **2**: pp. v-vi.

[139] See Appendix, No. V, p. 194. In 1932 in a lecture given before the Royal Historical Society Mr. H. G. Richardson pointed out how many exchequer clerks acted as attorneys. "William of Ely, The King's Treasurer," *Transactions of the Royal Historical Society*, 4th Series, **15**: pp. 66, 67.

lowly essoiner is ceasing to be a mere unnamed messenger, a relative, or fellow villager of the party, his cook, his forester or some chance merchant who has passed through his house. He is showing signs of becoming a professional man. The ebullient life of the courts will before long burst out into the open, demand cheap vernacular text-books for ambitious young men instead of the solemn Latin of Glanville and Bracton, and create in the Year Books the most remarkable series of contemporary law-reports any country has ever produced.

IV. KING JOHN AND THE COURTS OF JUSTICE *

"EDWARD I," said Professor Plucknett, opening his Ford Lectures, "meant to be a great king; and he was." [1] It would be equally true to say that Henry II meant to be a great king and that he, too, was, but it is unlikely that historians in general would say the same of King John, or agree with his latest biographer that he was "probably as good a king as his father." [2] Nevertheless, each of these three kings, Henry II, John, and Edward I, was alike in his regard for the common law, and each of them played a major part in its development. If historians have sometimes overstressed the achievements and good intentions of Henry II and the wide vision and legal acumen of Edward I, they have generally redressed the balance by concealing the activities of King John in a haze of moral disapprobation and commentaries on single clauses of the Great Charter. Yet it is in his reign that it is possible for the first time to look closely into the day-by-day activities of the King and trace his influence on every aspect of government. It is but an act of historical piety to recall the great work of Thomas Duffus Hardy in editing King John's chancery enrolments and working out the King's itinerary; of Francis Palgrave in initiating the publication of the records of his courts of justice; and of Joseph Hunter in attacking the pipe rolls and the feet of fines. Over a hundred years ago these three great archivists laid a sound foundation on which public parsimony and perhaps a failure of nerve prevented the next generation from building.

Now that one of Thomas Duffus Hardy's successors in office has sorted, dated, and edited the rolls of the central court of justice for King John's reign, and the printing of the rolls of the justices in eyre, the pipe rolls, and the feet of fines [3] is nearing

* Raleigh Lecture, British Academy, 1958.

1 T. F. T. Plucknett, *Legislation of Edward I* (Oxford, 1949), p. 1.

2 Sidney Painter, *The Reign of King John* (Baltimore, 1949), p. 238.

3 No series of public records has been treated by searchers during the last 120 years more unscrupulously than the feet of fines, and of none has a more continuous use been made, particularly by genealogists. It is only recently that these documents have come to be regarded as worthy of study in their own right as part of the history of the common law. It is perhaps optimistic to say that the printing of the feet of fines for John's reign is nearing completion, for many have been done in abstract and should therefore be done again. But Joseph Hunter printed in full those relating to counties beginning with the

completion, it is possible to take a more dispassionate, and perhaps a more accurate view of the part King John played in the organization and development of his courts of justice. He has never been regarded by historians as uninterested in his royal duty of hearing pleas, but few have credited him with any genuine respect for law or custom, or with any sympathetic understanding of the difficulties of litigants. Even Maitland prejudged the issue by writing in the *History of English Law* that "King John liked to do justice, or what he called justice." [4] As recently as 1948, after the publication of the *Curia Regis Rolls*, an eminent medievalist described it as "both strange and significant" that King John insisted that any action against his difficult archbishop must be preceded by a judgment "in his court" and "by process of law." [5] A reconsideration of the evidence is clearly overdue.

"Significant" such words coming from the King may be, but not "strange." From time to time throughout his reign King John can be heard voicing his respect for the customs of the land and insisting on the observance of the law. Cases from the *Curia Regis Rolls* can be called in evidence. In the Hilary Term 1201 he commanded that if an inquest had been taken "according to the custom of England, it should stand, but if otherwise it should be quashed." [6] In the Easter Term 1203 the King ordered an assize to proceed "unless reason and the custom of our kingdom stand in the way." [7] And again in the same term he ordered that the justiciar "without delay and according to the custom of England" shall cause a fine to be observed "inasmuch as it was reasonably made and ought to be held." [8] In the Michaelmas

letters B to D inclusive, and his invaluable introduction was based on an examination of all the feet of fines for the reigns of Richard I and John. Inevitably in working from unprinted material still in process of being tidied up after centuries of neglect he made a few slips which can more easily be rectified now. The Pipe Roll Society is trying to carry on his work. In this lecture I have used the unpublished fines when a printed text has not been available, but I have not inserted the precise manuscript reference to an unprinted fine save where the date of the fine affects my argument. In a forthcoming volume of the Selden Society I hope to include a table of the fines up to 1216 and the judges before whom they were made.

[4] 2nd ed. (1898), **1**: p. 170.

[5] V. H. Galbraith, *Studies in the Public Records*, p. 136.

[6] C.R.R. (1922 et seq.) **1**: pp. 375-376.

[7] *Ibid.*, **2**: p. 223.

[8] *Ibid.*, p. 202.

Term 1203 the King ordered the justiciar to "do nothing contrary to the custom of our kingdom" in regard to an order previously given on behalf of a litigant.[9] In the same term the King wrote to the justiciar from Exmes in the Argentan telling him to give plaintiffs "a record and reasonable judgment, unless anything had been done thereafter wherefore they ought not to have it." [10] In the octave of St. Martin the justiciar is to postpone a suit until the warrantor shall be of such age that he can and ought to warrant land "according to the custom of England." [11] In the Hilary Term 1207 the King instructed the justices of the Bench to cause an assize to proceed "according to the law and custom of England." [12] In a homicide case in the Michaelmas Term 1207 the sheriff is to do in regard to fugitives what he ought to do "according to the custom of England." [13] Words such as these are not merely common form. Like all his subjects King John was bred in an atmosphere created by long established law and custom. He understood as well as they the distinction between the custom of the land and the will of the King. He knew that each had its place.

Henry II had spent more than half his reign out of England; on two occasions he was abroad for several years together. Richard I visited England only twice in the ten years he was king. The government of the country had depended in the absence of the King on his justiciar and the little group of judges and financial experts who sat with him at Westminster or were dispatched on judicial or financial business about the land. These men were of necessity too powerful for their masters to trust them unreservedly, but they were indispensable. Since 1194 the general eyre with its carefully thought-out list of articles to be put to local juries had become a visitation recurring every four years or thereabouts, and at irregular intervals between the eyres the nearer and richer counties could expect judicial visits which involved taxation as well as the hearing of pleas. Sometimes a session held in vacation away from Westminster has all the appearance of a session of the Bench.[14] The

[9] *Ibid.*, 3: p. 27.
[10] *Ibid.*, pp. 56-57: not Exeter as in Index, p. 381.
[11] *Ibid.*, p. 64.
[12] *Ibid.*, vol. v, p. 33.
[13] *Ibid.*, p. 49.
[14] *Pleas before the King or his Justices* 1 (Selden Society, 67, 1953), p. 137.

necessity to look to the safety of the Welsh border might draw the justiciar to the border shires and if there were pleas awaiting attention he heard them then. The justiciar and judges, barons of the Exchequer, and sheriffs seem to be dancing an involved and recurrent measure between Westminster and the shires, and they knew the rules better than the King. Well might John move cautiously among them. But he showed a clear grasp of essentials in his determination to control the springs of justice. His determination is reflected in the bench roll of the Hilary Term 1200, which shows that writs were arriving at Westminster ordering that certain cases should be put before the King himself. His first visit to England lasted only from late February to mid-April 1200 and his next from October, 1200, to May, 1201, but throughout both visits he was accompanied by experienced judges; often the justiciar himself was with him, and he heard pleas as he moved about the land.[15]

There was nothing new in the men of the countryside pressing on the King to ask for favours as he moved from one royal lodging to another. Such behaviour is as old as the monarchy itself. Echoes of it can be heard throughout the previous centuries of English history. A new twist has been given to an old story by the development of writs of common form in the twelfth century, and particularly during its later years. On the other hand, not all grievances could be dealt with by a writ of common form, although the number of such writs was increasing and their range widening. At the end of the century, as when the Assize of Northampton was issued in 1176, some pleas were "so great that they could not be settled without the lord king and others for their dubiety must be put before the King himself." [16] The royal duty of settling disputes between his magnates and composing the uncertainties of the law was as apparent to King John as it had ever been to his father.

There were many pleas in which a strict observance of the law of the land and the customs of England was almost impossible either because of arbitrary royal action in previous generations, through the sheer complication of rules of inheritance, or because of obstinate political circumstances. Moreover, the close of the twelfth century seems roughly to have coincided with a

[15] *Ibid.* 1: pp. 56 ff.
[16] Stubbs, *Charters*, p. 180, cl. 7.

surge of business into the royal courts of justice as remarkable as it appears to have been unexpected. The ordinary freemen of the countryside were coming in increasing numbers to have their pleas heard before royal judges. Justice in their own shires was both quicker and cheaper than justice at Westminster, provided that there was no urgency to begin the plea.[17] Many therefore postponed bringing their actions until they knew that justices in eyre were about to appear in their own parts, and they hoped to finish their business while the judges remained near at hand. The increase in the number of feet of fines surviving from the last years of Richard I and the first years of King John, particularly the number made during the eyres, clearly proves this. The fact that judges time and again failed to keep to their time-table proves that business in the shires was greater than had been expected.[18] That the King should wish to keep in touch with this development of royal power was both natural and right.

The roll of proceedings before King John and his judges during his first progress as king opens a new chapter in the recorded history of the king's court of justice. Early in March, 1200, he set out for York by way of Woodstock, Nottingham, and Doncaster, and, after spending Easter at Worcester, returned to Westminster in time for the opening of the Easter Term. Although the roll recording the judicial business done in this journey was printed by Palgrave in 1835,[19] its peculiar interest has only recently been emphasized. Among the common-form entries of replevins, essoins, appointments of attorneys, and adjournments are cases which concern important feudal magnates and deal with problems which no one but the King, if even he, could settle. Some are reports of inquests into matters which might especially concern or interest the King. One is an early action of trespass, brought significantly enough by the

[17] Mr. G. J. Turner points out that in the thirteenth century the Common Bench at Westminster was "a court of luxury," in that it provided "an immediate hearing." Except in certain types of action, regarded as particularly urgent and in need of immediate attention, it was reasonable to make plaintiffs purchase the right to be heard there "at their own time": *Brevia Placitata* (Selden Society, **66**, 1951), p. li.

[18] *The Earliest Lincolnshire Assize Rolls* (Lincoln Record Society **22**), pp. xxxvi ff.; *Pleas before the King or his Justices* **1**: p. 146.

[19] *Rotuli Curiæ Regis* **2**: pp. 156-184. Reprinted, *Pleas before the King or his Justices* **1**: pp. 296-320.

King's seneschal, William de Cantilupe.[20] Other formless entries, of little moment in themselves, are valuable because they demonstrate the experimental character of the roll. When an entry begins "Speak with the lord King touching . . ." and ends with a judgment or precept in paler ink, it is safe to conclude that the King's own words are there recorded.[21]

Few of the judgments thus pronounced are in themselves remarkable. It is rarely, either in this first royal eyre or in the long royal eyre of the following winter and spring, 1200-1201, that the King can be seen going ahead of current practice.[22] His judgment in favour of a woman who complained that her husband, in collusion with the plaintiff, intended to lose by default land which was her inheritance has often been quoted. The King was "moved by pity" to receive the woman's offering of 40 shillings for permission to put herself on the grand assize, but it is also recorded that he took counsel before making this concession.[23] Similarly in a suit between the Earl of Chester and the advocate of Béthune, the clerk noted that a day was set for the hearing at Westminster because "the lord King with the counsel of his barons wishes to do to each what he ought."[24] The King was endeavouring to tread the narrow course between the letter of the rigid law and formless equity.

The King was in France from May, 1201, until 7 December, 1203. When he returned, Normandy was lost, although Château Gaillard did not fall until March, nor Rouen surrender until June, 1204. The justiciar and his fellow judges henceforward have to reckon with their master's continuous presence in England, and the office of justiciar must inevitably tend to decline in importance while its holder's duties as regent are in abeyance. The King and the justiciar came to Westminster together for the opening of the Hilary Term 1204 about 21 or 22 January.[25] At the end of the month they left to hold a prolonged

20 *Ibid.*, case 3159.

21 *Ibid.*, see illustration opposite p. 64.

22 *C.R.R.* **1**: pp. 254-268, 374-398, and 413-441. For the essoins of this eyre see *Pleas before the King or his Justices* **1**: 320-349.

23 *C.R.R.* **1**: p. 382: " . . . et dominus rex motus misericordia et per consilium recipit oblacionem ipsius Hawisie."

24 *Ibid.*, p. 392.

25 They were together for the greater part of the vacation: *Rot. Chart.*, pp. 114-117.

session at York.[26] The fines made at Westminster in this term relate to counties south of the Humber. They suggest that the business of the term had been prepared in two main divisions; northern pleas being generally directed to York, pleas from the southern, midland, and eastern counties to Westminster,[27] where a reduced bench of five judges finished off the term.

The King's presence at York gave occasion for the hearing of many northern pleas between people of the highest rank. But, as Sir Cyril Flower has pointed out, the king's court was accustomed to deal with ordinary cases awaiting a hearing in the shires through which it passed.[28] Not enough credit has been given to it for a practice which must have saved many litigants and jurors both time and money. In February, 1204, at York many assizes of novel disseisin and mort d'ancestor between people of no particular importance were heard. On the other hand, the apparent simplicity of these assizes was delusive, and a point might easily arise which the judges properly referred to the King. The jurors' verdict in an assize of novel disseisin that the complainant had been disseised by a third party who had given the land to the tenant meant that the complainant was in mercy for a false claim. A marginal note reads: "Speak with the lord King." An assize of mort d'ancestor brought by Holfrid daughter of Hugh for 8 acres of land in Balne should have been dismissed because the plaintiff had died, but her daughter was present and wished to sue. Again, a marginal note "Speak with the lord King" directs attention to the case, and the clerk later added: "The lord King ordered that the assize should not stand over for this reason, but should be taken, Emma daughter of Holfrid being present." Among the north-country pleas dealt with at York was a Cumberland murder case in which the duel was adjudged and the parties were ordered to be before the King

[26] The justiciar and Simon of Pattishall were both with the King at Nottingham in the octave of the Purification on their way north. Six final concords were made there, 4 relating to Nottinghamshire properties and 1 each to land in Derbyshire and Lincolnshire. At York 27 final concords were made between 18 February and 1 March. Richard of Herriard, the senior Bench Judge, was at York (*Rot. Chart.*, p. 120*b*) but did not sit as a judge. The presence of the King is not recorded in the final concords during this progress.

[27] An Essex case was put to York at this time, perhaps because of its difficulty. It concerned the soke of Downham and was not settled until November 1207: Assize Roll 1039, mem. 2; Feet of Fines Essex CP 25 (1), 52/13/237.

[28] *Introduction to the Curia Regis Rolls* (Selden Society 62, 1943), p. 23.

wherever he should be in England.[29] In the Michaelmas Term 1200 the King had instructed the judges to put certain duels before him because he wished to see them.[30] The frequency with which judicial duels were thereafter put before the King, both in rolls of pleas and of essoins, almost suggests that this writ was taken as a general directive.

That the reputation of the court *coram rege* stood high in 1204 is apparent from the large number of new fines recorded in the fine roll and the pipe roll for the privilege of having a suit heard before the King himself. The fines taken were generally not large and those who offered them were not always in a hurry to pay.[31] The King seems to have been less interested in the trickle of new income which might come to the Exchequer than in the cases themselves. Indeed, many cases came into his court for which there is no evidence that any special payment was made. The lists of points, or the single points, which the judges, both *coram rege* and of the bench, refer to the King merely indicate the inclusive character of the King's interest and the close attention which he wished to give to the work of his courts.[32] While he had been abroad the judges referred their difficulties to the justiciar.[33] On the King's return they were naturally placed before him. Some are matters of procedure which may seem inconsiderable, but it should be remembered that to Bracton, as to the judges of King John's court, the proper way to cast an essoin was part of "the custom and law of the land." Robert Morin, who had essoined himself for sickness, had been viewed not by knights but by freemen, and, summoned to hear his judgment, he had merely essoined himself for sickness again. The judgment to be pronounced in such a case would be, as the judges said, *litigiosum,* and a note on the roll appropriately reads "Speak with the lord King about Robert Morin." [34]

29 The Bench Roll of the Hilary Term 1204 is lost. The roll of proceedings *coram rege* at York, Lichfield, and Bridgnorth has been broken up. An English version of the Yorkshire cases in Assize Roll 1039 appeared in 1911 (Yorkshire Archaeological Society, Record Series **44**: pp. 1-30). Another section is printed in *C.R.R.* **3**: pp. 89-99. I hope to print the still unprinted cases and those only printed in English in a forthcoming volume of the Selden Society.

30 *C.R.R.* **1**: p. 279.

31 *Pipe Roll 6 John,* Pipe Roll Society, N.S., **18**: pp. xii ff.

32 *C.R.R.* **2**: p. 33; **4**: p. 287; **5**: pp. 53, 234-235.

33 *The Earliest Northamptonshire Assize Rolls,* cases 483, 485, 717, 793.

34 *C.R.R.* **3**: pp. 197, 211, 245.

The King's decisions in such cases are not necessarily recorded and are always laconic. Asked in 1204 about an assize of novel disseisin brought against an outlaw whose lands had been taken into the King's hands, the King ordered that the assize should go forward, and the complainant recovered his seisin.[35] Robert of Leicester's case was reserved for the King's opinion. Robert had bought a tenement in Northampton before the town and by the law of the town from a lady whose marriage portion the tenement had been. She had been divorced and had fallen into poverty. According to his own account, Robert had made the purchase unwillingly and after she had besought him "once, twice, a third time and often." Her husband returned and evicted Robert, who brought the assize of novel disseisin. This case came before the King at Northampton and he ordered that an inquest into the truth of the story should be made.[36] Not even a formal judgment is recorded about two ladies who had each appealed the same two men of her husband's death: [37] nor about Doding, who had led two men by night to a house in his father's garden, whence one of them fled and the other withdrew wounded and was found in the morning in the park decapitated.[38] But these are human as well as procedural problems, and there is no need to search about for reasons why the King should be interested in them.

When the King's itinerary, the feet of fines, and the rolls of essoins and pleas are all taken together, examined, and compared, certain features of the King's activities begin to stand out clearly. It is even possible to state some tentative conclusions about his intentions with regard to his courts of justice. The most striking fact which is revealed is the continuing close supervision by the King of his judges' work in the courts. John was as much beset with troubles as Æthelræd II or Harold II had been. He had lost his Norman and his Angevin inheritance, and his Poitevin inheritance was but insecurely held. His withdrawal from the Continent in 1203-1204 had lowered his prestige in

[35] *Ibid.*, p. 128, *Sumerset*. The complainant did not keep his seisin, for the jury which gave the verdict in his favour was attainted. With the exception of one juror who had refused to swear, they were all taken into custody a year later, also before the King: *Ibid.*, pp. 332-333.

[36] *Ibid.* 5: pp. 250-251.

[37] *Ibid.*, p. 234.

[38] *Loc. cit.*

the eyes of all Europe. He faced a recurring danger of invasion from his enemy in France. For his own self-respect he was bound to try to recover his continental lands. The quarrel with the Church, for which not all the blame must be laid on King John, was an unforeseen disaster, which affected everyone in England. The basis of the feudal order, loyalty between lord and man, was threatened. That amid such overwhelming misfortunes the King could still preserve a cheerful front and continue year by year to show the same interest in and concern for the details of judicial administration demonstrates a singular strength of character, a genuine *stabilitas,* which is wholly admirable whatever view is taken of King John as a man.

That he had a definite policy with regard to his courts of justice becomes increasingly clear as his steps are followed through the years up to the crisis of 1209. He desired that his own court which moved with him should form a core of expert judges to hear pleas which were summoned *coram rege,* to be dispatched in ones, twos, or threes to deal with individual cases away from the court,[39] or to carry out his orders about matters of general business.[40] Simon of Pattishall, already a judge of at least nine years' standing when John became king, and Ralf of Stokes, a master, were the first two judges thus singled out,[41] and Simon remained throughout the reign the chief of the judges *de curia.* Ralf was less regularly employed and before the end of the reign he has fallen out of view. Eustace de Faucunberg was tried out in the *curia* for a time in 1209, but he was always more of a bench than a *coram rege* judge. Moreover, he was in orders and when the last efforts to avert the King's excommunication failed

[39] E.g. the King wrote to the Sheriff of Lincoln from York on 28 May, 1207, informing him that he was sending Simon of Pattishall, Henry the Archdeacon of Stafford, and Simon of Kyme to deliver the Lincoln jail and hear the appeal of Agnes daughter of Richard the clerk against a group of Lincoln people touching the breaking of the king's peace and robbery: *Rot. Lit. Claus.,* p. 83*b*.

[40] E.g. the King sent "John Marshall and his fellows" to inquire into the debts of the county of Lincoln: *Pipe Roll 11 John,* p. 76. John Marshall was not a judge *de curia,* but a member of the King's household who was employed to hear the pleas of the *coram rege* court out of term time: *C.R.R.* **6**: p. 218. On 25 August, 1212, the King wrote from Kingshaugh to Walter of Preston and Simon of Pattishall telling them what to do if Earl David refused to give up Fotheringhay Castle as the King had commanded: *Rot. Lit. Claus.,* p. 122*b*.

[41] *Pleas before the King or his Justices* **1**: p. 78.

he disappeared for a time from the English scene.[42] The same is true of the brothers Joscelin and Hugh of Wells, who became bishops respectively of Bath and Wells in 1206 and Lincoln in 1209.[43] From 1204 James of Potterne became the almost inseparable companion of Simon of Pattishall during term-time. They were joined in 1205 by Henry Archdeacon of Stafford and the layman Richard de Mucegros, although the excommunication appears to have ended the Archdeacon's activities as a judge. Henry de Pont-Audemer, a Norman, joined the king's judges in 1207, and in 1210 two Oxfordshire knights, Robert de Aumari and Roger Huscarl, were added. The latter had possibly been a professional attorney in the bench. He came from John's own lands, the honour of Wallingford. The employment as the King's chief judge of such a man as Simon of Pattishall, master of Martin of Pattishall, to whose judgments Bracton looked with reverence, was proof that the work of the court held before the King himself would be based on a detailed knowledge of English law and long practical experience.[44] The King's control over his court is strikingly shown by the debt of 100 marks charged against James of Potterne in the pipe roll of 1207 for allowing Gilbert de Umfraville and Eustace de Vesci to come to an agreement in an appeal between them without the King's permission.[45] It was a salutary warning to all his colleagues.

[42] The justiciar and other barons held discussions at Dover with the bishops and came to a provisional agreement early in September, 1209. The King was at Canterbury before the Michaelmas Term began in the hope of coming to terms with the archbishop, but negotiations broke down. This failure meant that the process of excommunication could be no longer delayed: F. M. Powicke, *Stephen Langton*, p. 77. Eustace de Faucunberg was with the king through June and part of July 1209. He was also with him in the octave of Michaelmas at Canterbury, Havering atte Bower, and St. Bride's, but not later.

[43] Joscelin of Wells was presiding with the King on 8 July 1209 at Bristol and Gloucester: Feet of Fines Hampshire CP 25 (1) 203/3/23, Staffordshire CP 25 (1) 208/2/64 and Norfolk: *Feet of Fines, Norfolk and Suffolk*, nos. 239 and 240. He left England when negotiations with the Church failed. Hugh of Wells was authorising payments in the royal household as late as 20 October 1209, *Rotulus Misae*, p. 134. He joined Stephen Langton for consecration as Bishop of Lincoln, borrowing 300 marks from the Exchequer, doubtless to cover the expense of the journey: *Pipe Roll II John*, pp. xviii and xx.

[44] Of the twelve eyre rolls that survive from John's reign, eleven record business done before Simon of Pattishall; see *The Earliest Lincolnshire Assize Rolls*, pp. xxii-xxiii and *The Earliest Northamptonshire Assize Rolls*, p. xix. It is a fact worth remembering in this connexion that all the rolls preserved from the court *coram rege* in this reign were also rolls of a court in which Simon was the chief judge.

[45] *Pipe Roll 9 John*, p. 207.

The number of judges who sat regularly in the bench was declining from the early years of the reign. In John's first year death carried off Thomas of Hurstbourne, a survivor from the days of Henry II.[46] Richard of Herriard, who succeeded Thomas as first in precedence after the justiciar, ceased to sit in 1205, although he survived until 1208. Henry of Whiston had disappeared during the autumn of 1201. Osbert fitz Hervey died in 1206. William de Warenne, lord of the honour of Wormgay, did not long survive him, but he had ceased to sit as a bench judge before his death. Godfrey de Insula ceased to serve in 1205, but he was in orders and as a member of Hubert Walter's household owed loyalty to Canterbury. Apart from the justiciar, who was but intermittently present,[47] the bench was left by 1208 with three judges only, Eustace de Faucunberg, John of Guestling, and Walter of Creeping. But there is no hint before 1209 that the King had any intention of dispensing altogether with the bench at Westminster. The convenience of a standing court settled in one place, and that place opposite the Exchequer table, so that Exchequer and bench could support and supplement each other was as obvious to the King as to his subjects. What the King seems to have desired was what current practice provided—a flexible system with the King himself and his own court at its head, a small bench sitting at Westminster as a clearing house for pleas, and a succession of eyres dispatched through the country as the pressure of local business and the need for local taxation required.

It is evident during these years that both King and judges were well aware that "following the court" was a grievance which should be mitigated as much as possible. Since the King's itinerary must have been prepared some months ahead and the arrangements known both to the King's own judges and the bench, suits could often be adjourned to a date which would coincide with the King's appearance in the neighbourhood. An

[46] Thomas does not seem to have sat in the bench later than St. Edmund's day (20 Nov.), 1199: Bedfordshire, *Fines*, ed., J. Hunter, **1**: p. 25, His name has disappeared from the pipe roll of 1200.

[47] A careful reading of the rolls of proceedings in the Bench and an examination of the justiciar's activities recorded elsewhere suggests that, despite the recurrence of the justiciar's name in the feet of fines, he was often absent: *Pleas before the King or his Justices*, pp. 88, 142. An officer, Roger of Norwich, of higher status than a mere clerk, was the keeper of the justiciar's roll of proceedings: *C.R.R.* **3**: p. 334.

unforeseen happening might of course compel the King to change his plans. Early in July, 1205, he himself ordered that a case in which the Abbess of Shaftesbury was tenant should be before him on his coming into Dorset after his return from the parts of Northumberland,[48] but the death of the Archbishop of Canterbury on 13 July prevented the northern journey. The arrangements made in the Hilary Term 1207 offer a good example of the efforts the bench judges made to help litigants in this way. The King had been at Westminster before term began and left his senior judge, Simon of Pattishall, there to afforce the bench. The King himself had planned that work in his own court should not start until the octave of the Purification at Oxford, the week work stopped at Westminster. The roll of essoins and pleas heard at Westminster shows the judges putting a Didcot case before the King in the octave of the Purification at Oxford; [49] a Norfolk case before him in the quindene of Easter unless he shall previously go to Bury St. Edmunds; [50] Northamptonshire cases before him on dates when he is known to have been at Rockingham and Geddington; a Rutland case also to the time he was at Geddington.[51] A Salop case was put to the same day at Geddington, but the parties were also Norfolk landowners and must often have crossed England between East Anglia and the Welsh border.[52] It cannot be claimed that every adjournment in this term, or even a majority of them, was made as convenient to litigants. To achieve that would have been impossible, but some of those which on the surface look as though they would cause the maximum inconvenience—an Essex and a Derbyshire case, both put to Oxford—are part of what can be described as the hard core of long-standing cases which had been many times before the King since 1204.[53] The judges must have regarded the tenants as tough fighters who, with the aid of seasoned attorneys, were making every possible use of the law's delays before succumbing to the inevitable end of a final concord.

An examination of the King's activities as a judge during the

48 *C.R.R.* **4**: p. 38, *Wiltesir'*.
49 *Ibid.* **5**: p. 1.
50 *Ibid.*, p. 17.
51 *Ibid.*, pp. 24, 26, 16, and from the essoins cases 2554, 2591, my numbering.
52 *C.R.R.* **5**: p. 17.
53 *Ibid.*, pp. 2-3.

years before 1209 reveals neither oppression nor indifference. What it suggests is a hardworking king, well served by able judges and their clerks, trying to keep pace with an ever increasing volume of litigation and to ease as far as possible the difficulties of litigants and jurors required to attend a moving court. But the pipe rolls of 1208 and 1209 give support to the chronicles which reveal another side of the picture: a suspicious ruler, keeping his subjects in hand through fear.[54] The interdict and its repercussions and the looming excommunication of the King were endangering the relations between the King and his ministers and the clerks in his service. There were stirrings in Wales, and the King of Scots had given refuge to exiled English bishops. The feudal nobility was quiet, because the King was taking hostages for good behaviour and the fall of William de Braiose was an open threat. But if the barons feared the King, he in turn feared treachery. Treason was already in the air in 1209, although as yet impalpable. There is confirmatory record evidence for Matthew Paris's story that the King ordered the Michaelmas Exchequer of that year to sit at Northampton. The reason that Matthew Paris gave was the King's "hatred of the Londoners."[55]

The last eyre of the reign had gone out in the Michaelmas Term 1208. All the bench judges and all the *coram rege* judges took part in it. To find enough men to make up three companies, each seven or eight judges strong, it was necessary to commission many who had not acted as judges in recent years, some of them barons and some of them clerks. Even so, the southern midlands and the southwest were not visited. The practised professional judges were fairly evenly divided among the three groups. Both the bench and the *coram rege* court were kept open through the Michaelmas Term, but both courts were merely doing routine business, hearing essoins, and appointing days for suits to be heard in the octave or the quindene of Hilary, the quindene of Easter, or before the itinerant justices. Hugh of Wells, John Marshall, William Malet, and Walter Mauclerc were in temporary charge of the King's court.[56] One final concord made at the bench shows that the justiciar was

[54] See the Introductions to the Pipe Rolls of 10 and 11 John, Pipe Roll Society, N.S., **23**, **24**.

[55] *Pipe Roll 11 John*, p. 27; *Chronica Majora* (Rolls Series) **2**: p. 524.

[56] *C.R.R.* **5**: p. 304.

presiding there with two barons of the Exchequer, William Briwerre and Reginald of Cornhill, as well as John fitz Hugh and Richard Fleming.[57] Although the northern and midland circuits finished their work in eyre in December, the Lincolnshire, East Anglian, and east-midland circuit was still hard at work until after Easter 1209. Two of the three bench judges were on that circuit, so that work at the bench was still disrupted during the Hilary and Easter Terms. Nevertheless, John of Guestling was back there and brief rolls of essoins and pleas, as well as four final concords made in the Hilary and five made in the Easter term, show that the bench was sitting. The names of the judges recorded in these feet of fines prove that, as in the Michaelmas Term, the justiciar has called on barons of the Exchequer to man the almost empty bench.[58]

Sir Cyril Flower has described the changes in judicial organization made in these years as "dramatic," [59] but it is probable that they seemed less momentous to contemporaries, and less sudden. During a general eyre it was customary to close the bench and direct urgent business to barons of the Exchequer.[60] Since 1204 the King's presence in England has inevitably established a court of more importance than the bench. By bringing

57 Feet of Fines Hampshire CP 25 (1), 203/3/22.

58 Yorkshire Feet of Fines CP 25 (1), 261/9/, Nos. 27 and 29, made on 20 January, 1209, at Westminster before Geoffrey fitz Peter, William de Aubenny, William of Ely the Treasurer, William of Wrotham, Archdeacon of Taunton, William of Cornhill, Archdeacon of Huntingdon, John of Guestling, Robert Mauduit, and master Benedict of Ramsey. On 20 January also before the same judges, Essex Feet of Fines CP 25 (1), 52/13/14; and on the same day before the same judges and also Ralf de Arden, leader of the west-midland circuit, a Warwickshire fine, No. 352 (ed. Margaret O. Harris, unpublished thesis, Reading University). In the Easter Term: On 12 April (the quindene) Feet of Fines, Essex CP 25 (1), 52/13/23, before Geoffrey fitz Peter, William of Ely the Treasurer, William of Cornhill, Archdeacon of Huntingdon, master Benedict of Ramsey, and John of Guestling. On the same day a Gloucestershire fine, Feet of Fines Glouc. CP 25 (1), 73/3/10, before Geoffrey fitz Peter, William of Ely, William, Archdeacon of Huntingdon, John of Guestling, and Walter of Creeping and on the same day before the same judges a Staffordshire fine CP 25 (1) 208/2/55. On 10 May a Warwickshire fine, No. 354, before Geoffrey fitz Peter, William of Ely, William, Archdeacon of Huntingdon, John of Guestling, master Robert of Gloucester, and master Benedict of Ramsey; and a Staffordshire fine, CP 25 (1), 208/2/62, before the same judges, except that master Robert of Gloucester and master Benedict of Ramsey were absent. Walter of Creeping, whom fines show on the Bench in April and a party in the Essex fine made on 12 April, was still in eyre until the middle of May.

59 *Introduction to the Curia Regis Rolls*, p. 19.

60 *Pleas before the King or his Justices* 1: pp. 39, 59-60, 294-296.

his own judges to sit in London, either with or apart from the bench, the King has been giving another proof of the ascendancy of the city in the English social order. The decision that the bench should not be opened in the Trinity Term was probably taken at Easter 1209, when the King and justiciar were together at Northampton.[61] The decision to hold the Michaelmas session of the Exchequer at Northampton instead of at Westminster was probably taken at the same time. It is certain that the bench was not actually superseded until after the Easter Term. It was not until the quindene of Easter that the judges, both at the bench and on eyre, began to put cases "before the King in the morrow of Trinity." It was in the quindene of Easter in the bench that Roger la Zuche went so far as to vouch the King to warranty that no plea ought to be held at Westminster.[62] The last two fines of the Easter Term at Westminster were dated by the Sunday after Ascension day, 10 May.[63] The justices who were still on eyre in the Easter Term adjourned their cases before the King in the morrow, or in the octave of Trinity. The King opened the Trinity Term at Porchester on 26 May, moving on 28 May to Knepp in Sussex, a castle of William de Braiose, then in the King's hand. The essoin roll of the eyre was continued as the essoin roll of the Trinity Term *coram rege*.[64] But after holding the first full session of the term at Lewes the King sent his judges back to Westminster, where they sat under the chairmanship of Simon of Pattishall continuously for three return days. The King's name appears as a judge in one fine only made at Westminster during these three weeks. In the summer his judges accompanied him and his army to the borders of Scotland: twenty fines bear witness to their labours.[65]

Between the Sunday after Ascension Day 1209 and the morrow

[61] *Rot. Chart.*, p. 185*b*.

[62] *C.R.R.* 5: p. 327.

[63] See footnote 58.

[64] Curia Regis Roll, No. 49. The judges of the Lincolnshire, East Anglian, and eastern counties circuit visited so many counties in the course of their eyre that the roll has the appearance of a *curia regis*, rather than an eyre roll. Hence it has never been calendared with the Assize rolls. I hope to print this roll in a forthcoming volume of the Selden Society.

[65] These fines cover the period 24 June to 4 August; the first being made at Odiham and the last at Norham on Tweed. In the week before the Michaelmas Term the judges were with the King at Canterbury, see footnote 42. Through the Michaelmas Term the king's judges spent four return days, though not continuously, beside the Exchequer at Northampton.

of St. Martin's day 1212 the name of Geoffrey fitz Peter never occurs as a presiding judge at the making of final concords, even when the chirographs were written at Westminster. There is ample evidence that he was still chief justiciar and no evidence at all that he had lost the King's confidence, or ever did lose it before his death in October, 1213.[66] The King was still happy to enjoy the justiciar's hospitality at Ditton or Kimbolton,[67] to send roses to his mistress from the justiciar's manor at Ditton,[68] to feed paupers as a penance for the justiciar's consumption of meat when he should have fasted.[69] The justiciar's writ could still initiate pleas in the *coram rege* court.[70] He was presiding at the Exchequer[71] and bearing his full part in the negotiations between the King and the Pope, the Archbishop, and the bishops. But the King, or perhaps it might more truly be said the Pope, has brought the regular sessions of the bench to an end.

Nevertheless, this was not done without genuine efforts to meet the demands of litigants. Rolls of proceedings *coram rege* in the Hilary and Easter Term 1210 bear little evidence on their face that they are being compiled in a period of national distress, when the King was an excommunicate and the land had been for two years under interdict. The surviving feet of fines, twenty-eight from the Hilary and fifteen from the Easter Term, are as well written as ever. The Hilary Term lasted for seven weeks, during which sessions were held at Wilton, at London (partly at St. Bride's, partly at the Tower, and partly at Westminster), at Gloucester, at Winchester, and at London again. In each place the court sat long enough to allow the traditional number of

66 Professor Painter twice refers in *The Reign of King John* to a quarrel between the King and the justiciar in 1212. On p. 278 he calls it "a bitter quarrel" and on p. 262 he says that the king forced him "to offer a heavy fine for his goodwill." His authority is the *Histoire des ducs de Normandie* p. 116, but this is an account of floating gossip which should not outweigh record evidence. I am grateful to Dr. Bowen of Reading University for help with the translation. It is true that the custody of the great manor of Kirton in-Lindsey passed at the half year from Geoffrey fitz Peter to the Count of Boulogne, whose support the King desired: *Pipe Roll 12 John*, pp. 102, 103 and *Rot. Lit. Claus.*, 1: p. 116. But this does not justify the rumour in the Histoire.

67 *Rotulus Misae* (Cole's *Records*), pp. 232, 234, 250.

68 *Ibid.*, p. 234.

69 *Ibid.*, pp. 236, 243.

70 *C.R.R.* 6: pp. 80-81. The Abbot of St. Albans tried to get a writ brought against him quashed on the ground that although the King was in England he had been summoned by the justiciar's writ.

71 *Rot. Lit. Claus.*, p. 132 *b*.

days for the proper working of the sessions. The Easter Term lasted for two return days only, but they were both held at Westminster. A Gloucester session which had been arranged for the third week of the term was postponed because of the King's Irish expedition. The judges through both terms were the King, Simon of Pattishall, James of Potterne, Henry de Pont-Audemer, and, for part of the Hilary Term, Richard de Mucegros. Even if the King did not sit in court day by day, he was never out of touch with its work. His presence at an important Sussex case touching four manors is expressly stated.[72] It was the King himself who ordered that certain robbers should be detained in the Fleet prison,[73] and he was consulted about an essoin.[74]

The King was in Ireland between the middle of June and 26 August, so that there could be no Trinity Term *coram rege* and the Michaelmas Term started late, but during August most shires were visited twice by itinerant justices. Two writs entered in the cartulary of Reading Abbey refer to the first of these visitations.[75] On 3 August the justiciar instructed the Sheriff of Berkshire and his fellow justices itinerant in the county to allow the Abbot of Reading to enjoy his court in his forinsec hundred of Reading "touching all pleas and assizes and touching all pleas of the crown and all manner of liberties and customs." The second writ, also addressed to the itinerant justices in Berkshire, was sent by the Treasurer and the barons of the Exchequer and also affirmed the Abbot's right to his forinsec hundred. The writs were necessary on this occasion because no itinerant justices had visited Berkshire since the King had granted the hundred to the abbey.[76] The writs confirm the evidence of the pipe roll that the first of these anomalous eyres in each shire was generally made by the Sheriff acting as a judge in his own county together with other local men recruited for the purpose.[77] The

72 *C.R.R.* **6**: pp. 11-12.
73 *Ibid.*, p. 24.
74 *Ibid.*, p. 19.
75 See Appendix VI.
76 On 23 February, 1208, *Rot. Chart.*, p. 175.
77 In his introduction to the *Pipe Roll of 12 John*, pp. xix ff., Mr. Slade has set out the evidence the roll affords that the sheriff or under-sheriff generally acted on this occasion as a judge in his own shire together with local men, sometimes men of no particular importance and without previous experience. Curiously enough, the pipe roll, in recording the amercements imposed in Berkshire, omits the name of the Sheriff, John de Whichenolton, from the

second visit in each shire was made by what the pipe roll describes as "Autumnal Justices sent out by Geoffrey fitz Peter while the King was in Ireland." The sheriffs and their fellow judges had evidently been acting as vacation judges to hear assizes and deliver the jails.[78] The autumnal justices on the other hand were mainly occupied in detecting and amercing unspecified "transgressions" or "trepasses." Among those thus punished by the autumnal justices in many shires are men who had been acting as itinerant justices with the Sheriff earlier in the month.[79] The speed with which all this work was accomplished may be one reason why it has left no feet of fines behind it. No rolls made up before any of these judges has survived from any shire.

In addition to the amercements imposed by these two sets of judges itinerant the pipe rolls of 1210 and 1211 record new amercements by Simon of Pattishall, Richard Marsh, and the Earls of Winchester and Salisbury, all of whom had been with the King in Ireland.[80] Sometimes the amercements are said to be placed on "the convicted." It is probable that these sums are

heading giving the judges' names. Since the evidence of the justiciar's writ is clearly decisive it is at least arguable that even if the pipe roll omits the name of the sheriff from among the judges it is highly probable that he or his under-sheriff took part in the proceedings in every shire. The use of the sheriff as a judge on this occasion may have been due partly to the difficulty of finding enough skilled judges and partly to a desire to utilize to the full his local knowledge.

[78] The summer eyre of 1206 may be instanced as a parallel to the work done in early August, 1210. In 1206 the judges who sat in Somerset and Wiltshire are described in Feet of Fines as "itinerant justices to take assizes of novel disseisin" (Feet of Fines Wilts. CP 25 (1), 250/3/19 and 20): one of these fines ended a plea of dower and the other an assize of mort d'ancestor. The roll compiled before the judges itinerant in Lincolnshire in 1206 has survived: see *Earliest Lincolnshire Assize Rolls*, pp. xl-xlii and 235-277.

[79] Some of the judges who were amerced by the autumnal justices were men of far wider judicial experience than merely the August eyre of 1210. Alexander of Pointon (*P.R. 12 John*, p. 37) had served with Simon of Pattishall in 1202 and was with him again in 1208 (*Earliest Lincolnshire Assize Rolls*, pp. xxvii-xviii). Richard of Seething (*P.R. 12 John*, pp. 33, 34) was with the 1198 eyre in East Anglia (*Earliest Lincolnshire Assize Rolls*, p. 242) and on eyre with Simon of Pattishall in 1203 and 1206. Henry of Northampton (*P.R. 12 John*, p. 213) was on eyre with Simon of Pattishall in 1202 and 1208 (*Earliest Lincolnshire Assize Rolls*, pp. xxv-xxvi). He was a son of Peter son of Adam of Northampton who helped to put in writing the customary law of the town (*Leges Ville Norht*, published by the corporation of Northampton, ed. Councillor Frank Lee, mayor, 1951). Walter of Creeping (*P.R. 13 John*, p. 120) was a bench judge.

[80] *Rot. de . . . Praestitis*, ed. T. Duffus Hardy, pp. 188 (Simon of Pattishall), 177, 192 (Richard Marsh), 227 (Earl of Winchester), 192 (Earl of Salisbury).

debts resulting from work done by the *coram rege* judges who had not time to affeer all the amercements to be paid by those convicted before them. Members of the King's household and company may well have been deputed to do the work. The uneasy state of the country during the interdict had increased both crime and its violent, even extra-legal, suppression. As early as 11 April, 1208, the King had found it necessary to issue a writ for the protection of clerks and the religious in which the violence of the wording carries an echo of his living voice: he "will cause an offender to be hanged at the nearest oak." [81] The records both of the Exchequer and the king's court suggest that the conduct of judicial duels in counties as far apart as Yorkshire, Lincolnshire, and Gloucestershire needed correction.[82] It may well be that the Sheriff of Rutland was not alone among his fellows in hanging a criminal without the presence of the king's justices.[83]

In the Michaelmas Term 1210 the King opened his court at Westminster and sat at Northampton, Ely, Nottingham, Lichfield, and York, where he spent Christmas. The roll of proceedings shows that the judges were still doing their best to ease the burden of attendance. Many local cases were dealt with at Ely.[84] The parties to a Northamptonshire fine were told to receive their chirograph at Northampton.[85] Final concords often involved the appearance of tenants to express their agreement and do homage to a new lord. In this term a Lincolnshire, a Northumberland, and a Yorkshire concord each involved the appearance of tenants before the chirograph could be handed over. Each was accordingly adjourned until "the coming of the lord king into those parts." [86] The Lincoln fine was eventually dated at Nottingham and the Yorkshire one at Durham. The sureties of a Yorkshire man, who had been instructed to have him at Westminster at the opening session, but failed to do so, were

[81] *Rot. Lit. Claus.*, p. 111.

[82] *Pipe Roll 11 John*, p. 76; *Pipe Roll 13 John*, pp. 81, 92, 177; *C.R.R.* **6**: pp. 214-215, 67.

[83] *C.R.R.* **6**: p. 10. The King pardoned the sheriff: *Pipe Roll 10 John*, p. 213.

[84] *C.R.R.* **6**: p. 87.

[85] *Ibid.*, p. 84.

[86] *Ibid.*, p. 68, *Linc'* "in aduentu domini Regis in partes illas quando comitatus summonitus erit coram eo"; *Norhumb'* "in aduentu domini Regis in partes illas vel in aduentu justiciariorum, si prius uenerint"; p. 70, *Ebor'* " in aduentu domini Regis in partes illas etc."

given a day in the King's coming into the parts of York.[87] No rolls have survived from the Hilary or Easter Terms 1211, but the court circulated through Westminster, Southampton, Dorset, Winchester in the Hilary and Westminster, Norwich, Northampton in the Easter Term. The court accompanied the King for briefer sessions at Nottingham, Tutbury, and Chester, whence he began his summer campaigns against his son-in-law in North Wales. In consequence of these operations there was no Trinity Term. Nevertheless, in the course of the past year the King had opened each term with a Westminster session, had spent in all five return days there, and had taken his court to the north, the east, the Midlands, and the south.

A single roll contains the record of the Michaelmas and Hilary Terms 1211-1212. Sir Cyril Flower has pointed out that twenty-two of its membranes are written in the practised bench hand.[88] The first of them is even headed *Placita . . . capta apud Westmonasterium*. The other three, irregular in size, unorthodox in formula, and written by a household clerk untrained in legal reporting, contain cases heard in Dorset before the term began at Westminster and in Dorset and Wiltshire in the Christmas vacation. "The pleas of the court" were then in charge of "John Marshall and his fellows," vacation judges, acting as caretakers for Simon of Pattishall, James of Potterne, Henry de Pont-Audemer, Robert d'Aumari, and Roger Huscarl, the "judges of the court." [89] For all its mobility the court *coram rege* has developed its routine to a high degree of precision. The caretaker judges during vacations did not hear important cases. They adjourned them, but they did hear essoins, receive the appointment of attorneys, and appoint days for later hearings. They did valuable, but supplementary, work. Simon and his fellows of the court *coram rege* had organized the Michaelmas Term 1211 in two main sessions, at Westminster and at Hereford, with a brief session at Reading on the way west and a briefer one at Hanley in Worcestershire late in November, before the judges left the court for the vacation. The Hereford session had enabled the judges to dispose of an accumulation of business in the west. The Hilary Term opened at Kingshaugh in Nottinghamshire, and

87 *Ibid.*, p. 113.
88 *Ibid.*, p. 117.
89 *C.R.R.* 6: p. 322: *Sumerset'*, referring to day given at pp. 218-219, *Sumerset'*.

the court sat at York, Durham, and Newcastle before returning to Westminster through Lincolnshire. The many litigants who appeared by attorney and the many jurors who failed to appear at all illustrate the reaction of southerners to the prospect of a northern journey in winter. But some attempts were still being made to fix dates and places as convenient to litigants as the King's business permitted: a Nottinghamshire case to the next coming of the lord king to York after Easter; [90] a Middlesex case to the next coming of the lord king to London after Easter; [91] a Buckinghamshire case "at the prayer of the parties to the next coming of the lord king to London after Easter." [92]

Through the Easter and Trinity Terms 1212 the King was still moving in company with his judges, who were still as far as possible considering the convenience of litigants. In the Easter Term an Essex case was put at the prayer of the parties to the King's next coming to London; [93] the parties to a Surrey final concord were to receive their chirograph at the King's next coming to London; [94] a Middlesex case was put to the King's next coming to London after Whitsun.[95] "At the request of the parties and particularly of the tenants," a Yorkshire case was put to three weeks after Trinity: [96] the King is known to have reached Yorkshire in that week. At an early date in the Easter Term the judges began to adjourn cases to the Sunday after the Ascension; the court was then at Westminster. A Hampshire case was put to the King's next coming to Winchester [97] and many cases were put to that part of the Trinity Term in which the court sat in London before departing again to the north.[98]

Throughout the troubles of these years individual subjects of

[90] *Ibid.*, p. 210.
[91] *Ibid.*, pp. 234-235.
[92] *Ibid.*, p. 236 (Maud of Hedsor).
[93] *Ibid.*, p. 259.
[94] *Ibid.*, p. 286.
[95] *Ibid.*, p. 274.
[96] *Ibid.*, p. 275.
[97] *Ibid.*, p. 288.
[98] Like the justiciar in 1208-1209 the King was using the Exchequer and the barons of the Exchequer to supplement his judges' work. A final record was made before the barons at the Exchequer at Westminster "by command of the lord king" at the end of the Easter Term: Unknown Counties CP 25 (1) 282/5/60. The barons named were William the Treasurer; Richard Marsh, Archdeacon of Northumberland; William Briwerre; William, Archdeacon of Huntingdon; and Master Robert of Gloucester.

King John could still regard him as the fountain of justice, to be invoked when local officers and courts failed them. A man was robbed on his way from Yaxley market, his thumb and a bone in his chest broken. He failed to get his attackers into the shire court and when his brother, "whom they had likewise assaulted, saw that he could get no justice, he went to the court and secured that that suit should be put before the lord king." [99] At the request of a disseisor the King himself ordered a jury of twenty-four to report on the verdict of a jury of twelve, which had given in the complainant's favour. Since "the jury of twenty-four said the same as the jury of twelve" the disseisor was charged with an amercement of 100 marks.[100] The judges consulted the King about individual prisoners; a guiltless fool who said he was a robber; a boy who threw a stone and accidentally killed another; and the royal prerogative of mercy was extended.[101] It was certainly a tedious business for litigants from Cornwall, Kent, or Sussex to follow the court to Yorkshire or beyond, but the northern journey in the Trinity Term 1212 allowed the judges to dispose of a remarkable accumulation of local business, particularly novel disseisins and the delivery of jails. The fourteenth final concord of the journey was made at Durham on 25 June, and the King's return south was marked by more fines and little groups of local cases; [102] a fine at York on 1 July, three fines at Nottingham on 8 July, three at Northampton on 15 July. Some nineteen Buckinghamshire cases were probably heard when the King stayed, about the middle of the month, at Wakefield Lawn, a hunting lodge in Potterspury. The last fine is dated at Abingdon on 22 July. The heading *Oxon'* above six Oxfordshire cases may indicate that the judges sat in the city while the King went on to Woodstock for three nights, 19-22 July. Similarly the heading *Wigorn'* must mark their stay at Worcester while the King took help to Robert de Vipont beseiged in Wales.[103] The last entry of the term was made on 10 August at Lamport in Northamptonshire.[104]

99 *Ibid.*, p. 264.
100 *Ibid.*, p. 335.
101 *Ibid.*, p. 351.
102 The heading *Estreng*, not identified or indexed *ibid.*, p. 332, probably indicates a stay at Eastrington, Yorks, E.R.
103 *Rotulus Misae*, p. 237.
104 *C.R.R.* 6: p. 404.

Only a few days later, in the middle of August, the King had learned that many of his barons were plotting treason. It remains a striking tribute to his command of the situation that he allowed events to make so little immediate difference to his relations with his judges and his court. The essoins and feet of fines for the Michaelmas Term show that it was not until the morrow of St. Martin's day, 12 November, that he ceased to concern himself with the operations of his court. When the last seventeen final concords of the term were made at Westminster, although the king's judges are there, the justiciar has again replaced the King as president. But even then a membrane of essoins was made up at Flaxley by a household clerk and sent to Westminster to be inserted in the essoin roll of the term.[105] The judges at Westminster still wished to consult the King about Reginald of Cornhill's essoin, and cases were adjourned for the king's hearing when he came to London or in the Hilary Term.[106] Nevertheless, when the Hilary Term 1213 began the King was not at Westminster. His three judges sat there under the presidency of the justiciar, but no other record of their work survives than fifteen feet of fines.[107] The court did not sit in the Easter Term because of the general summons to defend the shores against the projected French invasion. The Trinity Term was suspended because of the settlement with the Pope and the solemn lifting of excommunication from the King. Thereafter the King, anxious to invade France, was distracted by the attitude of his irresponsive northern barons. No medieval king could have withstood the pressure of such events as caused King John at long last to break the routine of his judicial terms.

Despite these events, and although the justiciar was dying, the Michaelmas Term opened at Westminster in the octave. Between Geoffrey fitz Peter's death on 14 October 1213 and the appointment of Peter des Roches as his successor on 1 February, 1214, there was no justiciar. Feet of Fines show Simon of Pattishall and his fellow judges of the court sitting at Westminster

105 Curia Regis Roll (KB 26), No. 57, mem. 3.

106 *Ibid.* This essoin roll is unprinted. It is hoped to include it in a forthcoming volume of the Selden Society. By my numbering these cases are Nos. 4615, 4649, 4686, 4698.

107 A sixteenth fine was made before the King and his three judges. It is possible that his name replaces that of the justiciar because the plea had been before his court.

with the Earl of Winchester for the first session of the Michaelmas Term, and thereafter by themselves until they moved to Oxford at the beginning of November to be at hand during the discussions between the King, the Church, and the barons. They still expected the King to give attention to the work of his court. They adjourned a Middlesex case "until the King's coming to London" [108] and three Norfolk cases were adjourned until the morrow of All Souls at Oxford, one of them "by the lord King's command, because that matter touches the lord King." [109] The King's presence as a judge is recorded in the three fines made at Oxford on 2 November, in the four fines made at Westminster in the last half of November,[110] and in the five fines made at Reading on 7 December. Even while the King was engaged in hard bargaining over the compensation due to the Church for its losses during the interdict his interest in the proceedings of his court was still alive.

As the judges were gathering for the Hilary Term 1214 the King was leaving London to embark for Poitou. Nevertheless, the first thirteen final concords of the term were ostensibly made before him. Before the record of his presence is dismissed as fiction it should be noted that all these fines terminated suits which had been before the court in the previous term.[111] The parties might well be glad of the security of the King's name in their chirographs. The fourteenth fine of the term, in which the new justiciar's name replaces that of the King, ended a suit which had not been before the court in the Michaelmas Term.[112]

108 *Ibid.*, p. 7.

109 *Ibid.*, pp. 5, 6.

110 The King's itinerary shows that he cannot have been at Westminster during the two return days by which these four fines are dated. It is possible that, just as the justiciar's name was inserted in fines made at Westminster even in his absence, so during the vacancy in the justiciarship the King's name was automatically inserted to strengthen the authority of the court.

111 In the octave of Hilary 3 Bedfordshire, 2 Lincolnshire (Nos. 331 and 332), and 1 Divers Counties fine; in the quindene 2 Bedfordshire fines; in the morrow of the Purification 1 Middlesex and 1 Warwickshire fine. The thirteenth, a Lincolnshire fine (No. 333), made in the octave of the Purification, is wrongly stated (Pipe Roll Society, vol. xxix, N.S.) to be made at "Wilton." The reading is clearly "Westm." Although there is no mention of this case in any roll before that of the Hilary Term, when a day was set for the receipt of the chirograph (*C.R.R.* 7: p. 75), the fact that Simon of Pattishall was the complainant makes it highly probable that this case, like the others, had been at least technically before the King himself.

112 A Suffolk fine, made in a month from Hilary, the same week as the thirteenth fine of the term; *Feet of Fines, Norfolk and Suffolk*, Pipe Roll Society, N.S. **32** No. 563.

It is significant that one of the King's first acts after his return from Poitou in October 1214 was to instruct Simon of Pattishall and his fellows to put a plea before him in the state it was when it stood over because the tenant was crossing with the King to Poitou.[113] Only one more final concord records the King's presence as a judge. At the New Temple in the opening of the Easter Term 1215 with the Bishop of Winchester, Richard Marsh, and Roger Huscarl he presided at the making of a final concord touching the advowson of the church of Barney in Norfolk.[114] It may seem strange that, when his barons were already in arms against him, the King could still interest himself in a piece of judicial business. But even as late as 30 March, 1216, when the land was enduring foreign invasion and civil war was raging, the King appointed four men, of whom Simon of Pattishall was one, to hear a recognition of darrein presentment at Northampton in the quindene of Easter "according to the law and custom of the realm of England." [115]

Under Peter des Roches, the new justiciar, so much of the old order had been restored that justices had sat regularly through the usual terms at Westminster up to the outbreak of civil war. Another judge, Joscelin of Stukeley, steward of the Abbot of Ramsey, was even added to their number. No itinerant justices went out, but when business took the justiciar himself away from London he heard the assizes of novel disseisin awaiting settlement in the shires he visited.[116] The King had failed to satisfy his subjects' appetite for litigation, and the judicial clauses of the Great Charter point to the weaknesses in a system of judicial administration which had developed piecemeal in response to an ever increasing demand. Few, if any, of the abuses dealt with in the Charter were exclusively the result of John's policy, nor were they all satisfactorily corrected in the years which followed. The slowness of justice even in the new assizes could not easily be remedied, nor could untrustworthy sheriffs and local officers easily be kept from encroaching on the royal authority in the shire court. The judicial clauses of the charter were a genuine programme of reform for long-standing grievances.

In the long view it may well appear that in the matter of judicial administration King John deserves credit rather than

[113] *Rot. Lit. Claus.*, p. 175.
[114] *Feet of Fines, Norfolk and Suffolk*, No. 279.
[115] *Rot. Lit. Claus.*, p. 270.
[116] *Pipe Roll 16 John*, pp. 47, 133-136, 165-166.

blame. He should be credited with readiness to allow litigants access to the benefits of his court and the wisdom of his judges even if their pleas did not conform precisely with established rules. In this way the common law grew in volume and strength. He should be given credit for his readiness to fulfil his royal duty of ameliorating the rigour of the law for the helpless, women, children, the poor, and the idiot. He should be given credit for the real efforts made between 1209 and 1212 to create with a few judges the illusion of a stable court at Westminster and an itinerant court taking justice to the shires. The necessity of following the king's court was an old grievance when he became king. The attempts made in his reign to mitigate it by adjourning cases to his next coming to the litigants' own parts deserve acknowledgment. Moreover, the development of the legal profession was stimulated by the practice, increasingly common in his reign, of leaving the conduct of cases in his court to an attorney. Among the long list of "attorneys received before the King" in the Trinity Term 1212 are several who are certainly professional pleaders, forerunners of members of the bar.[117] The work of one of King John's judges was remembered with respect a generation later by a writer who had nothing good to say about the king himself. In recording the appointment of Hugh of Pattishall as Treasurer in 1234, Matthew Paris described him as "a man faithful and honest, son of Simon of Pattishall the judge, who at one time directed the government of all England, the father's fidelity bearing witness to the faith of the son." [118] Perhaps it may also bear witness to the part he and his master had played in the development of the English common law.

[117] Curia Regis Roll (KB 26), No. 55, mems. 9 and 10, e.g. Thomas Tutadebles, who once appears there as Thomas Tutatencenuledebles (case 4559, my numbering).

[118] *Chronica Majora (Rolls Series)* **3**: p. 296. Matthew Paris could not forbear another polite reference to Simon of Pattishall when Hugh was elected Bishop of Coventry in 1240: "by whose wisdom all England was at one time ruled" (*ibid.*, p. 542).

APPENDIX OF ILLUSTRATIVE MATERIAL

I. THE SANDWICH PLEA OF 1127

Collections for an History of Sandwich in Kent by William Boys, Canterbury (1792), p. 551.

Anno ab incarnacione Domini millesimo centesimo vicesimo septimo, ex precepto Henrici regis Anglorum, annuente Willelmo archiepiscopo Cantuariensi tocius Britannie primato et legato sancte Romane ecclesie, Habitum est placitum apud Sandewych de theolonio et consuetudine Sandewici portus. Siquidem rex Anglorum Cnut olim eundem portum et omnes exitus et consuetudines ex utraque parte ripe dederat ecclesie Christi Cantuariensi, cum aurea sui capitis corona que adhuc seruatur in predicta ecclesia in capite sancte crucis domini saluatoris: nuper autem quidam considerantes ex altera parte portus, in terra abbatis sancti Augustini que vocatur Stonore, esse locum abilem nauium stacionem sereno tempore, domunculas sibi propter naues aduectantes ibidem fecerunt: ex quo accidit, ut theoloneum et consuetudines a nauibus que ibidem applicuerant homines sancti Augustini ab exteris clancule acciperent, quas ministri de Sandewych et Sandewici portus accipere deberent: set hoc cum in noticiam veniret, transibant portum ministri, et ab hominibus abbatis theoloneum, siue quamlibet consuetudinem acceptam ab eis, auferebant, et nolentes intardum reddere violenter per iusticiam quam nitebantur extorquebant. Preterea erat nauicula in portu, qua vehebantur homines et res eorum ad mercatum venientes sive redeuntes, que Christi ecclesie erat, sicut portus et Sandewych; nec alius omnino ibidem nauem ad transfretandum habeat; sed postquam homines abbatis ceperunt habitare in terra ipsius ad Stonore, et rectitudines ad Sandewych pertinentes clanculo, ut supradictum est, usurpare, latenter eciam suam nauiculam frequenter sumpserunt ad transuehendos homines et sua, de insula Tanetos; habet enim ibi abbas plurimam multitudinem hominum. Qua ex re multe deceptaciones inter eos et discordie sepe numero contigerunt, dum ministri ecclesie Christi anticum morem veritatis racione constanter niterentur retentare, illi astuta calliditate et presumptuosa feritate studerent malecepta sibi tenendo firmare.

I. THE SANDWICH PLEA OF 1127

Collections for an History of Sandwich in Kent by William Boys, Canterbury (1792), p. 551.

In the year from the Lord's incarnation 1127 by the command of Henry King of the English, William Archbishop of Canterbury, primate of all Britain and legate of the Holy Roman See agreeing, a plea was held at Sandwich touching the toll and customs of the port of Sandwich. Cnut, King of the English, had in former days given the same port and all the issues and customs on each side of the water to Christchurch, Canterbury, with the golden crown from his head, which is still preserved in the aforesaid church on the top of the Saviour's cross. Of recent times some people thinking that the other side of the harbour on the Abbot of Saint Augustine's land called Stonar would be a convenient place for ships to tie up in fair weather, have built little houses there for themselves because of the ships coming there. Whence it happens that St. Augustine's men have secretly received the toll and customs from foreigners who have come there which the ministers of Sandwich and the port of Sandwich ought to have received. But when this became known the ministers of the port went over and justly took away from the Abbot's men forcibly whatever toll or custom they had wrongfully received. Furthermore, there was a little boat in the harbour, belonging like the port of Sandwich to Christchurch, in which men and their goods coming or going to the market were carried, nor had anyone else any right to a ferryboat there, but after the Abbot's men began to live on their land at Stonar and secretly to usurp the rights belonging to Sandwich, as is aforesaid, they secretly also used their ferryboat to carry men and their goods from the island of Thanet, for the Abbot had a great multitude of men there. Wherefore many disputes and quarrels without number broke out among them, while the ministers of Christchurch rightfully and consistently tried to retain the ancient custom, they, with cunning guile and daring fierceness, tried to strengthen their hold on what they had wrongfully seized. The King heard how the monks of Canter-

Taliter ergo cum monachi ecclesie Christi Cantuarie sua iura vellent tenere et abbas sancti Augustini cum suis eis conaretur auferre, audiuit rex, et volens utriusque ecclesie paci consulere, precepit, ut conuentus sapientum virorum, iuxta mare habitancium, apud Sandewych congregare, ubique quid iuris utraque haberet ecclesia dis-[p. 552] cuteretur, discussum sacramentum firmaretur, sicque deinceps firmum illibatumque teneretur. Itaque, conuentum congregatum, antequam edictum quod rex decreuerat legeretur, Willielmus archiepiscopus condigna sibi admonutacione breuiter populum allocutus est, mouens et contestans eos per fidem et christianitatem suam, ut omnes huius cause intentissime intenderent et sine ulla formidine vel passim fauore veritatem assererent. Regia quoque potestas hoc idem ipsis, per fidem et sacramentum quibus illi obligati, imperauit. Concorditer omnes dicta susseperunt seseque ita facturos promiserunt. Deinde cum omnes fere dicerent se nunquam sciuisse Sandewici portus redditum ad aliquem pertinuisse nisi ad ecclesiam Christi Cantuarie, petitum est, ut de hac re, quid rex decreuerat, audiretur. Itaque prolate sunt litere: Henricus rex Anglorum, archiepiscopo Cantuariensi et abbati sancti Augustini et vicecomiti de Kent, salutem. Facite recognosci per sacramentum duodecim legalium hominum de Douorre et duodecim legalium hominum de prouincia de Sandewico, qui non sunt homines archiepiscopi nec homines abbatis, veritatem de calumpnia consuetudinum que est inter eos, desicut fuerunt tempore patris mei et tempore Lanfranci archiepiscopi et Anselmi archiepiscopi, et tales habebat archiepiscopus consuetudines, et abbas tales, quales recognitum fuerit tunc temporis habuisse antecessores eorum; ita quod unaqueque ecclesia plene habeat rectum suum. Testibus episcopo Lincolniense et Roberto de Sigillo, et Galfrido de Clyntym, apud London. Hec cum in audiencia tocius conuentus lecta et intellecta fuissent, electi sunt, ut rex mandauerat, de hominibus regis et baronum qui rem optime nouerant, viginti quatuor maturi sapientes senes multorum annorum bonum testimonium habentes. Istis ergo a tota multitudine nominatis, quesitum est eis quid de hac re dicerent, ita quod dicerent scirent pro certo, quod sacramento probarent. Qui nichil hesitantes constanter affirmarunt, prefatum portum, theoloneum et consuetudines maritimas, esse monachorum ecclesie Christi Cantuarie, nec quen-

bury wished to retain their rights and the Abbot of St. Augustine's with his men wished to take them way, and, wishing to provide for the peace of both the churches, he commanded that an assembly of wise men, living near the sea should gather at Sandwich and there the rights which each church should have could be investigated, the findings could be confirmed by oath, and thus henceforward held firm and unshaken. And thus the assembly having come together, before the King's command had been read, William the Archbishop with an appropriate warning for his own part, briefly addressed the people, urging them and calling upon them by their Christian faith that all should consider most carefully the truth of this case and declare it without fear or favour. The royal power also laid this upon them by the faith and oath by which they were bound. All received his words with agreement and promised to do as they were bidden. Then when almost all said that they had never known the rent of the port of Sandwich to belong to anyone other than Christchurch, Canterbury, it was asked that what the King had commanded should be heard. And so the letters were produced: Henry, King of the English to the Archbishop of Canterbury and the Abbot of St. Augustine's and the Sheriff of Kent, Greeting. Cause the truth to be declared by the oath of twelve lawful men of Dover and twelve lawful men of the neighbourhood of Sandwich, who are neither the men of the Archbishop nor the men of the Abbot, touching the claim of customs which is between them as they were in the time of my father and in the time of Lanfranc the Archbishop and Anselm the Archbishop, and let the Archbishop have such customs and the Abbot have such customs as it is declared that their predecessors had at that time, so that each church shall fully have its right. Witnesses, the Bishop of Lincoln, and Robert de Sigillo and Geoffrey of Glympton, at London. When this had been read and understood in the hearing of the whole assembly, there were elected as the King had commanded, from among the men of the King and the barons, twenty-four wise old men full of years and having good testimony. These, therefore, having been named by the whole assembly, they were asked what they would say on this matter, so that they could say what they knew to be true and could prove on oath. Without hesitation, they firmly

quam hominem aliquid iuris in portu habere nisi ipsi et eorum ministri a loco qui dicitur ad Burgegate usque ad Merkesfliete ex utraque parte fluminis. His magna multitudo testimonium peribuit. Allatus est sibi textus sacrorum euangeliorum, et iurauerunt de Douorre homines regis duodecim. Wulfine filius Berewy. Wulfine Dod. Fadwyne. Canutus Kenward. Wulfinnus filius Wilnothi. Godwine Faber. Liofwinegille. Eadwine Clericus. Brinmane filius Lemay. Goldstan filius Brumig. Odo Monetarius. Baldewine filius Fike. Subsequentes vero sunt de prouincia circa Sandewicum, habens barones de Sancta Margareta. Blacsune. Sigar. Alfword filius Elnoldi. Alfword filius Blakemanno. Sirent filius Godwym. Wulfwi de Boklande. Ricardus homo Henrici de Port. Wulfwonord de Cilendenne. Fadwon de Eac. Wolfwyne filius Cake. Alfwyne de Eac. Hergod homo Alani Pirot. Primus itaque horum Wolfwyne filius Berewy, stans in medio multitudinis et tenens in manibus sacrorum librum euangeliorum pronunciauit sic: Ego iuro, theoloneum Sandewici portus, consuetudines omnes maritimas ex utraque parte fluminis ab Burgegate usque ad Merkesfliete, et nauiculam ad transfretandum, solomodo pertinere ad archiepiscopum et monachos ecclesie Christi Cantuarie; nec quenquam alium ius aliquod ibi habere nisi ipsi et ministri eorum; secuti ego accepi ab antecessoribus meis, et vidi et [p. 553] audivi ab adolescencia mea usque nunc; sic me deus adiuuet et hec sancta euangelia. Subsequentes socii qui assignati sunt hoc ipsum incuntanter prosecuti sunt. Huius placiti iusticiam tenuit Willelmus vicecomes Kancie, cui interfuerunt Willielmus archiepiscopus Cantuariensis, legatus ecclesie sancte Romane et primas tocius Britannie. Johannes episcopus Roffensis. Hugo abbas sancti Augustini. Robertus de Veer, Regis constabularius. Ruerent de Auerences. Hugo de Chilleham. Willielmus de Annisforthe. Hamo filius Vitalis. Rogerus de Welle et filius eius. Willielmus Reiner de Hesdynge et filius eius. Willelmus Asketur de Rettlynge. Raulf Pieoc. Raulf Camerarius. Vinufreid de Wicham. Hamo capellanus. Raulf Coffin. Rainolf frater Archiepiscopi. Raulf Cannel. Nigel filius Godfridi. Niel de Hwetacre. Giffard capellanus Limel. Henricus Jordan. Godfridus Presbiter. Wolfrik. Geldewin. Lyofwine. Wikemonde. Alanus Wiber de Sancto Gregorio. Adam de Hethe. Sprot.

declared that the aforesaid port, toll, and maritime customs belonged to the monks of Christchurch, Canterbury, and that no one else ought to have any right in the port save them and their ministers from the place called Burgegate as far as Merkesfliete on each side of the river. To these things the great multitude agreed. A copy of the holy gospels was brought and the twelve king's men of Dover swore, Wulfwine son of Beornwig, Wulfwine Dod, Eadwine, Cnut Kenward, Wulfig son of Wulfnoth, Godwin the smith, Leofwine Gille, Eadwine the clerk, Brunman son of Lemay, Goldstan son of Bruning, Odo the Moneyer, Baldwin son of Fike: afterwards those of the neighbourhood of Sandwich, including the barons of St. Margaret, Blacsune, Sigar, Alfword son of Elwold, Alfword son of Blacman, Siric son of Godwin, Wulfwig of Buckland in Woodnesborough, Richard man of Henry de Port, Wulfword of Chillenden, Eadwin of Each End in Woodnesborough, Wulfwine son of Cake, Alfwine of Each End, Hergod man of Alan Pirot. The first of these was Wulfwine son of Beornwig, standing in the midst of the multitude and holding in his hand the book of the sacred gospels he spoke thus: "I swear, the toll of the port of Sandwich, all maritime customs on either side of the river from Burgegate to Merkesfliete and the ferryboat belong only to the Archbishop and monks of Christchurch, Canterbury, nor has any other person any right there save they and their ministers, as I have received from my ancestors and I have seen and heard from my youth up to now, so help me God and these holy gospels. Those who had been chosen as his fellows without delay followed him. William Sheriff of Kent held the place of judge in this plea and with him there were present William Archbishop of Canterbury, legate of the Holy Roman See and primate of all Britain, John Bishop of Rochester, Hugh Abbot of St. Augustine's, Robert de Ver the King's constable, Ruelent of Avranches, Hugh of Chilham, William of Eynsford, Hamo son of Viel, Roger of Well and his son, William Reiner de Hesdin and his son, William Asketur de Rettlynge, Ralf Pieoc, Ralf the chamberlain, Humphrey of Wickham, Hamo the chaplain, Ralf Coffin, Rainolf the brother of the Archbishop, Ralf Cannel, Nigel son of Godfrey, Nigel of Whitacre, Giffard chaplain of Luvel, Henry, Jordan, Godfrey the priest, Wulfric,

Ricardus Robard de Tilman; plurimique alii de ordine clericali quam laicali, quorum multitudo non sunt enumerari.

Boys, in his Introduction to his *Collections for an History of Sandwich,* describes the Customal of Sandwich from which he derived this plea as "a small quarto volume, written on vellum, and bound literally in boards." This was in part copied from a more ancient manuscript, now apparently lost, which was written by Adam Champneys in the year 1301 and copied in the beginning of Edward IV's reign by John Serles, town clerk of Sandwich. There is no doubt of the general accuracy of the transcription. There are a few uncertainties in the text, but when Adam Champneys made his copy Old English names had already fallen out of use. The text here printed is the text of Boys, but in translating it I have made certain obvious corrections in personal names. The text of the writ of Henry I and the words of the oath taken by Wulfwine son of Beornwig are surely authentic.

Geldewin, Leofwine, Wikemonde, Alan, Wiber of St. Gregory, Adam de Hethe, Sprot, Richard, Robard of Tilmanstone, and very many others, both clerk and lay, of whom the multitude cannot be numbered.

II. DOCUMENTS ILLUSTRATING THE OFFICE OF SACRABAR

1. B.M. *Stixwould Cartulary*, Add. MS 46701, f. 134

Omnibus sancte matris ecclesie etc. Willelmus filius et heres Hugonis filii Hernisii de Pantona. Salutem in domino. Nouerit uniuersitas uestra me diuine pietatis et caritatis intuitu et pro salute anime mee at antecessorum et successorum meorum dedisse . concessisse et hac presenti carta mea confirmasse Deo et beate Marie et conuentui de Styk' . molendinum situm in feodo meo inter Magnam Pantonam et Paruam cum sede et stagno suo . et cum terra que dicto molendino adiacet . et cum omnibus pertinenciis suis et consuetudinibus . et proficuis et cum aliis exitibus et aisiamentis infra villam et extra . in pratis et pasturis . in viis et semitis . aquis et piscariis et cum omnibus aliis libertatibus predictum molendinum quod vocatum Northmilne cum sede et stagno suo et cum terra que dicto molendino adiacet . tangentibus. Habendum et tenendum predicto conuentui de Styk' . et successoribus suis libere et quiete bene et in pace , honorifice . integre et hereditarie . sine impedimento . calumpnia uel grauamine ab omni seculari seruicio et exactione . sectis curiarum . sacrabar . consuetudine et demanda . in liberam et puram et perpetuam elemosinam . adeo liberam . sicut aliqua elemosina viris religiosis dari uel confirmari potest. Et ego predictus Willelmus et heredes mei predictis magistro . priorisse et conuentui de Styk' . predictum molendinum cum suis pertinentiis predictis contra omnes homines warantizabimus . defendemus et in omnibus adquietabimus sicut puram et perpetuam elemosinam . inperpetuum. Hiis testibus.

2. P.R.O. Ancient Deeds (D.L. 25) 3005

Sciant presentes et futuri quod ego Peter filius Odonis Galle de Salfletby concessi dedi et presenti carta confirmavi Thome filio Roberti del Dick' de Skytebrock' et heredibus suis pro homagio et servicio suo octo acras et dimidiam acram terre arabilis in teritorio de Skytebrock' . jacentes in campo qui vocatur Melyngfeld' quarum scilicet quatuor acre et dimidia acra terre jacent inter terram Ricardi filii Walteri et terram Willelmi filii Galfridi ex est parte et terram predicti Willelmi et terram

II. DOCUMENTS ILLUSTRATING THE OFFICE OF SACRABAR

1. B.M. *Stixwould Cartulary,* Add. MS 46701, f. 134

To all sons of holy mother church etc. William son and heir of Hugh son of Ernis of Ponton. Greeting in the Lord. Let the whole body of you know that, at the impulse of divine piety and charity and for the safety of my soul and those of my ancestors and successors, I have given, granted and by this my present charter confirmed to God and blessed Mary and the convent of Stixwould the mill situated in my fee between Great and Little Ponton, with the site and the pool and with the land adjacent to the mill and with all its appurtenances and customs and profits and with other issues and easements within the village and without, in meadows and pastures, in ways and paths, in waters and fisheries, and with all the other liberties attached to the aforesaid mill, which is called North mill, with the site and pool and with the land adjacent to the said mill. To have and to hold to the aforesaid convent of Stixwould and its successors freely, quietly, well and in peace, honourably, wholly and hereditarily, without hindrance, claim or burden from any secular service and exaction, suits of court, the sacrabar, custom and demands, in free, pure and perpetual alms as freely as any alms can be given to any men of religion. And I, the aforesaid William, and my heirs will warrant and defend and in all things acquit the aforesaid mill with its aforesaid appurtenances to the aforesaid master, prioress and convent of Stixwould against all men for ever. These being witnesses.

2. P.R.O. Ancient Deeds L. (D.L. 25) 3005

Know present and future that I, Peter son of Odo Galle of Saltfleetby, have granted, given and by my present charter confirmed to Thomas son of Robert of the Dike of Skidbrook and his heirs for their homage and service 8½ acres of arable land in the territory of Skidbrook, lying in the field called Melyngfeld', of which 4½ acres of land lie between the land of Richard son of Walter and the land of William son of Geoffrey on the east part and the land of the aforesaid William and the land of

Willelmi filii Laurencii ex west parte et abbutat versus le north super terram Ade Goderig' et versus le suth super Duuedick' . et due acre et dimidia acra terre jacent inter terram Juliane filie Willelmi ex est parte et terram Willelmi filii Ade ex west parte et abbuttat versus le sut super Godwynegate et versus le north super terram Willelmi filii Ade . et una acra et dimidia acra terre jacent in Saltcroft inter terram Roberti filii Alexandri ex west parte et terram Willelmi filii Galfridi ex est parte et abbutat versus le north super terram dicti Thome del Dick' et versus le suth super Godwynegate . et quicquid habui in predictis placeis sine aliquo retenemento [*sic*] pro quadam summa pecunie quam predictus Thomas michi dedit pre manibus in negociis meis. Habendum et tenendum sibi et heredibus suis et suis assignatis . exceptis viris religiosis et Judeis et cui et quando dare . vendere . assignare siue in testamento legare voluerit . de me et heredibus meis libere quiete pacifice et hereditarie. Reddendo inde annuatim michi et heredibus meis quatuor solidos et undecim denarios et obolum ad quatuor anni terminos in soka de Gaython' statutos . pro omnibus secularibus serviciis conuetudinibus sectis curie et aliis demandis . hoc excepto quod predictus Thomas et heredes sui seu assignati facient duas apparencias ad curiam meam per annum apud Skytebrock' et per sacrabar' si contingat . scilicet ad proximam curiam post festum beati Michaelis et ad proximam curiam post Phasca [*sic*]. Et ego vero predictus Petrus et heredes mei omnes predictas octo acras et dimidiam acram terre arabilis cum pertinentiis suis predicto Thome et heredibus suis pro homagio et servicio suo et cuicunque et quandocunque ubicunque dare vendere et assignare sive in testamento legare voluerit . exceptis viris religiosis et Judeis predicto servicio faciente sicut predictum est in carta contra omnes gentes inperpetuum warantizabimus. In hujus rei testimonium presenti carte in modum cirograffi confecte et penes me remanenti sigillum dicti Thome est appositum. Hiis testibus . Domino Roberto de Sumercot' Willemo filio Ade de Skytebrock' Ricardo filio Walteri de eadem . . . et Johanne filiis . . . del Dick' . Andrea Pollard Willelmo filio Galfridi de Skytebrock' Adam Goderig' de eadem Thoma filio Hugonis de eadem Roberto Baron' de eadem . Willelmo de Salfleby . clerico et aliis. Ad hec predictus Thomas et heredes sui adquietabunt omnia honera communia ad pre-

William son of Laurence on the west part, and abut towards the north on the land of Adam Goderig' and towards the south upon Duuedick'; and 2½ acres of land lie between the land of Juliana daughter of William on the east part and the land of William son of Adam on the west part and abut towards the south on Godwynegate and towards the north upon the land of William son of Adam; and 1½ acres of land lie in Saltcroft between the land of Robert son of Alexander on the west part and the land of William son of Geoffrey on the east part and abut towards the north on the land of the said Thomas of the Dyke and towards the south on Godwynegate; and whatever I had in the aforesaid places without any reservation in return for a certain sum of money which the aforesaid Thomas has given into my hands for my affairs: to have and to hold to them and their heirs and assigns, except men of religion and Jews, and to whomsoever and whenever they shall wish to give, sell, assign or bequeath it by will, of me and my heirs, freely, quietly, peaceably, and hereditarily; Rendering thence annually to me and my heirs 4*s.* and 11½ *d.* at the four terms of the year appointed in the soke of Gayton, for all secular services, customs, suits of court and other demands; with this exception that the aforesaid Thomas and his heirs or assigns shall make two appearances each year at my court at Skidbrook namely at the next court after Michaelmas and the next court after Easter, and [they shall also come there] if it shall happen [that they are summoned] by the sacrabar. And I, the aforesaid Peter and my heirs will warrant the aforesaid 8½ acres of arable land with appurtenances against all people for ever to the aforesaid Thomas and his heirs for their homage and service and to whom so ever and whenever and wherever he shall wish to give, sell, assign or bequeath it, except to men of religion and Jews, by doing the aforesaid service as is aforesaid in the charter. In witness whereof the seal of the said Thomas is affixed to the present charter made in the manner of a chirograph and remaining in my hands. These being witnesses, Sir Robert of Somercotes, William son of Adam of Skidbrook, Richard son of Walter of the same place, . . . and John sons of . . . of the Dyke, Andrew Pollard, William son of Geoffrey of Skidbrook, Adam Goderig' of the same, Thomas son of Hugh of the same, Robert Baron' of the same, William of Saltfleetby, the clerk and others. In addition the aforesaid Thomas and his heirs will acquit and in all things

dictam terram spectancia et in omnibus sustinebunt pro me et heredibus meis in perpetuum.[1]

Endorsed cxl

Seal Fleur de lys [SIGILLUM] THOM[E FILII] ROBERTI

3. P.R.O. ANCIENT DEEDS L (D.L. 25) 2625

Sciant presentes et futuri [quod ego Petrus filius Odo Galle de Salfletby . . . . .] Gaske de Cuningesholm' et . . . . . placeam terram ad portum de Salflet' jac. . . . . . longitudine cum pertica sexdecim pedum et terram Thome . . . . pertica mensure predicte et abbuttans versus est super terram . . . . . Habend' et tenend' de me et heredibus meis . eis et eorum heredibus vel . . . . . .[here]ditarie integre et in pace cum longitudine et latitudine prescripta . Reddendo . . . . . . anni terminos videlicet ad Natale Domini novem denarios ad Pascha novem denarios ad festum sancti Bothulfi novem . . . . novem denarios pro omnibus secularibus serviciis accionibus consuetúdinibus sectis curie et demandis salvo sacrabar si contingat. Sustinebunt vero predicti Johannes et Hauwys' et heredes sui vel sui assignati omnes communitates et misas ville que ad dictam placeam pertinent et viginti pedes super fossatum maris proximo ex west parte Andree Pollard quociens necesse fuerit propriis suis sumptibus construent . rep. . et emendabunt. Et ego predictus Petrus et heredes mei dictam placcam terre cum longitudine et latitudine prescripta una cum omnibus pertinenciis libertatibus communis et aysiamentis predicte placee spectantibus prefatis Johanni et Hauwys' et eorum heredibus vel eorum assignatis exceptis viris religiosis et Judeis warantizabimus adquietabimus et contra omnes homines prout predictum est in perpetuum deffendemus. In cujus rei testimonium presentibus scriptis in modum cryograffi confectis uterque nostrum sigillum apposuit. Hiis testibus ; Andrea de Scupholm' Philippo debonayre Hereberto Galle Andrea Pollard Willelmo pastore Willelmo filio Hugonis Johanne fratre suo Roberto clerico de Skytebrock' Johanne clerico de Somercotes et aliis.

Endorsed Carta Johannis Gaske de Cuningesholm'

No seal survives on the tag.

[1] The last sentence was an afterthought and is written under the turn up at the bottom of the chirograph.

sustain all the common burdens belonging to the aforesaid land on behalf of me and my heirs for ever.

3. P.R.O. Ancient Deeds L (D.L. 25) 2625

Know present and future that [I, Peter son of Odo Galle of Salfleetby, have granted, given, and by my present charter confirmed to John son of] Gaske of Connisholme and [Hawisa his wife and their heirs for their homage and service] a place of land at the harbour of Saltfleet, lying . . . . [measured] in length with the perch of 16 feet and the land of Thomas . . . with the perch of the aforesaid measure and abutting towards the east on the land . . . . : to have and to hold to them and their heirs [and assigns except men of religion and Jews and to whomsoever and whenever they shall wish to give, sell, assign or bequeath it by will, of me and my heirs] hereditarily, wholly and in peace with the aforesaid length and breadth; Rendering [thence annually to me and my heirs 3 *s.* at four annual terms] namely at Christmas 9 *d.*, at Easter 9 *d.*, at the feast of St. Botulf [17 June] 9 *d.* [and at Michaelmas] 9 *d.* for all secular services, actions, customs, suits of court and demands, except [the summons of] the sacrabar, if it shall happen. The aforesaid John and Hawisa and their heirs or their assigns shall bear all the common burdens and charges of the village which belong to that place and they shall build, repair and renew twenty feet of the sea bank next on the west part to Andrew Pollard as often as it shall be necessary at their own expense. And I the aforesaid Peter and my heirs will warrant, acquit and defend the aforesaid place of land with the length and breadth aforesaid, together with all the appurtenances, liberties, commons, and easements belonging to the aforesaid place against all men as is aforesaid for ever to the aforesaid John and Hawisa and their heirs or their assigns, except men of religion or Jews. In witness whereof each of us has set his seal to the present writings made in the manner of a chirograph. These being witnesses, Andrew of Scupholme, Philip debonaire, Herbert Galle, Andrew Pollard, William the shepherd, William son of Hugh, John his brother, Robert the clerk of Skidbrook, John the clerk of Somercotes and others.

4. P.R.O. Ancient Deeds L (D. L. 25) 2743

Sciant presentes et futuri quod [ego Peter filius Odonis Galle de Salfletby] concessi dedi et hac presenti carta confirmavi Roberto filio Radulfi de Skytebrock' . . . . viris religiosis et Judeis totam terram quam habui vel habere potui jacentem inter . . . . . viam que ducit ad domum abbatis de Parco Lude ex north parte et abbuttans . . . . . super terram Andree Pollard ad portum de Sauflet que quedem terra continet in longitudine. . . . . quatuor pedes et octo fallas et decem pedes per north partem cum pertica sexdecim . . . . commoditatibus communis et aysiamentis ad predictam terram pertinentibus pro ho . . . . . . d' de me et de heredibus meis sibi et heredibus suis et suis assignatis . exceptis viris [religiosis et Judeis]. . integre bene pacifice et hereditarie cum libero introitu et exitu. Reddendo inde annuatim . . . . . argenti ad quatuor anni terminos . videlicet ad Natale Domini tres solidos ad pascha tres solidos ad. . . . . et ad festum beati Michaelis tres solidos pro omnibus secularibus serviciis consuetudinibus exactionibus et demandis . . . . sectis . exceptis duabus apparenciis in curia de Skytebrock' per annum . videlicet proxime curie post Pascha et proxime curie post festum beati Michaelis et sacrabar' si contingat. Sustinebunt etiam dictus Robertus et heredes sui aut assignati omnes communitates misas et expensas ville in omnibus locis ad dictam terram pertinentes et super fossatum maris quadraginta pedes proximo ex west parte Ade le Noreis. Et ego predictus Petrus et heredes mei predictam terram cum pertinentiis predictis predicto Roberto et heredibus suis et suis assignatis exceptis ut prius viris religiosis et Judeis warantizabimus pro predicto servicio contra omnes homines adquietabimus et deffendemus. In cujus rei testimonium presentibus scriptis bipartitis uterque nostrum parti penes alterum residenti sigillum suum apposuit. Hiis testibus Andrea de Scupholm' Philippo deboneyr Hereberto Galle Willelmo pastore Johanne filio Hugonis Johanne Gos Radulfo filio Hugonis Andrea Pollard Johanne filio Ade Johanne de Sumercotes clerico et aliis. Datum apud Saufletby in festo exaltacionis sancte crucis anno Domini M°CC° septuagesimo octavo.

Endorsed ccxlix

Seal with now illegible design and name.

4. P.R.O. Ancient Deeds L (D.L. 25) 2743

Know present and future that [I, Peter son of Odo Galle of Saltfleetby] have granted, given and by my present charter confirmed to Robert son of Ralf of Skidbrook [and his heirs or assigns, except] men of religion and Jews all the land which I had or could have lying between . . . . and the way which leads to the house of the Abbot of Louth Park on the north part and abutting . . . . . on the land of Andrew Pollard at the port of Saltfleet, which land contains in length 4 feet and 8 falls and 10 feet by the north part [measured] with the perch of 16 feet, together with all the conveniences, commons and easements belonging to the aforesaid land for their homage [and service] . . . ; to hold of me and my heirs to him and his heirs and assigns, except men of religion and Jews, wholly, well, peaceably and hereditarily, with free entry and exit; Rendering thence annually [to me and my heirs 12 *s.*] of silver at four terms of the year, namely at Christmas, 3 *s.*, at Easter 3 *s.*, [at the feast of St Botulf, 3 *s.*] and at Michaelmas 3 *s.* for all secular services, customs, exactions, and demands and suits of court, except two appearances each year in the court at Skidbrook, namely the next court after Easter and the next court after Michaelmas and [they shall come there] if it shall happen [that they are summoned] by the sacrabar. Also the said Robert and his heirs or assigns shall bear all the common charges and expenses of the village in all places belonging to the said land and forty feet upon the sea bank next on the west part of Adam le Noreis. And I, the aforesaid Peter, and my heirs will warrant, acquit and defend, the aforesaid land with the aforesaid appurtenances to the aforesaid Robert and his heirs and assigns for the aforesaid service against all men, except as before, men of religion and Jews. In witness whereof each of us has put his seal to the part of the present bipartite writings remaining with the other. These being witnesses, Andrew of Scupholme, Philip debonaire, Herbert Galle, William the shepherd, John son of Hugh, John Gos, Ralf son of Hugh, Andrew Pollard, John son of Adam, John of Somercotes the clerk and others. Given at Saltfleetby in the feast of the exaltation of the holy cross [14 September], 1278 A.D.

5. P.R.O., D.L. 42/5

Veredictum de inquisicione facta super seruicia et consuetudines portus de Waynflet' et libertates tempore domini Philippi de Kyma et predecessorum suorum per preceptum domini H. Regis filii J. Regis anno regni ipsius H. octo decimo per sacramentum Rannulfi de Friskenai . Galfridi de Thorp' . Simonis filii Wydonis . Antonii de Raeheby Ricardi de Haneby . Thome de Banburgh' Willelmi Chaff' . Radulfi Hardwyn' . Roberti de Wegland' . Johannis Hardebey . Alani Toller Godrici Frost . Lamberti nepotis Beatricis et Walteri filii Rogeri ad Trayngham apud Hydam die Mercurii in crastino sancti Benedicti . coram Philippo de Astill' tunc vicecomite. Scimus dicunt quod quelibet nauis ueniens ad portum de Waynflet carcata de blado uel sale causa uenditionis faciende dabit ij denarios de tolneto et j pro buss' domino portus et si ueniat ad carcandum dabit domino portus hoc idem. Et quelibet nauis ueniens cum pisce causa vendendi dabit ij denarios de tolneto. Et si nauis veniat ad portum et non emat neque vendat nichil dabit de consuetudine . set libere liceat recedere. Et quelibet nauis veniens ad portum cum marchandisa ancorabit ex utraque parte portus prout sibi necesse fuerit absque impedimento alicuius. Et si aliqua domus prope fuerit sita adeo prope portum quod nauis ibidem veniens et applicare volens non possit propter domum illam ibidem cum facultate ancorare . tunc licebit nauti [*sic*] nauis in domo illa libere ancorare et cordas circa postes domus ligare . et si necesse fuerit ancoram suam ultra domus proiecere ex altera parte domus ancorare sine impedimento alicuius. Item naute uenientes et applicantes ad portum libere bene et in pace faciant marchandisas suas a Limna usque crucem de Wlmeresty nec habebunt alios testes nisi corulos suos et si aliquis illorum infra dictas metas iniuratus fuerit super marcandisa sua uel emptionibus uel uenditionibus suis naute simul cum balliuo portus primo debent uenire ad dominum feodi uel ad eius balliuum ad rectum habendum et ad suscipiendum de tyda in tydam et si fuerit jus illis exhibitum infra terciam tidam dominus portus vel eius balliuus plenum rectum illis tenebit de quocunque sit infra dictas metas . et si balliuus portus aliquam fecerit festinatam summonitionem super aliquem infra dictas metas per querelam alicuius et dominus feodi vel eius

5. P.R.O., D. L. 42/5

The verdict touching the inquest upon the services and customs of the port of Wainfleet and the liberties in the time of Sir Philip of Kyme and his predecessors made by command of the lord King Henry son of King John in the eighteenth year of the reign of this King Henry by the oath of Rannulf of Friskney, Geoffrey of Thorpe, Simon son of Guy, Anthony of Raithby by Spilsby, Richard of Hagnaby, Thomas of Baumber, William Chafft, Ralf Hardwyn, Robert de Wegland', John Hardebey, Alan Toller, Godric Frost, Lambert nephew of Beatrice and Walter son of Roger ad Trayingham, at Hydam on Wednesday, the morrow of St Benedict [22 March, 1234] before Philip de Astill', then sheriff. We know, they say, that each ship coming loaded with corn or salt for sale to the port of Wainfleet shall give 2 *d.* in toll and 1 [*d.*] a bushel to the lord of the port, and if it comes to load up it shall give the lord of the port the same. And each ship coming with fish to sell shall give 2 *d.* in toll. And if a ship shall come to the port and neither buy nor sell it shall give no custom, but can freely depart. And each ship coming to the port with merchandise shall anchor on either side of the harbour as shall be necessary without hindrance from anyone. And if any house shall be situated so near the harbour that a ship coming there and wishing to tie up cannot conveniently anchor there on account of that house, then the sailors of the ship can freely anchor at that house and bind their ropes about the posts of that house and if it is necessary cast their anchor on either side of that house for anchorage without hindrance from anyone. Also sailors coming and tying up at the harbour freely, well and in peace shall make their sales from their landing place as far as the cross of Wolmersty, nor shall they have any other witnesses than their tallies. And if any one of them within the same boundaries shall be injured in regard to his merchandise, either in his purchases or sales, the sailors together with the bailiff of the port ought first to come to the lord of the fee or to his bailiff to have and receive right from tide to tide. And if right shall [? not] be done them within the third tide, the lord of the port or his bailiff shall do them full right touching whatever it is within the said bounds. And if the bailiff of the port shall make any hurried summons

balliuus veniat ad curiam domini portus et petat curiam suam ad horam et terminum habebit curiam suam et tenebit rectum conquerenti de die in diem quod si non fecerit . dominus portus vel eius balliuus in curia sua plenum rectum tenebit conquerenti. Item si quis infra dictas metas preocupauerit super alium super sandacris suis bene licebit illis hoc inter seipsos per amicos emendare si querela que fiat balliuo portus et non possunt hoc ınter se ipsos amicabiliter emendare. Et si querela veniat super hiis balliuo portus ipse balliuus in curia domini sui super hoc plenum rectum tenebit conquerenti . et ille qui conuictus fuerit deliquisse dabit domino portus pro misericordia sua xvj denarios . de quocunque feodo sit . Item si aliquid fossatum maris vel marisci fractum fuerit et ille cuius fossatum fuerit illud infra duas tydas non emendauerit dabit domino portus xvj denarios pro misericordia sua . et villate xvj denarios . de quocumque feodo sit et balliuus portus faciet illud fossatum et reparare et emendare. Et si aliqua via infra dictas metas fuerit carcata vel opturata per murum uel per aliquod fossatum leuatum uel per aliquod aliud . ille qui conuictus fuerit super hoc deliquisse dabit domino portus xvj denarios pro misericordia sua . de quocumque feodo sit . et villate xvj denarios et balliuus portus faciet illum illam viam iuste emendare. Item assisa panis et ceruisie debet fieri quolibet anno ad festum sancti Michaelis per commune consilium duarum villatarum et quocienscumque aliquis pistor vel braciator . vel braciatrix fregerit assisam panis vel ceruisie dabit domino portus xvj denarios pro misericordia sua . de quocumque feodo sit infra dictas metas excepto feodo domini Roberti de Tatesh'. Et omnes braciatores et braciatrices de Wayflet excepto feodo quod fuit domini Rannulfi de Praeres et tofto Holdani Palmeri . et tofto Godrici filii Himme dabunt domino portus viij denarios per annum de tolneto. Et quelibet patella buliens salem a limina usque crucem de Wlmersty dabit domino portus semel in anno unum funding salis . ET j satemel que debet esse de xviij pollicibus . excepto feodo domino Roberti de Tateshal'. quod nullum funding salis dat. Item dominus portus debet tendere rete suum primo . et loco primo in portu ad anguillas capiendas . et postea secundo loco heres domini Rannulfi de Praeres j rete . et postea quicunque voluerit de Waynflet. Item portus debet opturari et aperiri per commune consilium duarum villatarum quocienscumque ne-

on any one within the said bounds for the suit of any one and the lord of the fee or his bailiff shall come to the court of the lord of the port and seek his court at the hour and term he shall have his court and do right to the plaintiff from day to day. And if he shall not do it the lord of the port or his bailiff shall do full right to the plaintiff in his court. Also if anyone within the said boundaries occupies another man's place upon his sandbanks they may well settle the complaint by amends made through friends, but if they cannot settle the dispute in a friendly manner and complaint is made to the bailiff of the port that they cannot settle the matter in a friendly way between themselves, the bailiff of the port shall do full right to the plaintiff in the court of his lord and he who is convicted of doing wrong shall give to the lord of the port for his amercement, 16 *d.* whosever fee he shall belong to. Also if any bank of the sea or marsh shall be broken, and he whose bank that was shall not mend it within two tides, he shall give to the lord of the port for his amercement 16 *d.* and to the township 16 *d.* whosever fee he shall belong to, and the bailiff of the port shall cause [him] to repair and mend that bank. And if any way within the said boundaries shall be obstructed or stopped up by the building of a wall or bank or in any other way, he who shall be convicted of this shall give to the lord of the port for his amercement, 16 *d.* whosever fee he shall belong to, and to the township 16 *d.* and the bailiff of the port shall cause him justly to make that way good. Also the assize of bread and ale ought to be made every year at Michaelmas by the common counsel of the two villages, and as often as any baker or brewer, male or female, shall break the assize of bread or ale, he shall give to the lord of the port for his amercement 16 *d.* whose ever fee he shall belong to within the said boundaries, except the fee of Sir Robert of Tattershall. All the brewers of Wainfleet, except the fee of Sir Rannulf de Praeres and the toft of Holdan Palmer and the toft of Godric son of Himme, shall give to the lord of the port as toll 8*d.* a year. And every pan boiling salt from the shore to the cross of Wolmersty shall give to the lord of the port once a year one boiling of salt that is a piece of salt which ought to be 18 inches, except the fee of Sir Robert of Tattershall which gives no boiling of salt. And also the lord of the port ought to stretch his net first and in the first place in the harbour to catch eels, and after-

cesse fuerit ad emendacionem et comodum domini portus et duarum villatarum. Homines de Waynflet tunc debent portum opturare et aperire. Item omnes bussell' et omnes gallon' infra dictas metas debent signari de quodam signo ferri domini portus. Et signum illud debet tradi ad custodiam duobus hominibus legalibus per consilium duarum uillatarum. Item naute extranei qui non sunt de villa habebunt rectum de tida in tidam . si illis fuerit forasfactum vel iniuriam secundum usum et consuetudinem nautarum. Et naute qui sunt in villa eradicati et atrium habentes in villa habebunt rectum secundum usum et consuetudinem hominum ville vel prouincie si illis fuerit forasfactum vel iniuriam. Item nullus debet sequi placita portus nisi per sacrabar . et per vadium et plegium.

wards in the second place the heirs of Sir Rannulf de Praeres one net, and afterwards whoever wishes from Wainfleet. Also the harbour ought to be stopped up and opened by the common counsel of the two villages as often as shall be necessary for the improvement and welfare of the lord of the harbour and of the two villages. The men of Wainfleet then ought to stop up and open the harbour. Also all the bushels and all the gallons within the said boundaries ought to be marked with a certain iron mark belonging to the lord of the port; and that sign ought to be handed to the keeping of two lawful men by the counsel of the two villages. Also foreign sailors who do not belong to the village shall have right from tide to tide if wrong or injury is done to them according to the use and custom of sailors. And sailors who are born in the village and have a porch in the village shall have right according to the use and custom of the men of the village or shire if anyone does them wrong or injury. Also no one ought to sue pleas of the harbour save through the sacrabar and by gage and pledge.

III. THE CHARWELTON CASE
An early reference to the Process of Tolt

C.U.L. *Red Book of Thorney*, 2, f. 415[1]

De terra in Charwalton' quam Robertus de Stauertuna de abbate Gunterio uolelabat [sic] tenuisse

Sciant presentes et posteri quod Robertus de Stauert' requisiuit Gunterium abbatem per breuia Regis Henrici de Charuoltuna et uolebat eam de abbate tenere in feudo firmam. Abbas autem ei respondit quod eam nullo modo haberet quia nullum rectum inde habebat. Requisiuit inde saisitionem . set abbas noluit eum saisire nisi per iudicium . quapropter abbas precepit ut curia sancti inde rectum consideraret. Et curia sancti recto iudicio considerauit quod Robertus non debuisset saisiri nisi maius rectum super hoc monstraret . scilicet cartam uel testes qui hoc feudum sibi disrationarent. Inde ei diem abbas posuit. Robertus Regem Henricum iterata vice [f. 415 d] requisiuit . et Rex Hugoni vicecomiti mandauit ut homines prudentes et viros sapientes eodem die in curiam abbatis cum Roberto mitteret qui uiderent et audirent quod abbas eum omnino per rectum deduceret. Ascelinus de Wateruile et Willelmus Olifart et Walterus de Cloptuna cum Roberto missi ad diem venerunt et saisitionem sicut antea quesierat requisierunt. Et abbas respondit quod ei diem posuerat disrationandi feudum quod clamabat per cartam uel testimonium. Qui non habens cartam nec testimonium saisitionem requirebat. Abbas uero curiam sancti ad iudicium misit et precepit ut rectum iudicium considerarent . ad hoc judicium faciendum fuit Jolfridus senior de Traili . Rogerus de Gisneis . Herueius Monachus . Reginaldus et homines sancti . qui iudicauerunt Robertum et heredes suos calumpniam suam perdidisse cum cartam et testimonium non haberet unde disrationare posset . et quod abbas et ecclesia Thornensis eandem terram scilicet Cheruuoltun' solutam et quietam finaliter haberet.

[1] See *Facsimiles of Early Charters from Northamptonshire Collections*, ed., F. M. Stenton, Northamptonshire Record Society 4 (1930): pp. 12-15, where the actual writ of Henry I initiating the process of tolt in this case is facsimiled.

III. THE CHARWELTON CASE

An early reference to the Process of Tolt

C.U.L. *Red Book of Thorney,* 2, f. 415[1]

Let present and future know that Robert of Staverton impleaded Abbot Gunter by writs of King Henry touching Charwelton and he wished to hold it in fee farm of the Abbot. But the Abbot replied that he could in no wise have it because he had no right in it. He sought seisin thereof, but the Abbot refused to seise him save through judgment, wherefore the Abbot commanded that the court of the saint should declare the right therein. And the court of the saint declared by right judgment that Robert ought not to be seised unless he could show greater right therein, namely a charter or witnesses who could deraign this fee for him. The Abbot set him a day therein. Robert again sought King Henry and the King instructed Hugh the Sheriff that he should send prudent and wise men with Robert into the Abbot's court on the same day who might see and hear that the Abbot in every way treated him in accordance with right. Ascelin de Waterville, William Olifart and Walter of Clopton, sent with Robert, came at the appointed day and demanded seisin as he had sought before. And the Abbot replied that he had set him a day to deraign the fee which he claimed by charter or witness and he having no charter or witness demanded seisin. The Abbot sent the court of the saint to judgment and commanded that they should deliver a true judgment. Jolfrid the elder de Traili, Roger de Gisneis, Hervey Lemoyne, Reginald and the men of the saint made the judgment. They judged that Robert and his heirs had lost their claim since he had no charter and witness wherewith he could deraign it and that the Abbot and the church of Thorney should have the same land, namely Charwelton, whole and quit for ever.

[1] See *Facsimiles of Early Charters from Northamptonshire Collections,* ed., F. M. Stenton, Northamptonshire Record Society 4 (1930): pp. 12-15, where the actual writ of Henry I initiating the process of tolt in this case is facsimiled.

IV. THE CASE CONCERNING YAXLEY AND SIBSON BROUGHT BY THE ABBOT OF THORNEY AGAINST ROBERT OF YAXLEY, 1113-1127

C.U.L. *Red Book of Thorney* 3, f. 417

De quibusdam terris et tenementis in Jakel' et Sibeston' que quondam domnus Gunterius abbas dederat cuidam Roberto nepoti suo . sine consensu capituli . que postea dictus abbas Robertus recuperauit de eodem . ut patet in sequentibus memorandis.

Notum sit presentibus et posteris quod domnus abbas G. sine consensu tocius capituli huius ecclesie R. nepoti suo terram in Jakel' et in Sibestuna dedit. Quo defuncto pie memorie abbas R. regimen huius optinuit ecclesie. Qui audiens qualiter predictus abbas G. hanc donationem contra uoluntatem et prohibitum generalis capituli donauerat . homagium R. familiari usus consilio suscipere renuit . eique per monachos et homines huius honoris mandauit quatinus terram illam quam multis diebus et annis iniuste et contra uoluntatem tocius conuentus tenuerat . quantocius deliberaret . quem nolentem et superbe renitentem dissaisiuit . domos eius fregit . uirgultum extirpauit . et ut res maturius fieret . mare transiuit . et a domino nostro Rege per se et per amicos suos breue quesiuit ut de illa terra resaisari per iusticiarios Regis debuisset . eamque in firma pace teneret si R. nequiuisset disserere quod per concessionem capituli ei data fuisset . et quod dominica mensa non esset . et quod Rex eandem donationem sua auctoritate confirmasset. Videns autem R. quod nullo modo posset hec disserere . sciebant enim omnes vicini et conprouinciales nostri quod Sibestun ipsa die qua sibi data est in dominico huius ecclesie erat et quod concessionem capituli nunquam habuerat nec quod Rex hoc confirmauerat . deposita feritate qua satis superque intumuerat . dominum R. abbatem per vicinos suos requisiuit . eique ad ultimum terram de Sibestuna per baculum Odonis Reuelli qui in thesauro ecclesie reseruatur apud Neuuetune in grancia reddens homo eius efficitur eique fidelitatem iurauit quod sibi

IV. THE CASE CONCERNING YAXLEY AND SIBSON BROUGHT BY THE ABBOT OF THORNEY AGAINST ROBERT OF YAXLEY, 1113-1127

C.U.L. *Red Book of Thorney* 3, f. 417

Let present and future know that the lord Abbot Gunter without the consent of the full chapter of this church gave land in Yaxley and Sibson to Robert his nephew. On the death of Abbot Gunter of pious memory, Abbot Robert obtained the rule of this church. He, hearing how the aforesaid Abbot Gunter had made this gift contrary to the will and prohibition of the general chapter, with the support of his intimate advisers refused to take Robert's homage and ordered him through monks and men of this honour that he should immediately give up that land which for many days and years he had held unjustly and contrary to the will of the whole convent. Robert being unwilling and proudly refusing, the Abbot disseised him, broke his houses and stubbed up his holt and, that the matter might be the more quickly settled, crossed the sea and from our lord the King he sought through his own efforts and those of his friends a writ ordering that he should be reseised of that land by the King's justices and should hold it in peace if Robert was unable to show that it had given to him by grant of the chapter and that it was not appropriated to the support of the monks, and that the King had confirmed the gift by his authority. Robert, seeing that he could in no wise prove these things,—for all the neighbours and men of the countryside knew that on the day when Sibson was given him it was in the demesne of this church and that he had never had the consent of the chapter nor had the King confirmed the gift—laying aside the fierceness with which he was more than enough puffed up, through the intercession of friends sought the lord Abbot and at last, restoring to him the land at Sibson by the rod of Odo Revel which is laid up in the treasury of the church, in the grange at Water Newton he became the man of the Abbot and swore fealty to him, and

uidelicet et omnibus monachis huius ecclesie fidelis et seruiens pro posse suo esse deberet . et omnes calumpnias quibus eum impetiuerat de domibus uidelicet et de aliis rebus suis ita ei quietas clamauit ut nunquam per se uel per aliquem heredum suorum clamor inde uel calumpnia fiat. Huius rei testes sunt . Hugo de Wateruilla . Radulfus de la Mare . Willelmus de Burgele Gaufridus Burdun etc.

f. 17 d

Item de predicto Roberto qualiter in pleno comitatu Hunt' reliquit breue suum quod impetrauit et totam calumpniam suam quam habuit uersus prefatum abbatem Robertum.

Notum sit omnibus tam futuris quam presentibus quod abbas R. de Thorn' et Robertus de Jak' anno incarnationis dominice MCXXVII die festiuitatis sancti Mathei apostoli qua etiam die celebrabant iiij tempora conuenerunt coram me Fulcoio vicecomite apud Hunted' ubi erat quoque et plenus comitatus . ostenditque ibidem Robertus de Jak' breue suum et fecit clamores atque calumpnias suas de abbate Thorn'. Abbas uero Robertus auditis clamoribus eius atque calumpniis strenuissime monstratur [sic] per clericos et laicos qui inter eos fuerant testes quod nichil omnino ei deberet. Videns autem Robertus quod sua contentio nichil aduersus abbatem valeret . usus consilio mei Fulc' . uidelicet vicecomitis . et Rainaldi abbatis Ramesiensis in pleno comitatu omnes calumpnias quas aduersus abbatem et ecclesiam suam videlicet de terra Sibeston' siue de domibus aut uirgultis uel hominibus et omnibus aliis rebus habebat . per uirgam reddidit quietasque clamauit . preter terram suam de Jak' quam abbas sibi dedit tres scilicet uirgas et dimidiam . reddidit quoque mihi breue suum uidente toto comitatu. Et ut hec conuentio in posterum rata et firma perduraret . in presentia mei et abbatis Rames' et tocius comitatus . abbati Roberto fidelitatem sicut Herueius Monachus melius sciuit distinguere iurauit . quod ei uidelicet sicut legitimo domino suo et omnibus suis fidelis existeret . et quod nuncquam aduersus abbatem calumpniam aliquam uel querelam faceret . et quod nunquam sibi uel alicui suorum aliquando noceret . et prescriptas conuentiones inperpetuum teneret. Quo facto . ad confirmationem huius rei et testionem dedit ei abbas ij marcas

that to him and to all the monks of this church he would be faithful and serve them to the best of his power, and he has quitclaimed all the suits which he had brought against the Abbot touching his houses and other property, so that neither by himself nor any heir of his shall any complaint or claim be made therein. These are the witnesses of this settlement, Hugh de Waterville, Ralf de la Mare, William of Burghley, Geoffrey Burdun and others.

f. 17 *d*

Be it known to all as well future as present that Abbot Robert of Thorney and Robert of Yaxley in 1127 A.D. on the day of the feast of St. Matthew the apostle [21 September], which is also an ember day, have met before me Fulk the Sheriff at Huntingdon, where there was also a full shire court, and there Robert of Yaxley showed his writ and made his plaints and claims against the Abbot of Thorney. Abbot Robert, having heard his claims and complaints, most clearly showed through clerks and laymen who had been witnesses between them that he owed him absolutely nothing. Robert of Yaxley, seeing that his quarrel against the abbot would avail him nothing, taking my advice, that is, the advice of Fulk the Sheriff, and that of Rainald Abbot of Ramsey, has restored by the rod and quitclaimed in the full shire court, all his claims which he had against the Abbot and his church, namely touching the land of Sibson, whether touching houses or holts or men and all other property, except his land at Yaxley which the abbot has given him, namely 3½ virgates; and he has also, in the sight of the whole shire, given up to me his writ. And that this agreement may endure firm and stable for ever, in my presence and that of the Abbot of Ramsey and the whole shire, Robert of Yaxley has sworn fealty to Abbot Robert as Hervey Lemoyne best knew how to set it out, namely that he will be faithful to him and all of his as to his liege lord, and that never against the Abbot will he make any claim or suit, and that never at any time will he harm him or anyone of his men and that he will keep the aforesaid agreements for ever. This being done,

argenti unde ipse abbas Thorn' unam ei partem tradidit . et ego alteram . et abbas Rames' tertiam . et Herueius Monachus quartam . ut multiplex esset testimonium et res firma fieret et stabilis. Huius rei testes sumus ego Fulco uicecomes et abbas Rainaldus Rames' . et duo monachi sui Galterus et Daniel . Martinus prior Sancti Neoti . Henricus archidiaconus etc.

Item de predicto Roberto qualiter quietum clamauit cum Willelmo filio suo et herede abbati Roberto et toto conuentui totam terram suam in Jak' et Sibeston'.

Notum sit omnibus tam presentibus quam futuris me Robertum de Jak' et Willelmum filium meum per textum reddidisse et quietum clamasse deo et sancte Marie Thorn' totam terram meam de Jak' et terram meam de Sibeston' et omnes calumpnias meas quas habebam erga Thornensem ecclesiam siue iustas siue iniustas . ita quod deinceps nullus heredum meorum aut aliquis alius per me inde clamorem aut aliquam calumpniam faciet. Eet postquam eandem terram super altare dominicum per textum reddidi et quietumclamaui ne aliquis suspicaretur aliquam fraudem aduersus me iurauimus super idem textum et super idem altare tam ego quam Willelmus filius meus nos et omnes heredes nostros hoc idem pactum conseruaturos. Huius rei sunt testes . omnis conuentus Thorn' . Robertus presbiter de Stangr' . Willelmus filius Agamundi . Gilbertus portarius etc.

Testimonium personale Willelmi filii predicti Roberti de predicta quieta clamantia.

Sciendum est quod Willelmus filius Roberti de Jak' testificatus est in curia sancti apud Jakel' se presentem fuisse ubi pater suus et ipse reddiderunt totam terram suam de Jak' et de Sibestun' super altare dominicum et quod ibi forisiurauerunt eandem terram et quietamclamauerunt a se et ab omnibus heredibus suis et omnes calumpnias suas quas erga Thornensem ecclesiam habuerant siue iustas siue iniustas quietasclamauerunt . et ibi in curia Jakesl' iurauit idem Willelmus eundem finem quem pater suus et ipse sum abbate et [f. 418] toto conuentu fecerant se inperpetuum seruaturum. Huius rei sunt testes Radulfus filius Nigelli . etc. Item isti sunt testes in quorum presentia W. filius Robert de Jak' forisiurauit sicut legitimus heres patris

as confirmation and witness thereof, the Abbot has given him two marks of silver, whereof the Abbot of Thorney himself handed him one part, and I another and the Abbot of Ramsey the third and Hervey Lemoyne the fourth, so that there would be manifold testimony and the matter would be firm and stable. We are the witness of this settlement, I, Fulk the Sheriff and Rainald Abbot of Ramsey and his two monks Walter and Daniel, and Martin prior of St. Neots, Henry the Archdeacon [of Huntingdon] and others.

Be it known to all as well present as future that I, Robert of Yaxley and William my son have restored and quitclaimed by the gospels to God and St. Mary of Thorney all my land of Yaxley and my land of Sibson and all my claims which I had against the church of Thorney, whether just or unjust, so that henceforward none of my heirs nor any one else through me shall make any plaint or claim therein. And afterwards I have restored and quitclaimed the same land upon the high altar by the gospels lest any one should suspect any fraud on my part; and we have sworn upon the same gospels and upon the same altar, as well I as William my son that we and all our heirs will keep this agreement. These are the witnesses of this settlement, all the convent of Thorney, Robert the priest of Stanground, William son of Agamund, Gilbert the porter and others.

Be it known that William son of Robert of Yaxley has born witness in the court of the saint at Yaxley that he was present where his father and he restored all his land of Yaxley and Sibson upon the high altar, and that they have forsworn and quitclaimed the same land for themselves and all their heirs; and they have quitclaimed all the complaints which they had against the church of Thorney whether they were just or unjust, and there in the court at Yaxley the same William has sworn to keep for ever the same agreement which his father and he have made with the Abbot and the [f. 418] whole convent. These are the witnesses of this agreement, Ralf son of Nigel and others. Also these are the witnesses in whose presence Wil-

terram de Sibestuna scilicet duas hidas sicut pater suus Robertus antea forisiurauerat eas apud Huntend' coram quatuor comitatibus scilicet Willelmus archidiaconus de Hamton'. Rannulfus canonicus . Willelmus de Albenico . Rogerus de Torpel . Andreas Reuellus etc.

Item alia quietaclamantia predicti Roberti cum predicto Willelmo filio suo de predictis tenementis.

Sciant presentes et posteri quod R. de Jak' monstrauit in pleno comitatu apud Hunt' quod quietamclamauerat totam terram suam de Jak' et de Sibestun' et omnes querelas et calumpnias quas erga Thornensem ecclesiam habebat siue iustas siue iniustas quietasclamauerat et reddiderat super dominicum altare Thornensis ecclesie et quod iurauerat super iiij euangelia et super altare et super omnes reliquias eiusdem ecclesie quod nunquam amplius inde clamorem uel clamorem [*sic*] faceret nec aliquis heredum suorum. Monstrauit etiam in eodem comitatu quod W. filius suus qui legitimus heres eius erat . eandem adquietationem et idem iuramentum in Thornensi ecclesia super altare et super omnes reliquias iurauerat et post apud Jak' in curia sancti eandem adquietationem et idem sacramentum coram multis confirmauerat. Ibi presens fuit Gilebertus monachus Thornensis ecclesie qui inde testimonium accepit a toto comitatu et a Simone filio Petri constabulario Hunt' . et a Simone de Turri . et ab Anseled clerico etc.

Quietaclamantia iuratoria Radulfi filii Willelmi de terris et tenementis que fuerunt supradicti Roberti in Jakesle.

Ad memoriam presentium et posterorum scriptis signamus quod Radulfus filius Willelmi totam calumpniam suam de terra de Jak' que fuerat sicut dicebat Willelmi auunculi sui tempore Roberti abbatis quietam clamauit et iuramento apud Stangr' super iiij euangelia confirmauit quod ab illa die in reliquum nichil inde clamabit nisi in misericordia abbatis et capituli Thorn'. Huius autem forisiurationis testis est Robertus abbas et iiij monachi de Thorn' . Hugo scilicet secretarius . Gilebertus cantor etc.

liam son of Robert of Yaxley, as the lawful heir of his father, forswore the land of Sibson, namely two hides, as his father Robert had previously forsworn them at Huntingdon before four shirecourts, namely William Archdeacon of Northampton, Rannulf the canon, William d'Albini, Roger de Torpel, Andrew Revel, and others.

Let present and future know that Robert of Yaxley has shown in the full shire court at Huntingdon that he had quitclaimed the whole of his land in Yaxley and Sibson, and he had quitclaimed and restored upon the high altar of the church of Thorney all the suits and claims which he had against the church of Thorney, whether they were just or unjust, and that he had sworn upon the four gospels and upon the altar and upon all the relics of the same church that never would he or any of his heirs make any further plaint or complaint therein. He has shown also in the same shire court that William his son, who was his lawful heir, had sworn the same quittance and the same oath in the church of Thorney upon the altar and upon all the relics, and afterwards had confirmed the same quittance and the same oath before many people. There was present there Gilbert the monk of the church of Thorney, who received the witness thereof from the whole shire and from Simon son of Peter the constable of Huntingdon and from Simon de Turri and from Anseled the clerk and others.

We preserve in writing for the memory of present and future that Ralf son of William has quitclaimed all his claim to land at Yaxley which had been, as he said, the property of his uncle William in the time of Abbot Robert, and he has confirmed by an oath on the four gospels at Stanground that from that day henceforward he will claim nothing therein, save at the discretion of the Abbot and chapter. Of this oath of abjuration Abbot Robert is witness and four monks of Thorney, Hugh the sacristan, Gilbert the precentor and others.

V. THE CASE CONCERNING THE MARSH LYING BETWEEN THE ABBEY OF CROYLAND AND THE PRIORY OF SPALDING, 1189-1202

Of all the long pleas between individual fenland religious houses and their neighbours, lay and ecclesiastical, which occurred in the centuries from the tenth onwards, the following case, between the Abbot of Croyland and the Prior of Spalding, which began at the end of Henry II's reign and ended inconclusively early in John's, is of outstanding interest. The story, preserved in a now lost manuscript of Croyland abbey is, like so much of the Anglo-Saxon evidence about the law suits of those days, a unilateral account written down at Croyland. The beginning of the plea was in the days of Abbot Robert, who was himself responsible for telling the story. It is possible that his example encouraged his successor, Abbot Henry de Longchamps, on whom the burden of the main plea fell, to see that the tale was completed. Very little public information is interspersed in this particular continuation of the Croyland story, which goes on to recount other pleas and their conclusions when the successful end of the Spalding plea has been set down. There is no evidence of the date of the text, which is printed as the second part of the anonymous *Historiae Croylandensis Continuatio* in *Rerum Anglicarum Scriptorum Veterum Tomus* I (Oxford, 1684), pp. 451-470. The manuscript used by William Fulman was in part decayed and had itself been copied by someone who had supplied an occasional emendation in the margin, but could not always fill in the gaps. These emendations and others suggested, according to Fulman by himself, are printed as he printed them in the form of footnotes with an alphabetical reference to the text. My own footnotes are in the usual manner numbered, but I have not attempted to make emendations in the text. My translation contains such corrections as can easily be made. It is well worth reprinting this narrative and translating it into English because so many points mentioned in these lectures are here illustrated and I know of no other contemporary account which gives so vivid a picture of the royal court of justice at Westminster at work.

To the writer of this unilateral story, or perhaps it should be more correctly said, to the transcriber to whom Fulman owed his knowledge of the plea, the names of the judges who sat in the Bench during the reigns of Richard I and John were unfamiliar, so that they are often distorted, but it is easy today, when innumerable final concords have been correctly transcribed to make the necessary emendations. The bench judges stand out here as a clearly defined group, much concerned about points of procedure; withdrawing from the bench to discuss a point in doubt; sitting with nobles present on state business and consulting both with them and with the barons of the exchequer on difficult matters; inclined to set the dignity of the court as high as, if not higher than the royal prerogative. That the judges on the bench and the barons of the exchequer and the visiting nobility were separate entities is clear, but it is equally clear that one group alone would never venture to take a decision which might offend the King or powerful elements in the land without general consultation. The seeming unwillingness of the court, in particular of Geoffrey fitz Peter, its president, to allow the Abbot of Croyland the advantage of a royal warranty for his default can probably be explained by the powerful friends of the prior of Spalding. The court might well hesitate to offend the Earl of Chester, especially at a critical juncture in the reign.

Both the Abbot and the Prior evidently found the constant need to go to the King himself burdensome, but they never hesitated to undertake the journey over sea, either in person or through one of their monks. The Abbot complained greatly about the necessity of following the court in order to get a royal hearing. Like all other litigants of that time he wished for the advantages which only the highest court in the land could give, and had no understanding of the problems which beset a medieval king making war in a land separated by the English Channel from his main sources of supply.

This account throws a little light on one of the main problems of legal history—the origin of the profession of barrister. Professor Plucknett in his *Concise History of the Common Law* provides a fascinating account of the development of the legal profession, but he does not take it back behind the reign of Edward I. The Abbot had his own attorney, his seneschal John

de Sandon, who could appear for him when he himself was detained elsewhere. But when the Abbot himself appeared before the bench at least on one occasion, John Bucuinte, described as "a citizen of London, a man wise in the affairs of this world" spoke for the Abbot. John Bucuinte was frequently appointed by various parties as their attorney, as references to him in the *Curia Regis Rolls* show. His presence with the itinerant court can sometimes be proved.[1] It seems probable that one line of development leading to the profession of barrister springs from the attorneys of early days.

Finally it should be noted that the phrase "according to the custom of England," so frequently used by King John in giving directions to his judges, was by no means common form.

Since these lectures and the Appendix of Illustrative Material were set up in print I have learned from Mrs. Joan Varley, Archivist of the Lincoln Archives Office, that among the Cragg collection in her charge are two folios probably dating from the first half of the fourteenth century, being part of a manuscript of the *Second Continuation* of the History of Croyland, relating to the plea here printed from the text of Fulman. I owe gratitude to Mrs. Varley for drawing my attention to these fragments, and to Mr. Michael Lloyd for carefully describing them for me. I have been able to obtain a photograph through the assistance of Mrs. Varley and Mr. Lloyd so that I could check the text with that of Fulman. Unfortunately I learned of these fragments too late to incorporate the variant readings in the footnotes. The first fragment runs from the middle of page 453 of Fulman's text to the end of page 455, but a large triangular piece is torn out of the top of the parchment and the bottom of the fragment is torn irregularly right across. In the present volume this portion covers pages 154 to 162. The second fragment is in slightly better condition. It picks up the story two-thirds of the way down page 467 of the Fulman text and continues almost to the end of the case on page 471. Parts of the last six lines of the manuscript are torn off. In the present volume this portion covers pages 200 to 210. Both pieces of parchment are 10½ inches wide. Mr. Lloyd has noted signs of thread holes on one of the fragments which suggests that they may have come from a copy of the Croyland history written in roll form.

[1] *Curia Regis Rolls*, **1**: pp. 57, 74, 161, 232, 237, 272, 355, 477; **2**: p. 122; see Indexes, *Pleas before the King . . .* **1**: p. 322.

The fragments cover only a small portion of the account of the plea, but for that part they provide a medieval text, one remove nearer the original than Fulman and it is probably safe to assume that they are a direct copy of the master text at Croyland.

In his famous articles printed in *The Archaeological Journal* for March, 1862, at pp. 32 ff. and 114 ff. H. T. Riley demonstrated conclusively that the Saxon charters contained in the part of the history named after Abbot Ingulf are forgeries. From his list of the manuscripts of the *History of Crowland* mentioned by previous authors it is clear that there were in the seventeenth century certainly two, or probably, three copies of the work which contained that part of the *History* here under discussion, the so-called *Second Continuation:*

(i) Spelman was able to examine what he describes as a "very ancient" manuscript then at Croyland preserved under three keys in the care of the churchwardens in Croyland church. This manuscript seems to have disappeared about the middle of the seventeenth century. The date of this manuscript is uncertain. Selden knew of it, but could not gain a sight of it.

(ii) The manuscript used by Selden and mentioned by Camden which was completely destroyed in the Cottonian fire.

(iii) Sir John Marsham's manuscript which Fulman used and which is said to have been borrowed and never returned by Obadiah Walker, master of University College, Oxford. This, as Riley notes, could not have been identical with the copy at Croyland since there are 34 divergences between the text of the short extracts from the Croyland Manuscript and the text printed by Fulman. The other manuscripts of the Croyland history break off before they reach the part here printed. Too much stress should not be laid on the sheer number of divergences, for some of them are inevitably minor ones. The exact spelling of insignificant words or even the exact order of such words may not have seemed as important in the seventeenth as in the twentieth century. Fulman and the Cragg fragments do not always agree on precisely the same order for minor words, e.g. "prius nobis" for "nobis prius." Fulman tends to put "cum" where the Cragg text has "quando." But the differences between Fulman's text and that of the Cragg fragments are much more fundamental than can be explained by human frailty in

the seventeenth century. The more important of them are here listed:

(The pages and lines given below refer to this book)

The first fragment

Fulman		Cragg
p. 154 l. 17	arabilem bonam et fertilem	arabilem et fertilem bonam
p. 156 l. 1	Holdbeche	Hollebeche
p. 156 l. 7	esse	crescere—a reading which Fulman himself suggested was more likely to be correct than that of his manuscript
p. 156 l. 23	sicut gentes	figentes
p. 158 l. 3	quasi	quam—which, again, Fulman suggests as a more correct reading than that of his manuscript
p. 158 l. 4	warrantos	guarantos
p. 158 l. 22	etiam	autem
p. 158 l. 26	Fulveie	Fulneie
p. 158 l. 29	Gliat	Glinton
p. 158 l. 36	Westmonum	Westm'
p. 160 l. 35	eum	enim

Second fragment

p. 200 l. 3	Denique	Itaque
p. 200 last line	sed	si
p. 202 l. 10	utraque pars advenisset	utraque parstis uenisset
p. 204 l. 1	Patishill Sestinge	Pateshille Gestinges
p. 204 l. 18	scaccario	scacario
p. 206 l. 29	cum	sub
p. 206 last line but one	Post aliquot autem dies	Post [*blank*] autem dies

So much research has of necessity been expended on the Saxon part of the *History of Croyland* owing to the necessity of exposing the forged charters that the extreme importance of the later contemporary continuations has sometimes been overlooked. The importance of the *Second Continuation* for the working of the courts of justice in the last decade of the twelfth century and the early years of the thirteenth has seldom been stressed. It has been used to provide dates for the adventures and foreign wars of Richard I, particularly by the late Mr. Lionel Landon in his valuable Itinerary of Richard I. Riley noted that the fact that no charters earlier than the "great charter" of Henry II were produced in the plea against Spalding is evidence that no such charters existed at the end of the twelfth century.

It seems highly probable that the Cragg fragments at Lincoln are all that has so far been found surviving from the manuscript of the Croyland history which in the early seventeenth century was locked up in Croyland church in the care of the churchwardens. By what stages these poor remains journeyed from Croyland to the house of the late Captain Cragg at Threckingham, some twenty miles away as the crow flies, can only remain a matter of conjecture.

Rerum Anglicarum Scriptorum Veterum Tom. I, p. 453

Memoratus vero Abbas Robertus gravissima pro ecclesia sua toleravit placita contra priorem Spaldingiæ et homines Hollandenses, qui cum exercitu irruerunt in præcinctum Croylandiæ, etc. prout sequens processus per se idem editus prolixius declarabit.

Abbatia de Croylandia, quam incepit Beatus Guthlacus Confessor transactis quadringentis annis et eo amplius, qui et ibidem requiescit, propria eleemosyna est Regum Angliæ, de donatione eorum speciali ab antiquis temporibus Anglorum, postquam eam fundavit Ethelbaldus Rex, donando mariscum in quo sita est, sicut et continetur in vita ipsius sancti ab olim scripta; longius enim a cætera terra constituta est Abbatia, in medio marisci. Homines autem de Hoyland, qui ex aquilonari parte viciniores sunt, vehementer desiderant habere communionem marisci Croylande. Nam [a]priusquam desiccati sunt marisci eorum, quorum unaquæque villa proprium habet, converterunt in terram arabilem bonam et fertilem. Unde sit quod supra modum indigeant pascuis communibus ad animalia sua, quibus minus abundant.

Anno igitur Regis Henrici tricessimo quinto, ultimo videlicet anno vitæ suæ, ipso in transmarinis terris suis, guerris et aliis negotiis occupato, venit falsus rumor in Angliam de obitu eius. Quo audito Hoylandenses excogitaverunt quomodo possent mariscum violenter invadere et obtinere; putantes se facile posse abbatem de Croylandia pauperem et domum suam parvam superare, confidentes in virtute sua, et in multitudine divitiarum suarum. Gerardus itaque de Camvill, et Fulco de Oiri, et Thomas de Multon, pater Thomæ, et Conanus filius Heliæ, qui erga domum Croylandiæ et Robertum abbatem aliis de causis valde commoti erant; assumto etiam secum Ricardo de Flet, et Waltero, et aliis pluribus, convenerunt Nicholaum priorem Spalding, ut ipse hujus violentiæ se præberet ducem et primarium. [p. 454] Quid multa? Omnes potentiores de Ellou wapentak, preter paucos, conspirationem fecerunt adversus Croylandiam, convenientes in unum aliquando in horreo

a postquam

Rerum Anglicarum Scriptorum Veterum Tom. I, p. 453

The said Abbot Robert supported a most serious plea on behalf of his church against the Prior of Spalding and the men of Holland, who with an army attacked the precincts of Croyland as the following account set out by himself fully will show.

The abbey of Croyland, which the blessed confessor Guthlac, who rests there, founded four hundred years and more ago is the special alms of the kings of England from their personal gift in the Old English times after King Ethelbald founded the house by granting the marsh in which it is situated, as is contained in the life of the saint written in the old days, for the abbey is established far from other inhabited land in the middle of a marsh. But the men of Holland, the nearest neighbours on the north strongly desired to have common in the marsh of Croyland, for after their marsh had dried up, of which each village had its share, they had converted it into good and fertile arable, so that they have considerably less than the usual amount of common pasture for their stock of which they have little.

In the thirty-fifth year of King Henry, in the last year of his life, he being over seas occupied in wars and other affairs, a false rumour came into England of his death. Hearing this, the men of Holland thought how they could violently attack and gain possession of the marsh, considering that it would be easy to overcome the abbey of Croyland, a poor and small house, confident in their valour and the multitude of their riches. And therefore Gerard de Camville, Fulk de Oiri, Thomas of Moulton, father of the present Thomas, and Conan son of Elias, who had other reasons for anger against the house of Croyland and Abbot Robert, gathering in with them Richard of Fleet and Walter and many others, met Nicholas Prior of Spalding, so that he might offer himself as the leader and prime mover of this violence. What more? All the more powerful folk of Elloe wapentake, save a few, conspired against Croyland meeting sometimes in the barn of the Prior of Spalding at Weston and sometimes in Holbeach church.

When therefore in the usual way the Abbot of Croyland had put his marsh in defense, as he was accustomed to do about Rogation tide [14 May 1189], and this was publicly proclaimed on

prioris Spalding, apud Weston, aliquando in ecclesia de Holdbeche.

Cum ergo more consueto abbas de Croylande mariscum suum posuisset in defensione, sicut singulis annis fieri solet circa Rogationes, et acclamatum esset publice super pontem de Spalding, ut Hoilandenses et alii averia sua retinerent ab introitu marisci, ut foenum posset liberius [b]esse; noluerunt ipsi, sed tunc plusquam prius intrare compulerunt. Servientes vero abbatis ad hæc de more constituti, jussu ipsius, sicut aliis annis facere consueverant, animalia inparcaverunt. Super quo valde indignati Hoilandenses, die statuto, festo sanctorum Nerei et Achillei, venerunt in mariscum Croylande quasi ad bellum omnes armati omni genere armorum, ad tria millia virorum et eo amplius. Occurrit eis Robertus abbas cum paucis suorum ad fossam quæ dicitur Asendyke, ubi meta est marisci Croyland ea quæ pacis sunt, suppliciter rogans. Æstimabat enim tam ipse, quam alii quod ad subversionem totius abbatiæ venirent, superbe ei respondentes, et in faciem resistentes: sed mutavit Deus tantam illorum malitiam, et aliquantulum mitigavit de destructione abbatiæ; verum per medium marisci sic armati incesserunt, et diviserunt sibi mariscum, sicut sitæ sunt villæ suæ, licet longius in circuitu positæ, et circa abbatiam castrametati sunt, sicut gentes tentoria sua et logias facientes, et servientes armatos imponentes ad custodiendum singulas partes suas. Foderunt itaque turbam, et succiderunt in magna parte nemus et alnetum Croyland, et succenderunt, et prata depasta sunt; et asportaverunt vestam,[2] et alias violentias fecerunt per quindecim dies quasi in castris armati.

Interim autem in arcto positi sunt abbas et monachi Croylande, et servientes sui, in angustia et dolore, in tantum quod vix portas ecclesiæ egredi auderent. Disposuerunt autem facere querelam coram justiciariis domini Regis; et ad eum quem proprius invenerunt, Gaufridum videlicet filium Petri, qui tunc morabatur in Norhamtesire apud Clive, monachi transmiserunt; qui sex milites de Norhamt. ad videndum et plenius cognoscendum illud incomparabile ultagium transmisit. Qui venientes in orientali parte, primum tentorium et logiam invenerunt hominum de Sutton, qui sunt homines G. de Canvill, et viderunt in

b crescere.

2 *sic* for "vesturam."

Spalding bridge so that the men of Holland and others could keep back their stock from entering the marsh to let the grass grow more freely, they refused and then compelled more than before to come in. The Abbot's servants, appointed as usual for this purpose, by his command impounded the animals as they had been accustomed to do in other years. Upon which the men of Holland, very angry, on the appointed day, the feast of Saints Nereus and Achilleus [12 May, 1189], came into the marsh of Croyland as if to war, three thousand men and more, all armed with every sort of arms. Abbot Robert with a few of his men met them at the ditch called Asendyke, where the boundary of Croyland marsh runs, humbly speaking to them words of peace, for he thought, as others did, they they had come to overthrow the entire abbey, they replying proudly to him and resisting him to his face. But the Lord modified their malice and turned it from the destruction of the abbey, but they entered the midst of the marsh thus armed and divided the marsh in accordance with the site of their villages, although they were set around at some distance, and they encamped about the abbey like people putting up tents and huts and each setting armed servants to guard their part. They dug turves and cut down a great part of the grove and holt of Croyland and burned it and depastured the meadows and carried away crops and did other deeds of violence for a fortnight as if in armed camps.

Meanwhile the Abbot and monks of Croyland and their servants were in a difficult position, so anxious and troubled that they scarcely dared go outside the doors of the church. But they agreed to make their plaint to the justices of the lord king and they sent quickly to the one whom they found was nearest to them, Geoffrey fitz Peter, who was then at King's Cliff, in Northamptonshire. He sent six knights from Northamptonshire to view and fully report that extreme outrage. Coming in at the eastern side, they came first to the tent and hut of the men of Sutton, who are Gerard de Camville's men and saw there every sort of arms. On being asked, they replied that they were there by their lord's command and in this way all of each encampment, until they came last of all to the Spalding hut, vouched their lords to warranty.

Meanwhile Abbot Robert secretly hastened to London and before Hubert Walter, who then was acting on behalf of Ran-

omne genus armorum; qui ab eis inquisiti, responderunt, se ibi esse ex præcepto domini sui; sic et singuli de singulis logiis, usque ad logiam de Spaldinge [c]quasi postremam invenerunt, dominos suos vocaverunt warrantos.

Interim autem Robertus abbas clam Londinum festinavit, et coram Huberto Walteri, qui tunc illic locum tenuit Randulfi de Glanvull, qui in transmarinis partibus cum domino Rege morabatur, et coram sociis suis justitiariis conquestus est super tantis injuriis in pace domini Regis sibi illatis; et chartam domini Regis magnam, marisci limites nominantem, eis ostendit, qui vehementer illi condolentes, admirantes et irascentes, mandaverunt ex parte Regis, prædicto G. filio Petri, quatenus priorem de Spald. et omnes Hoilandenses illos ad se convocaret, et plenarium certum abbati de illis faceret. Quo audito, armati illi qui in logiis jam quindecim diebus excubias fecerant, easdem logias combusserunt, et recesserunt ad propriam.

Ad summonitionem itaque G. filii Petri venerunt cum priore illi Hoilandenses obviam illi apud Deping. Adduxitque G. filius Petri secum multos et magnos viros, et familiares domini Regis, hebdomadæ Pentec. feria sexta. [p. 455] Illic igitur ab abbate Roberto appellati sunt de pace Regis, et de omni prædicta violentia et injuria; surrexerunt etiam septem ex parte abbatis de ipsius hominibus, qui septem capitales homines appellaverunt, unumquemque de damno facto abbati viginti marcarum. Hugo Poll. Gilebertum de Peccebrig; Robertus Bee, Elfricum de Fulveie, fratrem eius: Hugo Molende, Conanum filium Helye; Robertus de Bastum, Fulconem de Oiri; Alfredus de Leveringt. Thomam de Multon; Willielmus de Gliat, Algerum de Colevill; Robinus Robet, Alexandrum de Quappelod. Eorum autem quidam qui appellati fuerunt, cum aliis pluribus, adducti et incarcerati sunt; Gileb. videlicet frater eius Elricus apud Norhamt, Willelmus Puleia et Hugo de Quappelod apud [d]Rothig. et alii alibi.

Postea autem constituit utrique parti diem nominatum adveniendi et standi coram capitali justitia apud Westmonum, per festum sancti Michaelis.

Inter hæc obiit dominus Henricus Rex Angliæ; coronatus est autem dominus Ricardus Rex tertia die Septembris; et

[c] quam.
[d] Rockingh.

nulf de Glanville who was overseas with the King, and before his fellow justices, he made complaint about such injuries put on him in the peace of the lord King; and he showed the great charter of the lord King setting out the bounds of the marsh. They, very much condoling with him, and surprised and angry, commanded Geoffrey fitz Peter on behalf of the lord King that he should summon before him the Prior of Spalding and all the Holland men and give full assurance to the abbot about these things. Having heard of this, those armed men who had been in the huts now for a fortnight, burned them and returned to their own parts.

And so at the summons of Geoffrey fitz Peter those Holland men came with the prior to meet him at Deeping. And in Whitsun Week [28 May-4 June, 1189] Geoffrey fitz Peter brought with him many great men, closely associated with the lord King. There they were appealed by Abbot Robert of the King's peace, and all the aforesaid violence and injury. Also seven of the Abbot's men stood up on his behalf and appealed seven of the chief men, each of damage done to the Abbot to the extent of 20 marks, Hugh Poll [appealed] Gilbert de Peccebrig; Robert Bee [appealed] Elfric of Fulney Gilbert's brother, Hugh the miller [appealed] Conan son of Elias; Robert of Weston [appealed] Fulk de Oiri; Alfred of Leverington [appealed] Thomas of Moulton: William of Glinton [appealed] Alger de Coleville; Robin Robet [appealed] Alexander of Whaplode. Some of those who were appealed with many others were taken and imprisoned, Gilbert, namely, and his brother Elfric at Northampton; William Pulleia and Hugh of Whaplode at Rockingham, and others elsewhere.

Afterwards he set both parties a day to appear before the chief justiciar at Michaelmas at Westminster.

While this was happening the lord King Henry died, the lord King Richard was crowned on 3 September; the justices were changed and the Holland men became more spirited, for if he had lived they feared condemnation. On the appointed day the Abbot of Croyland came with his friends and his champions to prosecute his plea and his appeals, and the Prior of Spalding was there with his accomplices. Thomas of Moulton was sick and sent his steward on his behalf. At that time Hugh Bishop of Durham was sitting as chief justiciar. But Conan son of Elias,

mutati sunt justitiæ; et Hoilandenses animosiores effecti sunt: nam si vixisset, damnari timuerunt. Die itaque constituto venit abbas Croyland cum amicis et campionibus suis ad prosequendam loquelam suam et appellationes suas; affuit et prior de Spald. cum complicibus; Thomas de Mulet æger, senescallum suum pro se destinavit. Residebat tunc temporis Dominus Hugo Dunelmi episcopus pro capitali justitia. Conanus autem filius Heliæ, et Fulco de Oiri, et dapifer Thomæ de Mult. et Alexander de Quappelod et Alger de Colevill timuerunt sibi, et amicis intervenientibus abbati supplicaverunt pro bono pacis et concordiæ; et ut brevietur oratio. Hi vero cum amicis affidaverunt abbati, se de cætero nunquam in æternum movere calumniam super marisco Croyland, et quod se ponerent in misericordia Regis pro injuria facta, et quod damnum quod intulerant per arbitrum amicorum redderent. Venerunt autem coram justitiariis et se reos confessi sunt, et amerciati sunt Thomas de Mult. quinque libras argenti, et Fulco quinque marcas, et Conanus totidem; duo reliqui qui pauperes fuerunt, abbate deprecante, non fecerunt illic finem suum. Prior autem et homines sui, G. et frater eius Elfricus, in contumacia sua perstiterunt.

Constitutus est itaque eis alius dies ad quem venerunt abbas et prior et sui secum. Conquestus est abbas de priore et hominibus suis, qui armati venientes in mariscum Croyland (quæ est de domino Rege) pacem regiam violassent. Prior autem respondit se quidem cum armis venisse in suum proprium mariscum, qui pertinet ad prioratum de Spald. de feudo Willelmi de Romar. et de hoc probando promisit domino Regi xl marcas pro habenda magna assisa. Abbas autem Croyland non bene sibi tunc prospexerat, quod nec chartam Regis secum detulerat, nec aliquem secum juvenem validum adduxerat, qui posset vadium pro abbate super proprietate marisci offerre, preter H. Poll, et Robertum Bee. Qui Gilebertum et Elricum fratrem suum appellaverunt; et quia duellum non potuit eligere, oportuit eum consentire in recognitionem, quamvis sibi periculosam. Milites eum[3] comitatus remotissimi sunt a marisco Croylandiæ, et nihil norunt de eius limitibus; et quod nullus fere extat in comitatu Lincoln. qui non sit aliquo modo obnoxius vel domui de Spald. vel Willelmo de Romar. vel alicui eorum calumniam moverant super marisco. Licet enim prænominati illi se retrahentes ca-

[3] *sic* for "enim."

Fulk de Oiri, Thomas of Moulton's steward, Alexander of Whaplode, and Alger de Coleville feared for themselves and through the intervention of friends prayed the Abbot for the blessing of peace and an agreement in order that the talk might be cut short. These with their friends pledged their faith to the Abbot that never to all eternity would they move a claim upon the marsh of Croyland; that they would put themselves in the King's mercy for the damage done; and that they would restore the damage by the judgment of friends. They came before the justices, pleaded guilty and were amerced; Thomas of Moulton, five pounds of silver; Fulk five marks; and Conan as much.[29] The remaining two were poor and at the Abbot's request did not make fine there. But the Prior and his men, namely Gilbert and Elfric his brother persisted in their contumacy.

And so another day was set at which the Abbot came and the Prior with his men. The Abbot complained touching the Prior and his men, who, coming armed into the marsh of Croyland, which is the alms of the lord King, had broken the royal peace. But the Prior replied that he had come with arms into his own marsh, which belongs to the priory of Spalding of the fee of William de Roumara, and he promised the lord King 40 marks for the grand assize to prove this. The Abbot of Croyland had not used due precaution, because he had not brought with him the royal charter nor any strong young man who could offer pledge upon the ownership of the marsh on behalf of the Abbot, except H. Poll and Robert Bee, who had appealed Gilbert and Elfric his brother. And because the Abbot could not chose the duel, he was bound to consent to a recognition, although dangerous to him; for the knights of the shire are very far away from the marsh of Croyland and know nothing of its boundaries; and there is hardly anyone living in the county of Lincoln who is not in some way bound either to the house of Spalding, or to William de Roumara, or to one of those who had moved a claim upon the marsh. For although those named above, withdrawing themselves, had remitted their claim, nevertheless, privately and secretly they were weighing out help, counsel and money to

[29] In 1190 the Sheriff paid in the royal treasury £5 on behalf of Thomas of Moulton for licence of concord with the Prior of Spalding and 5 marks each from Fulk and Conan. *Pipe Roll 2 Richard I*, p. 89. The clerk was in error over the form of the entry.

lumniam remiserunt, tamen private et secrete ad adjutorium et consilium . . . . .[4] pecuniam impenderent priori et suis. Electi sunt itaque milites de comitibus [5] in curia Regis et nominati et in scripto positi qui recognitionem facerent, et lætati sunt Hoilandenses se triumphasse, eo quod videbatur iis negotium jam perfici posse pecunia.

[p. 456] Dominus autem Rex Ricardus mandatum direxit ad vicecomitem Lincoln. in hac forma: Salutem. Præcipimus tibi quod summoneas Rogerum de Huntingfeld, Conanum de Kirket, Walterum [e]Maureunard, Radulfum filium Stephani, Alanum de Wichet, Willelmum de Foletebi, Alanum de Marc, Ricardum de Bracebrigg, Alveram de Hugwell, Robertum de Thorp, Alan Merscon, Hugonem de Nouilla, Hugonem de Bobi, Robertum filium Henrici, Radulfum de Reping, Gaufridum de la Mar, Robertum de Guing, qui nominati fuerunt per quatuor milites ad hoc electos, ad videndum mariscum de quo contentio fuit in curia nostra, inter abbatem de Croyland et priorem de Spalding; qui [6] sint ibi ad videndum mariscum illum proxima die lunæ ante natalem domini, et tu sis ibi cum quatuor aut sex ex legalioribus militibus de comitatu. Et summone prædictos milites post visionem factam, [f]quae fuit coram nobis quinto die post octab. sancti Hilarii, ubicunque fuerimus, vel coram justiciariis nostris eadem die apud Westmon. ad recognoscendum per sacramentum, quis majus jus habeat in eodem marisco, in quo logiæ factæ fuerunt, et combustio turbarum et alneti, vel abbas de Croyland, vel prior de Spalding, secundum seisinam quam iidem habuerunt a prima coronatione patris nostri Regis Henrici. Et habeas ibi hoc breve et summonitorem. Teste episcopo Dunelmi.

Die lunæ itaque proxima ante natalem [7] domini Nigellus vicecomes Lincoln. non venit in propria persona ad visum marisci, sed transmisit pro se Walterum de Sart. qui et fautor Spaldingensium extitit; paucissimi de militibus nominatis advenerunt, qui visum facientes, verumdictum suum sub hac forma scribi fecerunt.

[4] The manuscript was evidently decayed at this point.
[5] *sic* for "comitatu."
[e] Maureward.
[6] *sic* for "quod."
[f] quod sint coram.
[7] *sic* for "natale."

the Prior and his men. And so there were chosen in the King's court, knights of the shire, whose names were written down, to make the recognition and the men of Holland rejoiced because it seemed to them that the business could now be completed by money.

The lord King Richard sent his mandate to the Sheriff of Lincoln in this form, Greeting. We command you that you summon Roger of Huntingfield, Conan of Kirton, Walter Malreward, Ralf son of Stephen, Alan de Wichet', William of Fulletby, Alan de Marc, Richard of Bracebridge, Alver de Hugwell, Robert de Thorp, Alan Merscon, Hugh de Neville, Hugh of Boothby, Robert son of Henry, Ralf of Rippingale, Geoffrey de la Mar, Robert de Guing, who have been named by four knights chosen for this, to view the marsh touching which there was a plea in our court between the abbot of Croyland and the Prior of Spalding, that they shall be there to view the marsh on the Monday next before Christmas, and do you be there with four or six of the more lawful knights of the shire. And summon the aforesaid knights after the view has been made that they be before us on the fifth day after the feast of St. Hilary, wherever we shall be, or before our justices on the same day at Westminster to recognise by their oath whether the Abbot of Croyland or the Prior of Spalding has the greater right in the same marsh in which the huts were made and the turves and holt were burned, according to the seisin which the same had from the first coronation of our father King Henry. And have there this writ and the summoners. Witness, the Bishop of Durham.

On the Monday next before Christmas Nigel Sheriff of Lincoln did not come in his proper person to view the marsh, but sent on his behalf Walter de Essartis, who was also a supporter of the men of Spalding. Very few of the knights named came, who making the view, caused their verdict to be recorded in this form:

This is the verdict of the knights touching the view of the marsh whence the suit between the Abbot of Croyland [and the Prior of Spalding arose. The Abbot] says that the marsh where the huts were found, the burning done and the holt stubbed up is his own and part of the fee of the abbey of Croyland, so that the Abbot this year and ever since he became abbot has received the rent. The men of Holland say that that marsh is not the Abbot's, but is their own, from Munechelade towards

Hoc est verumdictum militum de visu marisci unde querela inter abbatem Croyland, dicta [g]quia mariscus ubi logiæ inventæ fuerunt, et combustio facta, et extirpatio alneti, est suus proprius, et de feudo abbathiæ Croyland. Itaque abbas hoc anno et semper postquam fuit dum receperit firmam ut dicit abbas. Homines Hoilandenses dicunt, quod mariscus ille non est abbatis, sed est illorum proprius, a Munechelade versus orientem; et nec combustionem nec extirpationem warrantizant, quæ facta fuit infra Munechelade. Homines Hoilandenses inquisiti utrum combustionem et extirpationem extra Munechelade vellent warrantizare, necne; dixerunt quod de his noluerunt respondere, quia justitiarii domini Regis habent recordiam [8] illorum inbreviatum.

Interim Hoilandenses, favente illis vicecomite, mutaverunt quos voluerunt de militibus nominatis, sine assensu abbatis, sicut Rogerum de Huntingfeld, Hugonem de Boebi, Gaufridum de la Mar. Appropinquante autem die placiti, abbas Croyland volens illuc ire, infirmitate detentus est, et fecit se essoniari de malo viæ. Et statutus est alius dies Westmonasterii, post purificationem sanctæ Mariæ. Abbas autem Robertus iter arripiens illuc eundi, apud Cotenham in tantum infirmatus est, quod fecit se essoniari de malo lecti. Quatuor autem milites ad videndum eum per præceptum justitiarii venerunt; qui statuerunt et [9] alium diem post octab. Paschæ. Ingravescente vero eadem infirmitate, defunctus est abbas Robertus in vigilia Paschæ: et seisita est Croylandia in manu Regis, et cancellarii, quem quando Rex transfretaverat, reliquerat capitalem justitiam totius Angliæ. Vacante itaque abbatia Croyland, et in manu Regis detenta, cessavit tempestas. . . . .

[The author here notes that King Richard disafforested the marshes of Holland and Kesteven between the Welland and the Witham.]

[p. 457] Interim dominus Willielmus de Longo campo Eliensis episcopus, domini Regis cancellarius, tunc apostolicæ sedis

g Deest quidd. The clerk who wrote the manuscript from which the editor was transcribing must have jumped from one "Croyland" to the next time it occurred, missing out several words, probably "et priorem de Spald. Et Abbas de Croyland venit et." He should have continued "dicit quod" instead of "dicta quia."

8 *sic* for "recordum."

9 *sic* for "ei."

the east, and that they were not responsible for either burning or stubbing up done within Munechelade. Asked whether they were prepared to warrant the burning and stubbing up outside Munechelade or not, said that they refused to answer touching these things because the lord King's justices have their record enrolled.

Meanwhile the men of Holland, by the favour of the Sheriff and without the Abbot's consent, made what changes they wished among the knights named, as for example, Roger of Huntingfield, Hugh of Boothby, Geoffrey de la Mar. When the day of the plea approached the Abbot was detained by sickness and caused himself to be essoined because he was ill on the journey and he was given another day at Westminster after the purification of St. Mary [2 February, 1190]. But Abbot Robert setting out to go there became so ill at Cottenham that he caused himself to be essoined because confined to his bed. Four knights came to view him by command of the justiciar and set him another day after Easter. Abbot Robert's illness grew so much worse that he died on Easter eve and Croyland was seised into the hand of the King and the Chancellor, who, when the King went over seas had remained as chief justiciar of all England. The abbey of Croyland being thus vacant and in the King's hand, the tempest ceased. . . .

Meanwhile the lord William de Longchamps, Bishop of Ely, Chancellor of the lord King, then apostolic legate, having sent messengers to the King in Normandy, where he was carefully arranging his journey to Jerusalem, obtained licence from him to appoint an abbot to the monastery of Croyland. And so with the King's assent and the choice of the brethren of Croyland, Henry, a monk of Evesham and the brother in the flesh of the aforesaid Chancellor was elected into the abbacy of Croyland.

While the Chancellor was acting as chief justiciar the Spalding folk made no claim against Croyland, but when owing to count John and the conspiracy against the Chancellor, nay rather against the lord King, now serving God in Judea, the Chancellor had been expelled from England and his brothers, Henry and Osbert, and many of his household taken and held in iron chains and most harsh prison, William de Roumara, a warm friend and now sworn to Count John, incited the persecution of Henry Abbot of Croyland owing to the hatred of his

legatus, directis nuntiis ad Regem in Normann. ubi iter suum Hierosolymitanum sollicite disposuit, licentiam obtinuit ab ipso abbatem in monasterio de Croyland substituendi. Itaque per assensum Regis, et electionem fratrum de Croyland, electus est in abbatem Croyland dominus Henricus, Evesham. monachus prædicti cancellarii frater carnalis.

Verum dum cancellarius pro capitali justitia resideret, nullam calumniæ mentionem fecerunt Spaldingenses adversus Croyland: cum autem per comitem Johannem, et per conspirationem contra cancellarium factam, imo contra dominum Regem jam in Judæa servitio Dei deditum, expulsus fuisset ab Anglia cancellarius, et fratres sui Henricus et Osbertus et plures alii consanguinei et familiares capti essent, et in vinculis ferreis et carcere durissimo detenti: suscitavit Willelmus de Romare, comiti Johanni valde familiaris et jam juratus, persecutionem in Henricum abbatem Croyland, in odium fratrum suorum; et jam accepta opportunitate, fecit summonere prædictum abbatem a justitiariis per breve Regis, quatenus die statuta ad Westmon. veniret, contra abbatem sancti Nicholai Andegavis, (nam supradictus Nicholaus prior Spalding jam depositus fuerat) ad audiendam recognitionem marisci sui. Ipse autem anxius, et quo se verteret, penitus nescius, nam undique sibi periculum imminere prospexit; non ausus est egredi septa monasterii sui, ne forte caperetur sicut fratres sui, aut etiam occideretur; jam in eum huiusmodi jam minæ processerant, sicut perceperat a multis. Essoniari itaque se fecit primo die a malo viæ: secundo die, de malo lecti. Unde mandatum est a curia Regis a justitiariis vicecomiti Lincoln. Gerardo de Camvill, inimico cancellarii, et præcipuo hujus factionis authori, quatenus quatuor milites legalioribus comitatus, ad visum abbatis die statuta mitteret. Nominati sunt autem quatuor milites, quorum hæc sunt nomina: Walterus de Braytoft, Reg. de Beniton. aliorum nomina exciderunt: qui ad diem præfixum non venerunt, sed tantum unus eorum, Reginus videlicet de Beniton. et alii viles [h]sp. de hominibus prioris Spald. cum aliis. Abbas autem H. arbitratus eos non fore venturos; nocte præcedente navem intravit in januis Croyland, nec dum enim plene convaluit, et ad quoddam manerium suum in Cantebrigesire se deferri fecit, versus curiam. Reginus autem præfatus, vocato priore de Croyland, dixit se

[h] praecipae, but more probably it should read "persones."

brothers; and now seizing the opportunity, he caused the Abbot to be summoned by the King's writ to appear on an appointed day at Westminster against the Abbot of St. Nicholas of Angers, for the aforesaid Nicholas Prior of Spalding had now been deposed, to hear the recognition of his marsh. The Abbot of Croyland, anxious, and not knowing which way to turn, for he saw peril threaten him on every side, dared not go outside the portals of his monastery, lest he should be taken like his brothers, or even killed. Already threats of this sort had been made against him as he had heard from many. And so on the first day he caused himself to be essoined for difficulties met on the journey; on the second, for being confined to his bed by illness. Wherefore the justices of the King's court ordered the Sheriff, Gerard de Camville, the Chancellor's enemy and the man who began this trouble, that he should send four lawful knights to view the Abbot on the appointed day; the names of the knights are these, Walter of Braytoft, Reginald of Bennington—the other names have been cut out—only one of whom, Reginald of Bennington, came at the appointed day, and certain other low fellows, men of the Prior of Spalding with others. Abbot Henry, considering that they would not come, on the preceding night entered a ship at the gates of Croyland, while he was not fully recovered, and caused himself to be borne to a certain manor of his in Cambridgeshire on his way to the court. The aforesaid Reginald, having summoned the Prior of Croyland, said that he had come by the King's command to view the Abbot's sickness, and although his fellow knights similarly instructed were not found there, he nevertheless sought to make his view, and those who had come appointed a day for the abbot [to appear before the justices].

When the day approached, the Abbot, more concerned for the perpetual disinheritance of his church than for his own safety, set out for London, where he arrived on Ascension Day and found gathered against him the chief men of the land, namely count John, Walter Archbishop of Rouen, Hugh de Nunant Bishop of Chester, William de Roumara and his accomplices, Gerard de Camville and Roger of Stixwould his undersheriff, the Abbot of Angers and others beyond numbering gathering against him in hatred of his brothers. William de Roumara and the Abbot of Angers, by many prayers, great gifts

venisse ad videndam infirmitatem abbatis, ex præcepto Regis; sed quia socios suos ad hoc nominatos illis non invenit, nequaquam solus ipsius quæsivit visionem; vevuntamen statuerunt abbati diem ex præcepto, ut dixerunt qui venerant, justit. . . .[10]

Appropinquante vero die, abbas Croyland magis super perpetua ecclesiæ sue exhæredatione, quam de periculo proprio solicitus, Londinum profectus est; ubi venit die Assensionis, illicque reperit adversus se congregatos principes terræ; comitem videlicet Johannem, Walterum archiepiscopum Rothom. Hugon. de Novanut episcopum Cestriæ, Will. de Romar. et complices suos, Gerard. de Camvill. et Rogerum de Stikelwald subvicecomitem suum, et abbatem Andegavum, et innumeros alios considentes adversus eum in odium fratrum suorum. Will. enim de Romar. et abbas Andeg. universos qui tunc temporis magni erant in terra, multis precibus et magnis muneribus et pravis suggestionibus commoverant adversus abbatem et domum Croyland, in tantum quod non videbatur iis plenam et perfectam obtinuisse victoriam de cancellario et de suis, donec abbatia de Croyland, cui fratrem suum præfecerat, in pace sine exhæredatione permaneret. Intendebat enim omnibus modis Willelmus de Rom. situm prædicti monasterii, quæ est propria [11]. . domini Regis de corona sua, et præde-[p. 458] cessorum suorum Regum Angliæ, ad suam baroniam et ad priorem Spald. convertere. Multis autem audientibus dixit quod abbatia de Croyland sita sit in feudo suo; quæ fundata fuit et regalis facta, priusquam aliquis de genere suo nosceretur, et antequam Spald. esset quæ olim aliquando dicitur fuisse manerium Croyland. Iste et W. cum aliquando super hoc a comite J. deprecaretur, respondisse fertur, Domine dilecte Will.[12] centum librarum in justitiam facerem et pro amore tuo.

Vocatus est tandem abbas Croyland ad scaccarium, coram omnibus præmissis considentibus contra ipsum, solus cum monachis tribus, et duobus tantum militibus mediocribus, quia nullus alius audebat stare cum ipso. Senescallus W. de Rom. facundus quidem et satis procax, cepit loqui contra eum valde versute et proterve et inique. Itaque multum visum est placuisse

10 The manuscript was decayed at this point.

11 The manuscript was decayed at this point; "elemosina" is missing.

12 *sic* perhaps "volens" or some such word; the whole of this last sentence of the paragraph is unintelligible as it stands, nor does any convincing emendation of the text come to mind.

and evil insinuations, had moved all who at that time were great in the land against the Abbot and house of Croyland so much that it did not seem to them that they would have acquired full and perfect victory over the Chancellor and his following so long as the abbey of Croyland, which his brother ruled, remained in peace without loss of its estates. For William de Roumara intended by all means to convert the site of the said monastery, which is the proper alms of the lord King and his predecessors, kings of England, to his own barony and the prior of Spalding. In the hearing of many he said that the abbey of Croyland is situated in his fee, although it was founded as royal alms before any one of his race was known and before the existence of Spalding, which at one time is said to have been a manor of Croyland. . . . [See footnote 12.]

At length the Abbot of Croyland was summoned to the exchequer before all the aforesaid assembled against him, alone with three monks and two very modest knights, because no one else dared stand with him. William de Roumara's steward, an eloquent and greedy man spoke against him very insolently, craftily and wickedly, and seemed to have given great pleasure to the Archbishop of Rouen and Count John and the others. When he had dragged out his case for a long time, blaming, reproaching and reviling the Chancellor and his [brothers] every one listening in complete silence, and he who ought to speak for the Abbot could scarcely be heard for the tumult. At length he replied sufficiently briefly on the Abbot's behalf that the marsh in which the abbey is set he ought to hold of the demesne and crown of the lord king, and that he held in peace and quiet when his lord the King, his advocate, set out to Jerusalem, and he has vouched the lord King to warranty, and that he may have an adjournment he offered forty marks to the lord King, but they refused to hear or understand. At length the Abbot produced the lord King's charter in which the limits of the marsh are set out, and another charter in which the King forbids that the Abbot of Croyland shall be impleaded except before himself. This was read last. For he first offered the charter of King Richard in the same words, but Count John rejoined that the Abbot's brother the Chancellor had made this charter according to his own will. But after he had heard his father's charter Count John blushed. These charters being read and understood, the

archiepiscopo Rotom. et J. comiti, et aliis. Qui cum rationem suam diu et multum in convitiis et reprehensionibus et opprobriis cancellarii et suorum cum summa tranquillitate silentii omnibus attendentibus, protraxisset, et ille qui respondere pro abbate deberet, vix potuit audiri propter tumultum; tandem respondit nimis breviter pro abbate quod mariscum illum qui sedem abbatiæ de dominio domini Regis et corona ipsius teneret, et quod in pace et quiete tenuit quum dominus suus Rex et advocatus iter suum Hierosolymitanum arripuit; et vocavit super hoc dominum Regem Gavant.[13] et ut inducias possit habere, obtulit ad opus Regis quadraginta marcas quod noluerunt audire vel intelligere. Tandem abbas protulit chartam domini Regis, in qua determinati sunt limites præfati marisci; et aliam chartam, in qua prohibet Rex ne abbas Croyland ponatur in placitum nisi coram seipso; que postrema lecta est. Nam primo chartam Regis Richardi in eisdem verbis protulit; sed comes J. respondit, quod Cancellarius frater suus fecerat ei hanc chartam pro voluntate sua. At postquam chartam patris sui audierat, erubuit. His lectis et intellectis, confusi sunt adversarii supra modum, vix habentes quid rejicerent.

Quod videns Robertus de Fentefeld,[14] unus justitiarius adjutor eorum, inquisivit alta voce, si milites qui fecerunt visum abbatis, illic essent, produxerunt igitur quatuor satis viles personas, quos ad hoc, ut dicitur, mercede conduxerant, Gaufridum videlicet de Thurleby, qui de tenemento Andeg. tunc erat; et Willelmum filium Alf. et Walterum Rufum de Hamnebi, et Gilebertum filium Justi de Beningt. nec milites, nec feudum habentes militarem; Respondit abbas, eos non esse milites nominatos; et quod neque ipsi, neque illi, ad visum suum faciendum venerunt, et de hoc obtulit probationem: et voluerunt[15] eum audire; sed falsum testimonium, quod alii tulerunt contra eum, scribi fecerunt; et nihil veritatis quod abbas proposuit, scribere voluerunt. Veruntamen omnes qui intererant, præter adversarios et alios malevolos, et compatientes et condolentes abbatis oppressioni, existimaverunt quod judicium abbatis in bonum ei verteretur, eo quod non erant de militari ordine, nec accincti gladio, illi qui se visores esse dicebant; et tertius eorum

[13] *sic* for "warrant."
[14] *sic* for "Witefeld."
[15] *sic* for "noluerunt."

Abbot's adversaries were beyond measure confused not having anything to reply.

Seeing this, Robert of Wheatfield, one of the justices who supported them, asked in a high voice if the knights who had made the view of the abbot were present, and they produced four low fellows who it was said were hired for the occasion, namely Geoffrey of Thurlby, who held a tenement of [the Abbot of] Angers, William son of Alfred and Walter Rufus of Hamby and Gilbert son of Justi of Bennington, neither knights nor holding a knight's fee. The Abbot replied that these were not the knights named and that neither they nor the others came to make the view, and he offered proof of this. They refused to hear him, but the false witness which the others bore against him they caused to be written down and nothing of the truth which the Abbot put forward were they willing to write. Nevertheless, all who had been present, except the Abbot's adversaries and ill-wishers, sympathising and pitying the oppression of the Abbot, thought that judgment would be in his favour because those who claimed to have been the viewers [of his sickness] were not of the knightly order nor girt with the sword, and the third of them did not know how to speak French. Another day was appointed for him after the octave of Whitsun to hear judgment.

At that day the Abbot of Croyland returning found his adversaries and ill-wishers now sure of [a favourable] judgment. Judgment was put off on the Monday, Tuesday, and Wednesday and at length the Abbot, called to it once, twice and a third time came and stood with Benedict Abbot of Peterborough and Baldwin Wake. The aforenamed Robert of Wheatfield pronounced [the judgment] that the Abbot of Croyland, who essoined himself against the Prior of Spalding for lying in his sick bed at Croyland was not found there in bed when the view of him should have been made, should for the time being lose seisin, but not right, that is, possession, but not ownership; and the Prior of Spalding should have seisin which was in contention between them. The Abbot, not daring to reply, withdrew confused and sad.

His adversaries, returning quickly, were put in seisin by the Sheriff of Lincoln of all the marsh of Croyland within Munechelade, which they have never claimed, and without and

Gallice loqui non noverat; verum positus est ei alius dies post octavas Pentecostes ad audiendum judicium.

Ad illum igitur diem revertens abbas Croyland, invenit adversarios et malevolos jam securos de judicio. Dilatum est ergo judicium die lunæ et martis et mercurii; tandem vocatus abbas ad illud semel, et secundo, et tertio, tandem venit, et astitit, cum Benedicto abbate de Burgo, et Baldewino Wake. Robertus prænominatus de Fentfeld [16] pronunciavit, quod abbas Croyland qui se essoniavit contra priorem de Spald. de malo lecti apud Croyland, et illic non est inventus in lecto, quando visus deberet de eo fieri, amitteret ad tempus seisinam, et non rectum: hoc est, possessionem sed non proprietatem. Et prior Spald. haberet seisinam idem de quo [p. 459] contentio fuit inter eos; abbas non audens mutire, recessit confusus et tristis.

Adversarii festinanter redeuntes seisinaverunt sibi per vicecomitem Linc. totum mariscum Croyland infra Munechelade, quia [17] nunquam clamaverunt; et extra et ultra Croyland duas leucas usque ad Namansland, et solummodo alnetum modicum in circuitu abbatiæ stantem, proprium ei reliquerunt; et furcas in quibus suspensi fuerant latrones capti in villa Croyland per judicium curiæ abbatis, asportaverunt; et ex alia parte Spald. statuerunt, ad approbrium [*sic*] sempiternum Croylandiæ.

At postquam divulgatum est per universas terras, quod dominus Rex Richardus captus est in Alemania, et in captione Imperatoris detentus; abbas Croyland arrepto laborioso itinere in medio hyemis in Alemaniam profectus est statim: qui invenit dominum Regem apud Spiram quindecim dies ante liberationem suam. Conquestus est igitur ei super injuriis et damnis illatis, non tam sibi quam coronæ Regi, et ostendit ei chartam patris sui. Secunda denique die liberationis suæ confirmavit dominus Ricardus Rex chartam patris sui, et præcepit fieri literas ad archiepiscopum Cantuariensem Hubertum, qui tunc pro justitia resedit, ut abbas Croyland habeat seisinam marisci sui, secundum chartam patris sui, et sicut habuit quum iter Hierosolymitanum arripuit, quod et factum est in hac forma;

Richardus Rex Angliæ archiepiscopo Cantuariensi salutem. Præcipimus vobis quod sine dilatione faciatis habere abbatem de Croyland seisinam marisci sui de Croyland, secundum quod

[16] *sic* for "Witefeld."
[17] *sic* for "quod."

two leagues beyond Croyland as far as Namansland, and only a little holt standing about the abbey did they leave him for his own; and the gallows on which the robbers taken in the village of Croyland were hanged by judgment of the Abbot's court, they carried away and put up on the other side of Spalding to the eternal shame of Croyland.

And after it spread through every land that the lord King Richard had been captured in Germany and detained in the Emperor's hands, the Abbot of Croyland immediately set out on a laborious journey into Germany in midwinter, and he found the King at Speyer fifteen days before he was freed. He complained to him about the injuries and losses put on him, not so much on himself as on the crown of the King and showed him his father's charter. The lord King Richard on the second day that he was free confirmed his father's charter and commanded that letters should be directed to Hubert, the Archbishop of Canterbury, who was then acting as justiciar, that the Abbot of Croyland should have seisin of his marsh according to the charter of his father and as he had it when the King set out for Jerusalem, which was done in this form:

Richard King of England to the Archbishop of Canterbury, Greeting. We command you that without delay you cause the Abbot of Croyland to have seisin of his marsh of Croyland according as the charter of King Henry our father bears witness that he ought to have, whence he has been disseised after our crossing over. Witness, me myself at Speyer on 22 January in the fifth year of our reign.[30]

And so having returned from Germany Abbot H. found the Archbishop at London and presented to him the King's command, to which he immediately gave effect, directing it to the Sheriff of Lincoln, in whose place Eustace of Leadenham was then acting. The undersheriff, Eustace, therefore solemnly reseised the Abbot and the house of Croyland of their marsh on behalf of the King and the justiciar at the beginning of Lent and peacefully and quietly the Abbot possessed it for the whole of that year and another.

Nevertheless about the kalends of July the abovesaid Abbot of St. Nicholas of Angers obtained revocatory letters against us and sent them to Joslen, then Prior of Spalding, in this form:

[30] Landon *Itin.* no. 393.

charta H. Regis patris nostri testatur, quod habere debeat, unde dissauseitus[18] fuerat post transfretationem nostram. Teste meipso apud Spiram, die vicesimo secundo Januarii, anno quinto Regni nostri.

Regressus itaque ab Alemania abbas H. invenit archiepiscopum Londini, et porrexit ei præceptum Regis; qui statim mandavit illud effectum, dirigens illud ad vicecomitem Lincoln. in cujus loco Eustachius de Ledenh. tunc inventus est. Subvicecomes Eustachius igitur solenne fecit abbati et domui Croyland, ex parte Regis et justitiarii, reseisinam marisci sui, in initio quadragesimæ; pacifice vero et quiete possedit illo anno toto et alio.

Verumtamen circa calendas Julii abbas superius dictus sancti Nicholai Andeg. literas domini Regis revocatorias contra nos impetravit, et transmisit ad Joslemium tunc priorem Spald. sub hac forma:

Richardus Dei gratia Rex Angliæ, Cantuariensi archiepiscopo salutem. Questus est nobis abbas sancti Nicholai Andeg. quod occasione quarundam literarum quas abbas de Croyland tanta veritate impetravit, ut dicit, a nobis dum in Alemania fuimus in captione, disseisiatus est injuste et sine judicio de quodam marisco inter Croyland et Spaldinge, pertinente ad prioratum de Spald. qui est de domo sancti Nicholai Andeg. unde idem abbas sancti Nicholai in curia nostra per judicium curiæ nostræ seisinam recuperavit, ut dicit, et dedit nobis quadraginta marcarum argenti pro judicio curiæ nostre habendo de eodem marisco: unde vobis mandamus quod super hoc veritatem diligenter inquiri faciatis; et si vobis constiterit hoc ita esse, tunc faciatis eidem abbati sancti Nicholai talem seisinam habere de eodem marisco, qualem habuit per judicium curiæ nostræ; et cum idem seisinam habuit, ab eodem abbate recipiatis viginti marcarum quas nobis pro habenda saisina sua promisit. Teste meipso.

Porro lætati sunt Spaldingenses, et arbitrati pro certo, se statim habituros resaisinam, quia multa promiserunt multis adjutoribus. Cum ergo hoc mandatum illi detulissent apud Westmonasterium inquisivit veritatem ab his qui pro justitia residebant, qui recordabantur abbatem de Croyland pro defectu quodam disseisitum fuisse, et abbatem sancti Nichol. sai-

18 *sic* for "dissaisitus."

Richard by the grace of God King of England to the Archbishop of Canterbury, Greeting. The Abbot of St. Nicholas of Angers has complained to us that by reason of certain letters which he says the Abbot of Croyland truly sought, as he says, from us while we were in captivity in Germany, he is unjustly and without judgment disseised of a certain marsh between Croyland and Spalding belonging to the priory of Spalding, which is of the house of St. Nicholas of Angers, whence the same abbot of St. Nicholas in our court, by the judgment of our court, has recovered seisin, as he says, and he has given us forty marks of silver to have the judgment of our court touching the same marsh; wherefore we command you that upon this you cause diligent enquiry to be made and if it is clear to you that this is so, do you then cause the Abbot of St. Nicholas to have such seisin of the same marsh as he had by judgment of our court; and when he has had the same seisin, do you receive from the same abbot the twenty marks which he has promised to us for having his seisin. Witness, myself.

Then the Spalding folk rejoiced and thought for certain that they would immediately have reseisin, because they had promised much to many helpers. When therefore they brought this mandate to the Archbishop at Westminster, he asked the truth from those who were presiding as justices. They recorded that the Abbot of Croyland was disseised for a default which he had made and the Abbot of St. Nicholas was seised, and that the Abbot of Croyland again recovered seisin without a judgment of the king's court [so that] it seemed to some that the Spalding folk ought immediately to be put in seisin. But because the command was conditional and the Abbot of Croyland was not present, the Archbishop put the case in respite until the quindene of Michaelmas. Hearing this, the Abbot went to the Archbishop to ask his advice. He replied that unless he received another command before the appointed day he would give seisin to the Spalding folk according to the King's command. Therefore the Abbot, troubled, and with the advice of the convent and his friends, prepared to cross the sea, for he was summoned not to plead, but to hear the King's command in these words:

Hubert Archbishop of Canterbury to the Sheriff of Lincoln, Greeting. Summon the Abbot of Croyland by good summoners to be before us at Westminster in the quindene of Michaelmas

siatum, et abbatem de Croyland sine judicio curiæ Regis re-saisinam iterum recuperasse; [p. 460] visum aliquibus, quod Spaldingenses statim mitti deberent in saisinam. Sed quia præceptum sub conditione factum fuit, et abbas Croyland non fuit præsens, posuit archiepiscopus in respectum usque post quindecim dies post festum sancti Michaelis. Abbas autem his auditis, adivit archiepiscopum, ut sciret consilium ejus, qui respondit ei quod nisi aliud præceptum audierit ante diem statutum, saisinam faceret illis de Spald. secundum præceptum Regis. Anxius igitur abbas præparavit se ad transfretandum juxta consilium conventus et amicorum suorum. Nam summonitus fuit non ad placitandum sed ad audiendum præceptum Regis sub hæc forma:

Hubertus archiepiscopus Cant. vicecomiti Lincoln. Salutem. Summonite per binos [10] summonitores abbatem Croyland, quod sit coram nobis apud Westm. a die sancti Michaelis in quindecim dies, auditurus præceptum dom. Regis de marisco inter Croyland et Spald. unde contentio fuit inter ipsum et priorem de Spald. et interim facias mariscum illum cum omnibus pertinentiis ex eo provenientibus, sine destructione et vasto esse in pace. T. Simone de Pattishill.

Proxima igitur die dominica, die sancti Hippolyti mart. ante assumtionem beatæ Mariæ virginis, valefaciens fratribus, statutis orationibus tam privatis quam communibus, et missarum celebrationibus, in conventu, cum omni benedictione, dominus abbas Croylandiæ recessit, iter propositum constantissime arripiens. Cum autem appropinquasset Wint. audivit sæpedictum H. archiepiscopum, totius Angliæ primatem, et apostolicæ sedis legatum et domini Regis Angliæ in toto regno capitalem justitiam, illic propter regni negotia advenisse. Accedens itaque ad ipsum, necessitatem transfretandi illi insinuavit, et licentiam impetravit, et benedictionem petens accepit. Denique ad mare apud Portismum properavit.

Quo quidem magnam optimatum Angliæ, comitum videlicet et baronum et militum invenit confluentiam, maris tranquillitatem operientium, et transire omnimodo affectantium, propter urgentissimam domini Regis citationem. Mortalis siquidem discordia et funesta perturbatio agitabatur inter ipsum et Philippum Regem Franciæ, qui domino nostro Richardo Regi maxi-

[10] *sic* for "bonos."

to hear the command of the lord King touching the marsh between Croyland and Spalding, whence a quarrel arose between him and the Prior of Spalding; and meanwhile cause that marsh with all the appurtenances coming thence to be in peace without destruction and waste, Witness, Simon of Pattishall.

Therefore on the Sunday next before the assumption of the blessed Virgin, the day of St. Hypolitus the martyr [13 August], taking leave of the brethren with the accustomed prayers, as well in privacy as with the convent, and the celebration of the mass and blessing his brethren, the lord Abbot of Croyland departed with the greatest courage, beginning his journey. When he approached Winchester he heard that the said Archbishop H., primate of all England, legate of the apostolic see and chief justiciar of the lord King of England in the whole realm had come there on account of national business. And so going to him, the Abbot pointed out the necessity for his journey, obtained licence and seeking his blessing, received it.[31] At last he hastened to the sea at Portsmouth.

There he found a great gathering of the greatest men of the land, earls, barons, and knights, awaiting a tranquil sea and urgently desiring to cross on account of a most urgent summons from the King. Mortal discord and a grievous quarrel had arisen between the King and King Philip of France, who fraudulently rather than violently had stolen the greatest and best part of Normandy while our lord King Richard was held in Germany. Hence the lord King desiring to be avenged had summoned the greatest men of England, whom the Abbot joined as they waited to cross. And so, boarding the ships they had a prosperous journey to Barfleur and landed on the feast of St. Augustine, the doctor, [28 August]. Thence the Abbot came to Rouen in the company of the same nobles who held him in no little veneration. The King of France, leading an army into Normandy, had wasted it almost to its borders, wherefore the lord King of England was in such straits and so anxious that he could attend to nothing but expeditions, the ordering of camps, and the custody of castles, so that the Abbot postponed setting out to the King the business on which he had come.

Meanwhile the lord King's Chancellor, the Bishop of Ely, who had been sent by the King to Germany to get the Emperor's

[31] Landon *Itin.*, p. 104.

mam et optimam partem Normaniæ, dum in Alemannia teneretur, fraudulentus potius quam violenter surripuit. Ulcisci itaque se dominus Rex desiderans, optimos Angliæ summonuerat. Quibus ad transfretandum expeditis, se abbas associavit. Naves itaque ascendentes prospero cursu apud Barbeflet in festo sancti Aug. Doctoris applicuerunt. Deinde in comitatu eorundem nobilium qui ipsum nimiæ venerationi habebant, ad civitatem Rotomagi pervenit. Rex autem Franciæ exercitum in Normanniam ducens, funditus fere illos vastaverat fines. Quapropter dominus Rex Angliæ in tam arto constitutus est, tamque angustiatus, quod ad nihil aliud potuit intendere, nisi expeditionibus, et castrorum ordinationibus, et castellorum custodiis. Quocirca distulit abbas negotium suum pro quo venerat, Regi propalare.

Interea episcopus Eliensis, domini Regis cancellarius, per Angliam ab Alemania, quo ipsum Rex ad Imperatorem pro suppetiis impendendis transmiserat, rediit: audito ejus reditu, abbas ei occurrit, summam negotii sui exprimens. Tempore autem modico transacto postea die sancti Lamberti, venit Rex ad manerium Ponsarche vocatum. Abbas vero illic festinans cancellarium cum Rege invenit, nec differre voluit amplius, quin Regi domino, pro negotio supplicaret. Humiliter itaque et obnixe coepit enarrare causam pro qua venerat. At cancellarius verbum accepit de ore ipsius, et totius rem negotii exposuit. Rex vero respondit, se optime recordari, abbatem pro hac causa ad ipsum in Alemanniam venisse, et quod justitiæ plenitudinem libenter illi exhiberet; sed sequere me, inquit, [p. 461] quousque possim tibi intendere. Cancellarius vero cum abbate et aliis benevolis gratias egerunt. Ipse cancellarius statim iterato iter arripuit ad Imperatorem Alemaniam.

Abbas autem et qui cum illo erant, secuti sunt Regem per vicos et castella et civitates, donec tandem ad Falesiam Rex veniret. Obnixe et suppliciter deprecatus est eum dominus abbas, et ad jussum Regis totius negotii summam succincte et breviter ore proprio coram Rege perstrinxit. Itaque videbatur placuisse Regi et constantia animi et brevitas verbi: et quod adversarii sui, sicut in brevi Regis superius edito, quod attulerunt, manifestum est, viginti marcarum promiserant; se easdem marcas domino Regi reddituurum promisit. Rex breviter respondit, se super his velle cum concilio suo agere. Facta autem sunt hæc die sancti Mauricii Martyris.

advice, returned, and hearing of his coming the Abbot went to meet him, setting out the point of his business. After a little time, on St. Lambert's day [17 September] the King came to Pont-de-l'Arche. The Abbot hastening there found the Chancellor with the King and did not want to put off any longer supplicating the King on his business, and so humbly and urgently he began to tell him the reason why he had come, but the Chancellor took the words from his mouth and set out the whole business. The King replied that he very well remembered the Abbot coming to him for this reason in Germany and that he would willingly do him full justice; but "Follow me," he said, "until I can attend to you." The Chancellor with the Abbot and his other well wishers thanked him. The Chancellor immediately set off again to the Emperor in Germany.

The Abbot and those with him followed the King through villages, castles and cities until at last the King came to Falaise. Resolutely and humbly the lord Abbot entreated him, and at the King's command set out before the King succinctly and briefly by his own mouth the account of the whole business. The firmness of his mind and his brief speech seemed to please the King, and because his adversaries, as appears in the King's writ quoted above, had promised the King twenty marks, he promised to pay the same amount. The King replied briefly that he would take council about these things. This was the day of St. Maurice the martyr [22 September].

Afterwards the Abbot followed the King for many days through many places until he came to Gorron on Michaelmas eve. On the morrow at the solemnity of mass he went to him a humble suppliant and was heard. The King, having summoned master Eustace his seal-bearer, said "Hasten to complete this Abbot's business, setting out our mandate to the archbishop of Canterbury in these words:

Richard by the grace of God King of England to the venerable father in Christ, H. by the same grace Archbishop of Canterbury. The Abbot of Croyland coming to us in Germany told us that by reason of the default, when because of his brother he did not dare appear, he was disseised of a certain marsh between Croyland and Spalding; we found out by enquiry from him and others that he had hidden for fear because his brother had been chased from the kingdom, and so fallen into default,

Postea secutus est abbas Regem per multa loca multis diebus, donec veniret Gorham in vigilia sancti Michaelis. In crastino vero ad sacram missæ solennitatem accessit ad ipsum supplex exorator et exauditus est. Accitoque magistro Eustachio sigillario suo, Accelera, inquit, negotium hujus abbatis perficere; Mandatum nostrum ad archiepiscopum Cantuariensem formans in hæc verba:

Ricardus Dei gratia Rex Angliæ venerabili patri in Christo H. eadem gratia Cantuariensi archiepiscopo. Veniens ad nos abbas Croyland in Alemaniam, nobis proposuit, quod occasione defectus, cum causa fratris sui apparere non auderet, de quodam marisco qui est inter Croyland et Spald. dissaisiatus fuit; nos autem per eundem et per alios inquisivimus, eum præ timore, quod causa fratris sui ab . . . [20] fugati habuit, latuisse, et ita in defectum venisse; quem defectum ei remisimus. Nos autem literis nostris, cum essemus in Alemania, mandavimus, quod idem abbas de prædicto marisco plenariam saisinam haberet, sicut charta H. patris nostri testatur. Adhuc idem vobis mandantes volumus, et mandavimus quod secundum tenorem chartæ patris nostri continentis [21] secundum consuetudinem Angliæ de marisco illo deducatur, quod chartam nostram et remissionem defectus ei warantizamus. Et si forte prior de Spald. viginti marcarum ad scaccarium reddidit, quas vobis [22] promisit pro habenda saisina prædicti marisci, illas ei reddere faciatis; et si non reddiderit illas, non recipiatis; quod literas illas per falsam suggestionem episcopi conventum [23] a nobis impetravit. Nec remaneat propter literas quas abbas sancti Nicholai Andegav. impetravit de prædicto marisco. Et hoc faciatis cum mandatum Will. de Sanctæ Mariæ Ecclesia super hoc habueritis. Teste meipso apud Gorham, trecesimo die Septembris.

Ei eidem Willelmo scripsit sic:

Richardus Dei gratia etc. Will. de Sanctæ Mariæ Ecclesia Salutem. Mandamus tibi, quod cum abbas Croyland plegios bonos dederit de quinquaginta marcis vobis reddendis ad terminos quos ei assignamus; hæc archiepiscopo Cantuariensi significes, ut prædicto abbati tunc faciat de marisco Croyland quæ

[20] The manuscript was decayed at this point.
[21] *sic* for "contentio."
[22] *sic* for "nobis."
[23] *sic* for "Couentr."

which default we remitted. We ordered by our letters while we were in Germany that the same Abbot should have full seisin of the aforesaid marsh as the charter of our father King Henry bears witness. We still wish the same, commanding you as we commanded, that according to the tenor of our father's charter the quarrel touching that marsh should be settled according to the custom of England, because we have warranted our charter and remitted his default. If perchance the Prior of Spalding has paid the twenty marks at the exchequer which he promised for having seisin of the marsh, cause them to be repaid to him, and if he has not paid them, do not receive them, because he obtained the letters from us by a false suggestion of the Bishop of Coventry. Nor should this matter stand over on account of letters which the Abbot of St. Nicholas of Angers has obtained touching the aforesaid marsh. And do this when you shall have a mandate on it from William de Ste. Mère Eglise. Witness, myself at Gorron on 30 September."

And to the same William he wrote thus:

Richard, by the grace of God etc. to William de Ste. Mère Eglise Greeting. We command you that when the Abbot of Croyland shall give you good pledges to pay fifty marks at the terms we have set him, do you inform the Archbishop of Canterbury so that he can then act touching the Abbot in regard to the marsh of Croyland as we have ordered by our letters. Witness, myself at Gorron on 30 September.

The Abbot having received these mandates left the court with haste, seeking the port so that he could appear against his adversaries in the quindene of Michaelmas at London. But when he came to Barfleur he waited there a long time, not able to cross on account of the high seas. Wherefore on the appointed day, as is said above, he could not appear before the justices at London. Nevertheless, the bailiffs whom he had left in England, namely Nicholas the monk and William the clerk, coming on the appointed day, essoined their lord the Abbot for difficulty of crossing the sea. Respite of forty days and one day was given him, according to the custom of England.

On St. Wulfran's day [15 October] the Abbot landed at Portsmouth, and hastening to complete his business, by which he was fatigued, he set out as soon as possible to London, for he heard that the lord Archbishop had either come or was about to come

ei literis nostris mandavimus. Teste meipso apud Gorham tricesimo die Septembris.

Abbas autem cum his mandatis acceptis cum festinatione a curia recessit, portum petens quatenus decimo quinto die post festum sancti Michaelis Londinum posset venire contra adversarios. Sed cum ad Barbefl. venisset expectavit illic diutius, transfretare non valens præ confusione maris et fluctuum: quocirca die statuta, sicut superius dictum est, non potuit Lond. coram Justitiariis apparere. Verumtamen ballivi quos in Anglia reliquerat Nicholaus videlicet monachus, et Will. clericus, coram justitia die statuto venientes, dominum suum abbatem de malo viæ de ultra mare essoniaverunt. Et datæ sunt ei induciæ, secundum consuetudinem regni, quadraginta dierum et unius diei.

[p. 462] Abbas autem die sancti Welfranni applicuit apud Portismum, festinansque negotium, pro quo tamen fatigatus fuit, consummare, Londinum quantocius tetendit. Illic enim audierat dominum archiepiscopum aut venisse aut citius venturum. Invento archiepiscopo porrexit mandatum domini Regis, quo [i]inscripto vel audito, inquisivit utrum Will. de Sanctæ Mariæ Ecclesia de quo mentio fuit in mandato, testimonium haberet. Quodque præsto non fuit, nihil illa vice facere voluit. At vero in brevi ipse W. advenit; abbas autem causæ suæ nequaquam oblitus, cognito ipsius adventu, statim illum adiit, salutem ex parte Regis, et ipsius mandatum porrexit; quo lecto et intellecto, quæsivit si haberet plegios secundum præceptum domini Regis, de quinquaginta marcis ad terminos solvendis; ipse quidem dominum W. de Albeng. et magistrum Stephanum archidiaconum [j]Buchanch. fidejussores produxit: actumque est hoc ante solennitatem omnium sanctorum, et prædictus W. terminum ei primum statuit ad dimidium solvendum ad Pascha, et secundum terminum ad reddendum ad festum sancti Michaelis. Scripsit ergo domino archiepiscopo literis continentibus præceptum domini Regis ad se directum, et quod ei satisfecerit inveniendo plegios optimos, et obnixe rogavit ut negotium abbatis non differret amplius.

Postquam hæc audivit dominus archiepiscopus, dixit quod vellet conferre conjustitiariis suis super negotio isto. Decem

i inspecto.
j Buckingh.

there. Having found the Archbishop he presented the King's mandate and the Archbishop, having inspected and heard it, asked whether he had the witness of William de Ste. Mère Eglise of whom mention was made in the writ, and because he was not at that time present the Archbishop would do nothing on that occasion. Soon this William came. The Abbot mindful of his suit, immediately went to him, and offered him greeting on behalf of the King and produced his mandate. Having read it and understood it, William asked whether he had pledges according to the King's command to pay fifty marks at the appointed terms and the Abbot produced as sureties William d'Albini and master Stephen Archdeacon of Buckingham. And this was done before the feast of All Saints and the aforesaid William appointed Easter as his first term when he should pay half and the second term of payment at Michaelmas. Therefore he wrote to the Archbishop in letters containing the command directed to him by the lord King, that the Abbot had satisfied him by finding the best of sureties and urgently requested that he should not longer delay the Abbot's business.

After he heard this the lord Archbishop said that he wished to confer with his fellow justices about this business. And so the Abbot waited there ten days and on each day when he could have access to the Archbishop he urged him, even to weariness, that he should attend to him and his suit. But the Archbishop was in such a weight of business that he could in no wise find time for the plea. At length the Abbot's reproaches caused the Archbishop to send two of his familiar counsellors with him before the justices sitting in the bench with the King's command, so that they should hear, understand and declare what ought to be done therein. Therefore having read, as well the Abbot's charters, as the royal letters, it seemed to them that the seisin of the marsh ought to remain in peace to the Abbot. But because it was contained in the King's command that that plea should be settled according to the custom of England, it was on this point in particular that the Archbishop wished to be assured what he ought to do. To this doubt the justices replied that in as much as the Abbot was disseised on account of a default and the King has remitted and remits that default to him and warrants his charter and default, by the custom of England he should recover the seisin which by that default he had lost. Those who had

itaque diebus sustinuit illic abbas, singulis diebus quum accessum habere potuit, archiepiscopum solicitando, usque ad tædium, ut sibi et causæ suæ intenderet. Sed tanta erat multiplicitate negotiorum implicatus, quod loquelæ huic vacare nullatenus potuit; propter improbitatem abbatis tandem cum ipso transmisit duos de familiaribus consiliaribus suis coram justitiariis in banco residentibus, cum mandato domini Regis, ut audirent, intelligerent, et quid super hoc fieri deberet, pronunciarent. Lectis ergo tam chartis abbatis, quam literis domini Regis, visum est illis ut saisina marisci remanere deberet in pace abbatis. Verum quia in mandato Regis continebatur, quod secundum consuetudinem Angliæ loquela illa de marisco diduceretur; de hoc præcipue verbo certiorari voluit archiepiscopus quid facto opus esset. Cui dubitationi responderent judices, quandoquidem abbas propter defectum dissaisiatus fuit, et dominus Rex illum defectum illi remisit et remittit, et chartam suam et defectum warantizat per consuetudinem Angliæ saisinam recuperare dicitur, quam per defectum illum amiserat. Reversi qui missi fuerant, quæ audierant a justitiariis, archiepiscopo insinuaverunt. Actum est in die sancti Germani. Archiepiscopus vero mandavit abbate se debere inquirere, utrum defectum illum incurrerat per timorem, sicut dominus Rex ait in literis suis, an per despectum Curiæ Regis. Et hoc modo pertraxit dominus ille negotium usque in crastinum omnium sanctorum.

Residente denique ipso pro tribunali in die animarum, et justitiariis circumcirca assidentibus, astitit abbas super negotii sui consummatione indefesse supplicans. Archiepiscopus vero fecit recitari præceptum domini Regis. Quibus in aure omnium perlectis, inquirere coepit ab his qui tunc temporis in banco residebant, quæ causa, timoris videlicet, an contemtus curiæ Regis, defectus acciderit. Cumque super hoc judices mutuo loquerentur secretius, surrexit unus eorum fidelis vir et prudens nomine Richardus de Heriet; et ait archiepiscopo, sufficere debere ad hanc rem, inquisitionem, quam dominus Rex literis suis præsentibus testatur se fecisse, sicut aperte in mandato continetur inter cætera. Huic autem sententiæ assenserunt tam archiepiscopus quam cæteri judices quorum hæc sunt nomina, Rogerus Bigot, Will. de Warenna, Will. de Brinner, Rich. Harte archidiaco-[p. 463] nus Eliensis, Rich. Heriet, Simon de Pateshill, Osb. filius Hernei, Henricus de Chastill'. Scripsit

been sent returned and informed the Archbishop about what they had been told. This was done on St. German's day [30 October]. The Archbishop informed the Abbot that he must inquire whether he had made that default through fear, as the lord King said in his letters, or in contempt of the king's court. And in this way that lord dragged out the business to the morrow of All Saints.

At length on the day of all souls [2 November] the Archbishop sitting in the judgment seat, the justices sitting all around, the Abbot stood up an unwearied suppliant for the consummation of his business. The Archbishop caused the command of the lord King to be recited and when it had been read through before them all he began to enquire from those who sat in the bench at that time the reason why the Abbot fell into default, namely whether it was fear or contempt of court. And when the judges wished to speak together secretly about this, one of them stood up, a faithful and wise man named Richard of Herriard, and said to the Archbishop that the enquiry which the lord King bears witness by his present letters that he made, as is openly contained in the mandate, among other things, ought to suffice for this matter. To this opinion the Archbishop agreed as well as the other judges, whose names are these, Roger Bigot, William de Warenne, William Briewerre, Richard Barre archdeacon of Ely, Richard of Herriard, Simon of Pattishall, Osbert fitz Hervey, Henry de Chastill', and so the lord Archbishop wrote to the Sheriff of Lincoln in this form: H. by the grace of God etc to the Sheriff of Lincoln, Greeting. Know that the lord King warrants to the Abbot of Croyland the default which he made when the King was on his pilgrimage, by reason of which default the Abbot was disseised of his marsh between Croyland and Spalding, and he commands that the Abbot should fully have seisin thereof. Therefore we command that without delay you cause him to have such seisin as he had before he was disseised thereof by reason of that default.

And so Abbot H. in 1193 [32] returned with full seisin of the marsh. But at the day appointed to his proctors as is above related, he wished for the greater security, to be present and he was at London on the morrow of St. Edmund, King and martyr [21 November]. But prior Joslen of Spalding refused to labour

[32] *recte* 1195.

itaque dominus archiepiscopus vicecomiti Lincoln. sub hoc tenore:

H. Dei gratia etc. vicec. Lincoln. Salutem. Scias quod dominus Rex warantizat abbati de Croyland defaltam quam fecit tempore quo dominus Rex fuit in peregrinatione sua, occasione cujus defaltæ dissaisiatus fuit de marisco suo qui est inter Croyland et Spald. et præcepit quod inde saisinam haberet plenarie; et ideo tibi præcipimus, quod sine dilatione talem inde ei habere saisinam facias, qualem inde habuit antequam occasione prædictæ defaltæ inde dissaisiatus fuit.

Abbas itaque H. anno incarnationis dominicæ M centesimo nonagesimo tertio, reversus est cum plenaria saisina marisci. Verum ad diem procuratoribus suis, sicut superius relatum est, statutum, ad majorem cautelam interesse voluit et in crastino sancti Edmundi Regis et Mart. affuit Londini. Prior autem Spald. Gos, noluit ibi incassum laborare; pro certo intelligens, quod abbas Croyland in causa obtinuisset; sed direxit illuc quendam de monachis suis, Hugonem cognomento Grull. qui in omnibus pro posse suo nobis adversabatur. Cui coram justitiariis se offerenti, dictum est ab eis, abbatem Croyland per præceptum Regis, et communem ipsorum assensum, possessionem marisci sui obtinere, et quiete et pacifice debere possidere; nisi aliud dominus Rex præciperet: ipso vero Grull. supra modum tristis et confusus discessit; juxta illud, Confundantur et erubescant qui volunt nobis mala.

Anno autem subsequente, necessitate debiti domini Regis compulsus, vendidit abbas maximam partem alneti, quod et anno præmisso in parte non minima inchoaverat. . . . . [Translation of St Guthlac and renovation of the high altar.]

Dominus itaque Henricus abbas et sibi commissa ecclesia Croyland mariscum suum sæpedictum per novem circiter annos pacifice possiderunt, priore de Spalding. Nicholao nomine, et monachis suis, et multis aliis fautoribus de Hoyland dolentibus multum et indignantibus, et tempora vindictæ tam expectantibus quam considerantibus. Tandem postquam Rex Richardus decesserat, et frater suus Johannes ei successerat, arbitrati [p. 464] sunt sibi feliciter accidisse, et fortunam familiarius arrisisse, quia sicut superius insinuatum est, per ipsum Johannem tunc temporis comitem de Moret. saisinam qualemcunque adquisierant.

there in vain, knowing for certain that the Abbot of Croyland would have won his suit, but he sent there one of his monks named Hugh Grull who did his utmost against us in all things. When he appeared before the justices he was told that the Abbot of Croyland by the King's command and their common consent had obtained possession of his marsh and ought quietly and peacefully to possess it, unless the lord King should otherwise command. This Grull departed, sad and confused beyond measure; according to that text "They are confounded and brought unto shame that seek to do us evil."

In the following year, forced by the need to pay the King's debt, the Abbot sold the greatest part of the holt, of which he had begun the sale in no small part in the previous year . . . .

And so the lord Henry the Abbot and the church of Croyland committed to his charge for about nine years peacefully possessed his aforesaid marsh, the Prior Nicholas of Spalding and his monks and many other supporters of Holland, much lamenting and indignant, and both looking forward to and planning times of vengeance. At length after King Richard had died and his brother John had succeeded him they judged that it had happened happily for them and that friendly fortune had smiled, because as is suggested above, they had acquired some sort of seisin through this John, then Count of Mortain.

Therefore in the year of grace 1202, which was, unless I am deceived, the third year of King John's rule, they sent messengers over sea, namely Hugh the said monk and others whose names I know not, who went to Abbot Joslen of Angers and set out the cause of their coming and asked for counsel. He went with them to King John and by a careful tale tried to recall to his memory how he had obtained seisin of a certain marsh before him by judgment of the court of King Richard against the Abbot of Croyland; adding that afterwards the same abbot recovered seisin through the violence of his brother the Chancellor. At length he promised the lord King John forty marks to have the record and reasonable judgment of this matter.[33] And so the lord King John wrote to Geoffrey fitz Peter, who then presided in England as chief justiciar, whose favour and grace

[33] *Pipe Roll 3 John*, p. 20. The debt of the Abbot appears on the roll made up to Michaelmas, 1201.

Anno igitur gratie Millesimo ducentesimo secundo qui erat, ni fallor, tertius annus imperii Regis Johannis, nuntios destinaverunt ad transfretandum, Hugonem videlicet monachum superius nominatum, et alios nescio quos, qui ad abbatem suum Joslenum Andegav. accesserunt, et causam et consilium adventus sui insinuaverunt. Ipse vero G. una cum illis Regem J. adiit, et diligenti relatione ei ad memoriam reducere studuit, qualiter coram ipso per judicium curiæ Regis Rich. seisinam cujusdam marisci obtinuerat contra abbatem Croyland; adjungens quod postea sine judicio idem abbas per cancellarii sæpedicti fratris sui violentiam, saisinam recuperavit. Spospondit tandem domino Jo. Regi quadraginta marcarum pro habendo recordo hujus rei et rationabili judicio. Scripsit itaque dominus Rex Jo. Gaufrido filio Petri, qui tunc pro capitali justitia in Anglia residebat: cujus etiam favorem et gratiam Spaldengenses multis et magnis obsequiis adquisierant in hæc verba:

Jo. Dei gratia Rex Angliæ dilecto et fideli suo G. filio Petri, comiti Essex Salutem. Sciatis quod veniens ad nos abbas sancti Nicholai Andeg. promisit nobis quadraginta marcarum pro habenda saisina cujusdam marisci inter Croyland et Spald. unde placitum fuit inter priorem suum de Spald. et abbatem de Croyland in curia Regis Rich. fratris nostri apud Westm. et qua ipsi priori adjudicata fuit per recordum et rationabile judicium ejusdem curiæ, ut dicit; et ideo vobis mandamus, quod accepta ab eo securitate de illis quadraginta marcas reddendis ad terminos competentes, tunc coram vobis audiri faciatis recordum ejusdem loquelæ, et per recordum et rationabile judicium prædictæ loquelæ ei juste et secundum consuetudinem Angliæ plenariam saisinam præfati marisci sine dilatione habere faciatis. Walterus.

Galfridus autem filius Petri convertit hoc mandatum sub sigillo suo, scribens Gerardo de Camvill' qui tunc temporis vicecomes erat Lincolnia, sub hoc tenore:

Gaufridus etc. vicecomiti Lincoln. Salutem. Scias quod prior de Spald. fecit nos securos per Simonem de Lima de quadraginta marcis solvendis domino Regi, quas ei promisit pro habenda saisina marisci inter Croyland et Spald. unde placitum fuit in curia domini Regis, inter ipsum et abbatem Croyland; et ideo summone per bonos summonitores ipsum abbatem quod

the Spalding folk had acquired by much obsequiousness, in these words:

John by the grace of God King of England to his beloved and faithful G. fitz Peter, Earl of Essex, Greeting. Know that the Abbot of St. Nicholas of Angers, coming to us has promised us forty marks to have seisin of a certain marsh between Croyland and Spalding, whence there was a plea between his Prior of Spalding and the Abbot of Croyland in the court of our brother King Richard at Westminster, and which was adjudged to the same prior by record and reasonable judgment of the same court as he says. Therefore, we command you that, having taken security from him to pay those forty marks at suitable terms, then cause the record of the same plea to be heard before you and, by the record and reasonable judgment of the aforesaid plea, justly and according to the custom of England cause him without delay to have full seisin of the aforesaid marsh. [by] Walter.

Geoffrey fitz Peter enclosed this mandate under his seal, writing to Gerard de Camville who was then Sheriff of Lincoln in these terms:

Geoffrey etc. to the Sheriff of Lincoln, Greeting. Know that the Prior of Spalding has given us security by Simon de Lima to pay forty marks to the lord King which he promised for having seisin of the marsh between Croyland and Spalding whence there was a plea in the court of the lord King between him and the Abbot of Croyland, and therefore summon by good summoners this Abbot to be before us at Westminster in the octave of St. Martin [18 November] to hear his record and reasonable judgment; and have there the summoners and this writ.

This summons was made at Croyland on the morrow of the apostles Simon and Jude [29 October] [34] within the ninth hour and the lord Abbot of Croyland had departed in the morning. The writ of summons was sent after him, and having heard it, he went to Geoffrey fitz Peter to get his advice, who among other things advised him to cross over to the lord King. Wherefore the Abbot appointed before Geoffrey fitz Peter, John de Sandon, then seneschal of Croyland abbey, as his proctor in the whole plea.[35] He also presented him at London before the appointed

[34] Presumably 1201.

[35] *C. R. R.* **2**: p. 51. In the morrow of St Martin, 1201.

sit coram nobis apud Westm. in octavis sancti Martini, auditurus recordum et rationabile judicium suum: et habeas ibi summonitores, et hoc breve.

Hæc autem summonitio facta est apud Croyland in crastino apostolorum Simonis et Jude, intra horam nonam; dominus vero abbas a Croyland discessit mane. Missum est post ipsum breve summonitionis; quo audito iter convertit ad Gaufridum filium Petri ut ejus uteretur consilio; qui inter cætera consuluit ei ut ad dominum Regem transfretaret. -Quocirca abbas constituit coram ipso G. procuratorem totius loquelæ Johannem de Sandon. tunc senescallum abbatiæ Croyland. Præsentavit etiam eum Londinum ante diem sibi constitutum justitiariis in banco illic residentibus, quorum hæc sunt nomina, Ricardus Heriet, Simon de Patishill, Johannes de Cestling, Walterus de Crepinges, Eustathius de Fautub, Magister Godefrei de Insula. Inde profectus est abbas ad dominum Cantuar. archiepiscopum, quod ipso residente in Anglia pro capitali justitia, seisinam marisci sui recuperaverat per præceptum domini Regis Richardi, sicut superius dictum est, et ad dominum episcopum Eliensem Eustachium tunc ejusdem Regis cancellarium, et negotii illius usquaque conscium, ut ipsorum uteretur consilio: qui condolentes ipsius injustæ vexationi, rei veritati quam plenius ad memoriam duxerant, testimonium perhibentes, scripserunt pro ipso. Dominus Cantuariensis in hæc verba:

[p. 465] Henr.[24] Dei gratia Cantuariensis archiepiscopus etc. G. filio Petri comiti Essex Salutem. Mittimus vobis scriptum verissimum literarum a bonæ memoriæ Rich. Rege pro abbate Croyland nobis transmissum, super quodam marisco, qui inter Croyland et Spald. unde contentio inter eundem abbatem et priorem Spald. Credimus quod si ad notitiam domini Regis pervenisset quod idem frater ejus tales literas super hoc nobis transmisisset, tale mandatum ab eo accepissetis, quale nunc contra memoratum abbatem accepistis. Quod igitur rationi consonum ex discretione vestra super hoc decreveritis, statuere curetis. Vale.

Tenor autem literarum illarum Regis, scilicet superius transcriptæ inveniuntur. Dominus vero E. Eliensis episcopus sub hoc tenore scripsit:

[24] *sic* for "H[ubertus]."

day to the justices then sitting in the bench, whose names are these, Richard of Herriard, Simon of Pattishall, John of Guestling, Walter of Creeping, Eustace de Faucunberg and master Godfrey de Insula. Thence the Abbot set out to the Archbishop of Canterbury because when he was presiding in England as chief justiciar the Abbot had recovered seisin of his marsh, and to the lord bishop Eustace of Ely, then the lord King's Chancellor, who knew all this business, that he might have their advice, who condoling with him for this unjust affliction, fully recalled to memory the truth of the matter and supplying testimony the Archbishop wrote on his behalf in these words:

H. by the grace of God Archbishop of Canterbury etc. to G. fitz Peter Earl of Essex, Greeting. We send you an authentic copy of the letters sent to us on behalf of the Abbot of Croyland by King Richard of good memory, touching a certain marsh between Croyland and Spalding, whence there is contention between the same Abbot and the Prior of Spalding. We believe that if it had come to the notice of the lord King that his brother had sent us such letters upon this matter you would [not] have received such a mandate from him as you have now received against the said Abbot. Take care that what your discretion shall decree upon this matter is consonant with reason. Farewell.

The tenor of those royal letters, namely as they are found transcribed above:- The lord E. Bishop of Ely wrote in these words:

E. by the grace of God Bishop of Ely to his friends . . . the justices of the lord King sitting in the bench, greeting and affection. As we well remember King Richard of good memory while he was alive and the abbot of Croyland went to him at Gorron, fully remitted to him the default which he had made in the plea touching the marsh between himself and Spalding; which we have caused to be made known to you so that the truth may be more fully known to you upon this matter.

In this year died Hugh of saintly memory Bishop of Lincoln in London and his body was borne to Lincoln and buried with honour by King John, who had newly come in to England, together with archbishops, bishops, and other great men of the kingdom.

Meanwhile the term of the plea appointed to the Abbot of Croyland in the octave of St. Martin approached. The afore-

E. Dei gratia Eliensis episcopus amicis suis . . .[25] Justiciariis domini Regis de banco residentibus, salutem et dilectionem. Sicut bene recolimus, dum adhuc viveret bonæ recordationis Richardus Rex, accessit autem abbas Croyland apud Gorham et ipse defaltam in qua fuit pro placito de marisco inter ipsum et priorem de Spald. ei plenarie remisit: quod vobis duximus intimandum, ut vobis super hoc veritas plenius innotescat.

Hoc in anno obiit sanctæ memoriæ Hugo Lincoln. episcopus London. et corpus ejus Lincolnam delatum est, ubi a Rege Johanne, qui noviter in Angliam transfretaverat, una cum archiepiscopis et episcopis, cæterisque proceribus regni, honorifice tumulatur.

Interim terminus placiti præfixus in octab. sancti Martini, abbati Croyland appropinquavit: prænominatus vero Johannes procurator abbatis, se fecit essoniari de malo viæ; justitiarii vero per præceptum G. filii P. dederunt ei alium diem brevissimum in quindecim dies, diem scilicet post festum sancti Andreæ. Quo audito abbas Croyland et sui amplius angustiati fuerunt: speraverant enim quod prolixius tempus eis præfigeretur, post octabas videlicet sancti Hillarii, ut interim possent ad dominum Regem J. tranfretare, et ei rei veritatem insinuare. Paraverat enim se ad transfretandum, quum ultimo discessit a Croyland ante festum omnium sanctorum: itaque conventus Croyland existimaverat eum jam transfretasse, quod medio tempore nec ipse rediit, nec nuncium domi misit. Ex insperato igitur affuit nuncius ipsius præcipiens ut prior suus Nicholaus de Toft, et Gauf. de Horva celerarius, et procurator totius abbatiæ, domino abbati occurrent Londini ad diem statum. Qui illic accelerantes invenerunt dominum abbatem in provincia Cantabr. ad manerium suum de Draiton: pariter ergo tendentes, Londinum petierunt. Occurrerunt ergo illis illuc Osb. de Longo campo, frater domini abbatis et quidam miles sapiens et discretus, Reginaldus nomine de Argento; quorum consilio fretus dominus abbas, potentibus curiæ supplicavit singillatim, domino videlicet Johanni de Gray, tunc episcopo Norwic. Regi valde familiari, et Sim. de Patishill et Richardo de Heriet, et aliis pluribus, ut ipsius negotio benignius intenderent.

Affuit et Nicholaus prior Spaldingiæ, cum fautoribus suis et amicis multis et magnis, quia amici divitis multi. Ipse deinceps

[25] The manuscript was decayed at this point.

named John, the Abbot's proctor, caused himself to be essoined for difficulty upon the journey and the justices by command of G. fitz P. appointed him another, very early day in a fortnight's time, namely the day after the feast of St. Andrew. Hearing this, the Abbot of Croyland and [his supporters] were much troubled, for they had hoped that a longer time would have been fixed for him, namely after the octave of Hilary, so that in the meantime he could cross over to King John and tell him the truth. For he had prepared himself to cross over when he had last departed from Croyland before the feast of All Saints, so that the convent of Croyland had thought that he had already crossed, since he had neither returned nor sent a messenger to the house. Therefore an unwelcome messenger came commanding that his prior, Nicholas of Toft and Geoffrey de Horva the cellarer and proctor of all the convent, should meet the lord Abbot in London on the appointed day. They hastening on their way found the lord Abbot at his manor of Drayton in Cambridgeshire and they went on to London together. There they met Osbert de Longchamps, the lord Abbot's brother, and a certain wise and discrete knight, Reginald de Argentan, on their counsel the Abbot very much relied. He approached certain powerful men of the court individually, namely John de Gray, then Bishop of Norwich and very friendly with the King, Simon of Pattishall and Richard of Herriard and many others, so that they might consider his business favourably.

And Nicholas Prior of Spalding was present with his supporters and many and great friends, for he had many rich friends. On the appointed day of the plea he stood before the justices sitting in the bench, setting out his case against the Abbot of Croyland, who being called, immediately appeared and, as the custom is, asked that the writ might be heard. The writ of summons was produced and read because the original writ could not be heard because it spoke only of the Abbot of St. Nicholas of Angers. To that also the Abbot of Croyland was not bound to reply since he of Angers was not present, nor had he appointed anyone in his place. And so it was judged that he should reply to the last writ which G. fitz Peter had sent under his seal to the Sheriff of Lincoln. The Abbot of Croyland, drawing apart with his friends and counsellors and having had a brief word of advice, returned. The Prior at

die litis statuto, stetit coram justitiaris in banco residentibus, causam suam proponens contra abbatem Croyland, qui vocatus statim apparuit et auditionem brevis, sicut mos est, requisivit: prolatum est breve summonitionis et lectum, quia originale audire non potuit, quod loquebatur solummodo de abbate sancti Nicholai Andegavis. Cui etiam non debuit abbas Croyland respondere, cum abbas ille præsens non fuerit, nec alium loco sui constituerit. Judicaverunt itaque ipsum ultimo brevi debere respondere, quod G. fil. Petri sub sigillo suo direxerat vicec. Lincoln. Abbas vero Croyland in partem secedens cum amicis et consiliariis suis, habito brevi consilio reversus est. Astitit et prior instans ut præceptum domini Regis manciparetur effectui; viz. ut daretur sibi recordum et rationabile judicium de quodam marisco [p. 466] inter Croyland et Spald. Respondens quidam sapiens hujus sæculi, qui pro abbate loquebatur, Johannes Gluccente [26] civis Londoni, dominum abbatem Croyland nolle declinare recordum curiæ, nec rationabile judicium; sed ipsum illud breve requirere quod initium litis continet, ex quo et judicium et recordum formari debent: quod si nullo modo habere posset, visum illius marisci requirere inter Croyland et Spald. quod plura habentur illic de quibus placita multoties fuerunt. Deinde justitiarii sciscitaverunt, quo tempore motum fuerit placitum illud: Responderunt Spaldingenses quod tempore Regis Richardi, quum Walterus archiepiscopus Rotomag. capitalis justitia fuit in Anglia; assidente ei Roberto de Witefeld. de quo mentio superius facta est. Attestati sunt abbas et sui, sic esse, et gavisi sunt vehementer; tum quod iniuste et contra juris civilis ordinem trahebatur in causam per illud breve quo antecessor suus abbas Robertus citatus fuerat; tum quod remissio defaltæ quam Rex Richardus ei fecerat, et charta ipsius marisci illum confirmans abbati posterior fuit tempore; et posterius mandatum præjudicat. Justitiarii autem hæc audientes, surgentes de bancho cum baronibus scaccarii, et domini Regis fidelibus illuc residentibus consilium habuerunt.

In crastino residentibus in banco affuerunt et partes. Tunc Simon de Patishill pronunciavit, quod loquela majori consilio indigeret, et quod conjustitiarii sui plures tunc illic non interfuerunt, quia tunc Adventus Dominicus celebrabatur, et nullum aliud placitum tunc tenebatur nisi illud; et idcirco necessario

[26] *sic* for "Bucuinte."

once stood up and asked that the King's order be put into effect: namely that he should be given his record and reasonable judgment touching a certain marsh between Croyland and Spalding. John Bucuinte, a citizen of London, a man wise in the affairs of this world, who was speaking for the Abbot, said that the Abbot did not wish to refuse a record of the court and a reasonable judgment, but to ask for that writ which contains the beginning of the plea, on which the judgment and record ought to be founded. And if in no way he could have it he sought a view of that marsh between Croyland and Spalding, because there are many things there about which there were often pleas. Then the justices enquired when that plea was begun. The Spalding folk replied that it was in the time of King Richard when Walter Archbishop of Rouen was chief justiciar in England, Robert of Wheatfield, of whom mention is made above, sitting with him. The Abbot and his supporters agreed that this was so and very much rejoiced, as well because it would be unjust and contrary to the order of civil law for him to be drawn into a suit by that writ in which his predecessor, Abbot Robert, had been cited, and because the remission of the default which King Richard had made for him, and his charter confirming it to the abbot, was later in time and would be prejudicial to the previous mandate. But the justices hearing this, rising from the bench took counsel with the barons of the exchequer and lieges of the lord King there sitting.

When they sat in the bench on the next day the parties were present. Then Simon of Pattishall declared that the plea needed more consideration and that many of his fellow justices were not present there then both because Advent was being celebrated and there was no other plea in hand then except this; and therefore it was necessary to accept a delay for more weighty hearing and deliberation.[36] Therefore they set another day in the octave of Hilary so that in the meantime the original writ of the whole case might be sought and those also might be sought and summoned under whose hearing that case was ventilated, because none of them except Simon himself was then sitting in the bench, and he would not alone, because he ought not to make the record then. The Abbot and his party rejoiced at such

[36] *C. R. R.* 2: p. 89. The last plea but two heard at the end of the Michaelmas term, 1201.

oportere jam accipere dilationem, ad majorem audientiam et deliberationem; et idcirco constituerunt alium diem, post octabas sancti Hillarii in octo dies; ut interim breve illud totius causæ originale quæreretur, et illi etiam quærerentur et convocarentur, sub quorum examine causa illa ventilata fuit, quod nullus eorum præter ipsum Simonem, tunc in banco residebat; et ipse solus noluit quia non debuit tunc recordum facere. Exultaverunt abbas et sui propter tantam dilationem, quia penitus paratus fuit ad transfretandum: verum breve illud domini Cantuariensis, et breve domini Eliensis præfatum dimisit Johanni de Sandon. et suis citra remanentibus, ut valere possent; si forte non possit ad diem placiti præfixum revertenti in Anglia; et profectus est statim; sed aliquandiu moratus est apud Portesmum, mare tranquillum et ventus operiens prosperum. Sed et prior Spaldingensium nuntium suum contra eum direxit, monachum quendam satis sagacem, Godefridum nomine, qui tunc celerarii officium gerebat.

In illa etiam tempestate dominus Cantuariensis et dominus Eliensis per urgentissimum Regis mandatum ad transfretandum invitabantur, expectantes apud Shorham transeundi prosperitatem. Abbas autem Croyland in festo sancte Luciæ navem ascendit super Portesmum, et prospero cursu applicuit sequenti die Barbeflet. Dominus autem Cantuariensis jam quarta die præterita venerat in Normanniam, sæpedictus vero abbas iter tetendit ad Montem fortem, quod dominus Rex et archiepiscopus illuc tunc venerant. In vigilia beati Thomæ apostoli locutus est cum domino Rege, præsente archiepiscopo, et supplici relatu et simplici causam suam in auribus domini Regis exposuit, succincte enarrans quomodo disseisiatus [est] fuerit de suo marisco, propter quandam defaltam quam fecerat propter timorem, non ausus comparere coram justitia, quod frater suus [k]Cantuariensis fugatus jam fuerat de Anglia, et alii fratres sui incarcerati, dum dominus Rex Richardus moraretur in terra Syriæ; et quomodo idem Rex ei ad se venienti in Alemaniam, et conquerenti, illam defaltam plene remiserat. Qualiter etiam dominus archiepiscopus per mandatum domini Regis, ipsum in saisinam et possessionem miserat. Archiepisco-[p.467] pus vero præsens et hoc audiens, testimonium perhibuit rei veritati, et preces abbatis erga Regem commendavit, videlicet ut remis-

k Leg. Eliensis.

a delay, because he was quite ready to cross. He left that writ of the lord of Canterbury and the writ of the lord of Ely with John de Sandon and his supporters remaining on this side the sea so that they could use them if perchance he could not return to England on the day fixed for the plea. He set out immediately, but was delayed a little time at Portsmouth awaiting a tranquil sea and favourable wind. The Prior of Spalding sent his messenger to oppose him, a sufficiently wise monk named Godfrey, who then held office as cellarer.

At that time the lord of Canterbury and the lord of Ely were asked by urgent summons of the King to cross the sea and were awaiting a favourable crossing at Shoreham. The Abbot of Croyland went aboard at Portsmouth on the feast of St. Lucy [13 December] and after a good crossing landed at Barfleur the next day. The lord of Canterbury had reached Normandy on the fourth day before and the Abbot set out for Montfort because the King and the Archbishop had come there. On the eve of blessed Thomas the apostle [20 December] he spoke with the lord King in the presence of the Archbishop and set out his case in the hearing of lord King in a humble and simple story, succinctly telling how he had been disseised of his marsh on account of a default which he had made for fear, not daring to appear before the justiciar because his brother the Bishop of Ely had been chased from England and his other brothers imprisoned while the lord King Richard was in the land of Syria, and how the same King on the Abbot's going to him in Germany and complaining, had fully remitted that default to him. He also set out how the lord Archbishop, by command of the lord King had put him into seisin and possession. The Archbishop, being present and hearing this, bore witness to its truth and commended the prayers of the Abbot to the King, namely that he should hold firm and should warrant the remission of the default which his brother the King had made. The lord King graciously promised to show him the fullness of justice, but commanded the abbot to follow him until he could give more attention to his case.

About the same time a certain monk named Godfrey, sufficiently crafty and shameless, sent by the Prior of Spalding against the Abbot of Croyland, opposed him in everything and before the King and elsewhere stood up to him to his face and hindered

sionem defaltæ, quam ei frater suus Rex, ratam haberet et warantizaret. Dominus autem Rex se ei justitiæ plenitudinem exhibiturum satis benigne pollicebatur; sed ut se sequeretur, quousque posset causæ melius intendere, ei præcepit.

Sub eodem tempore monachus quidam, Godefridus nomine, satis versutus et protervus, a priore de Spaldingensibus contra abbatem Croyland transmissus, ei in omnibus adversabatur, et coram Rege et alibi in facie restitit, et omnimodis negotium ejus impedivit. Ita quod diu protelatum est. Verumtamen abbas Croyland circumiens per vicos et castella dominum Regem sequendo, et causam suam prosequendo, indefessus perseveravit.

Interim dominus Rex J. instantem dominicæ nativitatis festivitatem apud Argentomachum regio more et magnificentia, convocatis itaque terræ suæ principibus et magnatibus, statuit celebrare. Inter alios et præ aliis comes Cestriæ nominatim invitatus affuit. Qui partes Spaldingensium sicut ipsorum patronus et advocatus, diligenter fovebat. Quocirca et Regi et familiaribus ejus et consiliariis attentius supplicavit, quatenus monachorum suorum negotium promoverent. Quod enim eis factum fuit sibi ipsi asseruit fieri. Commendavit itaque universis et singulis G. monachum et causam ejus, et a curia discessit. Ipse igitur G. animosior effectus, Regem sæpe et multum sollicitabat, quatenus literis iteratis præciperet justitiariis Angliæ, ut sine occasione et dilatione loquelam prioris Spaldingiæ secundum tenorem priorum literarum superius scriptarum deducerent: pollicitusque est domino Regi viginti marcarum argenti, præter quadraginta marcas primo illis promissas.

Abbas autem Croyland his auditis plurimum anxiatus est, tum quia dominus Rex negotium suum in tantum protraxerat, tum quia curiales propter petitionem comitis, non sicut heri et nudius tertius, hilarem ei faciem prætendebat. Tandem vero cognoscens quod in curia illa vix ullum potuit expediri negotium nisi donis vel promissis intercedentibus, habito cum benevolis consilio, Regi obtulit pecuniam non modicam ea conditione quod remissionem illius defaltæ sæpedictæ, quam Rex Richardus ei fecerat, ipse per chartam suam warantizaret; quod quidem Rex facere supersedit usque ad sanctam Susannam veniret. Ubi abbas consueta constantia Regem rogavit, ut ipsius preces exaudire dignaretur. Sed G. monachus non minori dili-

his business in every way so that it was protracted for a long time. Nevertheless, the Abbot of Croyland, going round through villages and castles following the lord King and prosecuting his suit, persevered unwearied.

Meanwhile the lord King John determined to celebrate the coming Christmas feast [37] at Argentan in a royal manner and in magnificence, having summoned his chief men and magnates. Among and above the rest, the Earl of Chester was present by special invitation. He diligently favoured the Spalding party as their patron and advocate. Wherefore he urgently prayed both the King and his household and his councillors that they would promote the cause of his monks, for what they did for them he declared would be done for himself. And so he commended to one and all this G. the monk and departed from the court. This G. therefore became more spirited and often and much prayed the King to command his justices of England by letters that without hindrance and delay, according to the tenor of the former letters written above they should settle the suit of the Prior of Spalding; and he promised the lord King twenty marks of silver beyond the forty marks promised before.

Having heard these things, the Abbot of Croyland was very troubled, as well because the lord King dragged out his business so much, as because the men about the court on account of the Earl's request, no longer as yesterday or three days ago showed him a cheerful face. At length, indeed recognising that in that court he would hardly be able ever to finish his business unless through the offer of gifts or promises, taking counsel with those who wished him well, he offered the King no small sum on condition that he should warrant by his charter the remission of that often mentioned default which King Richard had made him, but the King caused it to be postponed until he should come to Ste. Suzanne, where the Abbot, with his accustomed consistence, asked the King that he would deign to hear his prayers. But the monk G. with no less diligence prayed the King to the contrary. Then the lord King, taking the counsel of his wise men and wishing to please both sides at the moment, each party having made promises which he had agreed to accept granted letters to the monk G. under this form:-

J. by the grace of God King of England etc. to G. fitz Peter,

[37] 1201.

gentia Regem in contrarium sollicitavit. Tunc dominus Rex prudentium suorum usus consilio, utrisque ad tempus volens satisfacere, facta ex utraque parte promissa decrevit accipere. Denique G. monacho concessit literas suas sub hoc tenore:

J. Dei gratia Rex Angliæ etc. G. fil. Petri Salutem. Sciatis priorem Spaldingensium præter quadraginta marcas quas prius nobis promisit, finem fecisse nobiscum pro viginti marcarum argenti, pro habendo recordo et rationabili judicio suo usque [27] abbatem de Croyland, de loquela quæ est inter eos de marisco: et ideo vobis mandamus, quod si ipse fecerit vos securos de pecunia illa reddenda ad terminos quos scitis, tunc eidem priori sine dilatione secundum consuetudinem Angliæ faciatis habere recordum et rationabile judicium suum, secundum formam aliarum literarum nostrarum quas inde habuistis, et secundum quod loquela illa inter eos rationabiliter deducta est. Teste meipso etc.

Concessit etiam literas abbati Croyland in hunc modum:

J. Dei gratia Rex Angliæ etc. G. fil. Petri Salutem. Mandamus vobis quatenus audiatis loquelam quæ est inter abbatem Croyland et priorem de Spaldinge de marisco quodam, et abbati Croyland locetis hoc quod in loquela illa locari debet, et priori Spalding. similiter et processum totius ne-[p. 468] gotii, et consilium vestrum super hoc, nobis per literas vestras significetis. Teste meipso apud Fescham decimo die Januarii.

Godefridus igitur monachus Spalding. acceptis literis suis cum exultatione a curia discedens, festinavit in Angliam reverti, sperans se posse totum negotium suum sine contradictione ad effectum perducere, antequam abbas Croyland repatriare possit. Quippe sciebat eum in causa sua parum adhuc vel nihil erga Regem profecisse. Nam et ipse abbas tunc a curia discesserat. Post hoc aliquantulum moratus est in partibus illis, tam circa hæc quam alia plura negotiosus; noluit enim nimium festinare in revertendo; quia dies datus fuerat ipsi et adversariis suis coram justitia in banco apud Westmon. in octabas sancti Hillarii, et ipse prudenter sibi præviderat, priusquam transfretaverat, in loco suo quendam ponens attornatum Johannem scilicet de Sandon. qui causam suam sustineret; sed [28] ipse die statuto

[27] *sic* for "versus."
[28] *sic* for "si."

Greeting. Know that the Prior of Spalding in addition to the forty marks which he promised us before, has made fine with us for twenty marks of silver to have his record and reasonable judgment against the Abbot of Croyland, touching the suit for a marsh which is in progress between them. Therefore we command you, that if he gives you security to pay that money at the terms which you know, then without delay, according to the custom of England, cause the same Prior to have his record and reasonable judgment according to the form of our other letters which you have had therein and according as that plea has reasonably proceeded between them. Witness, myself etc.

To the Abbot of Croyland he granted letters in this form:-

J. by the grace of God King of England etc. to G. fitz Peter, Greeting. We command you that you hear the plea which is in progress between the Abbot of Croyland and the Prior of Spalding touching a certain marsh, and that you allow to the Abbot of Croyland in that plea what ought to be allowed and to the Prior of Spalding likewise, and let us know by your letters the process of the whole business and your counsel on this. Witness, myself at Fécamp on 10 January.

Therefore Godfrey the monk of Spalding, having received his letters with delight, leaving the court, hastened to return to England, hoping that he would be able to bring his whole business to an end without hindrance before the Abbot of Croyland could return, because he knew that the Abbot had profited little or nothing in his case in regard to the lord King. For the Abbot had then left the court. After this he stayed for a little in those parts, busy as well with this as with much other business, for he was unwilling to be in too much haste to return because a day had been set to him and his adversaries in the bench at Westminster in the octave of Hilary and he had prudently arranged, before he crossed the sea that his attorney, John of Sandon, should appear in his place if on the appointed day he himself could not. And so his attorney caused himself to be essoined on the aforenamed day and another day in three weeks was appointed for him.

Meanwhile the Abbot of Croyland, God willing, safely returned and, coming to Westminster at the appointed day presented himself before the justices. His adversaries were also present and with them several others, wise in the affairs of this

apparere non posset. Attornatus itaque suus ad diem prænominatum se fecit essoniari, et alius dies datus est ei in tres septimanas.

Interim abbas Croyland Deo disponente prospere remeavit, et ad diem præfixum veniens apud Westm. se coram justitiariis præsentavit. Affuerunt etiam adversarii sui, et cum ipsis plures alii sapientes hujus seculi, quos prece et pretio adduxerant et conduxerant, certo certius arbitrantes, se illa vice totum velle suum ad effectum perducturos. Cum igitur justitiariis in banco residentibus utraque pars advenisset, precatus est prior Spald. justitiarius, [sic] ut præceptum domini Regis recitaretur, et judicium sine dilatione, sicut Rex præceperat, ipsi redderetur. Abbas vero Croyland distulit proferre literas suas, competentem ad hoc neque locum neque tempus esse considerans. Cum igitur justitiarii cum nobilioribus regni tractarent de hoc negotio, venit abbas Croyland coram ipsis, et protulit eis literas domini Cantuariensis archiepiscopi, quas ipse justitiariis direxit in hunc modum scriptas:

H. Dei gratia Cantuar. archiep. etc. G. fil. Petri Salutem. Mittimus vobis transcriptum verissimum literarum a bonæ memoriæ Rege Richardi pro abbate de Croyland nobis transmissarum, super quodam marisco, quod est inter Croyland et Spald. unde contentio est inter eundem abbatem et priorem de Spald. Credimus quod si ad notitiam domini Regis pervenisset, quod idem frater ejus tales literas super hoc nobis transmisisset, tale mandatum minime ab eo suscepissetis. Quod igitur rationi consonum ex discretione vestra super hoc decreveritis, statuere curetis.

Miserat etiam dominus Cantuariensis archiepiscopus literas quas ipse receperat tempore Richardi Regis, cum ipse justitiarius totius Angliæ fuerat, sc. de warantizatione defaltæ quam fecerat abbas de Croyland, sub una et eadem sigilli sui impressione inclusas. Cumque lectæ essent literæ Regis Richardi, in quibus processus totius negotii continebatur, et insuper literæ domini Cantuariensis, in quibus testimonium perhibebat, quod ipsas ex mandato Regis Richardi suscepisset; Post multas altercationes consideraverunt omnes justitiarii, qui tunc præsentes ibi erant simul cum consilio sapientum regni, quod warantizatio a Rege facta, rata deberet esse et stabilis; nec propter hoc abbas de Croyland aliquid damnum incurrere deberet. Nomina autem justitiariorum qui tunc in banco sederent, hæc sunt, Simon de

world, whom by prayer and price they had brought and hired, considering that for certain they would achieve their end. When therefore both parties approached the justices sitting in the bench, the Prior of Spalding prayed that the King's command should be read and judgment pronounced for him without delay as the King had commanded. The Abbot of Croyland put off proferring his letters, considering neither the time nor place suitable. When therefore the justices had discussed this business with the greater men of the land, the Abbot of Croyland came before them and produced the letters of the Archbishop of Canterbury which he had addressed to the justices in these words:

H. by the grace of God Archbishop of Canterbury etc. to G. fitz Peter Greeting. We send you an authentic copy of the letters sent to us by King Richard of good memory on behalf of the Abbot of Croyland about a certain marsh between Croyland and Spalding touching which there is a quarrel between the same Abbot and the Prior of Spalding. Because we believe that if it had come to the notice of the lord King that his brother had sent us such letters, you would not have received from him such a command. What therefore, consonant with reason, your discretion shall have decided upon, this take care to command.

Also the lord Archbishop of Canterbury had sent the letters enclosed under the same impression of his seal which he had received in the time of King Richard when he had been justiciar of all England, that is, touching the warranty of the default which the Abbot of Croyland had made. And when these letters of King Richard were read, in which the process of the whole matter was contained, and moreover the letters of the lord of Canterbury, bearing witness that he had received them by command of King Richard, after much discussion, all the justices then present, with the advice of the wise men of the realm, judged that the warranty made by the King should be firm and stable, and that the Abbot of Croyland should not suffer any loss in this matter. The names of the justices who then sat on the bench are these, Simon of Pattishall, Richard of Herriard, John of Guestling, Walter of Creeping, Eustace de Faucunberg, and Godfrey de Insula. Moreover many nobles had come to the court on business of state and on that day were present at that judgment; and these are their names, the lord John Bishop of

Patishill, Rich. Heriet, Johannes de Sestinges, Wal. Crepi, Eustachius de Faucumberg. Godfridus de Insula. Præterea etiam multi nobiles pro utilitate regni ad curiam venerant, et ipso die illi considerationi interfuerunt; quorum hæc sunt nomina, dominus Johannes Norwic. episcopus, Rogerus comes de Clare, Robertus filius Walteri, Gaufr. de Bouchlande, Willelmus de Warenna, et multi alii: qui omnes sine contradictione consenserunt in unum. Sed tamen ad ipsum diem non est judicium publice prolatum quia G. filium Petri, qui summus justitiarius tunc in Anglia fuerat, [p. 469] præsens ibi non erat; visum est enim omnibus, desicut ipsi G. capitali justitiæ literæ domini Regis de prædicto negotio missæ fuerant, ita coram ipso judicium redderetur. Vocati sunt igitur abbas et prior, et dies datus est eis, scilicet octo dies ab illo die.

Ad illum itaque diem venit prædictus G. filius Petri, et ceteri justitiarii cum eo. Cumque recitaretur loquela coram eo, quæ erat inter prædictum abbatem et priorem, contendebat contra omnes, volens judicium quod justitiarii et barones de scaccario fecerant, subvertere et in irritum revocare. Et omnes una voce responderunt se nolle, nec debere aliam considerationem facere, quia rectum judicium eis videbatur esse, quod fecerant. Cumque diu multumque super prædictis contendissent, videns G. filius Petri, quod non solus contra omnes posset obtinere, distulit loquelam in crastinum.

Mane itaque præcepit ut omnes justitiarii coram eo venirent, ut de prædictis tractarent. Cumque iterum de his contenderent, respondit Gaufr. filius Petri, sibi justum videri, quia contentio de hoc negotio inter eos orta fuit, ut processus totius negotii in Normanniam Regi constituto ab initio usque ad diem illum mandaretur, et dominus Rex quod sibi rectum videretur, faceret. Hoc autem dicebat, quia fovebat partem prioris de Spalding. Tandem autem consenserunt omnes justitiarii in hoc, quod abbas de Croyland et prior de Spalding haberent literas sub una forma, et mitterent nuncios suos ad dominum Regem, qui literas justitiarii de isto negotio illi portarent; et quod dominus Rex ipsis rescriberet, justitiarii libenter exequerentur. Forma literarum hæc erat:

Reverendo domino suo Johanni Dei gratia, illustri Regi Angliæ etc. G. filius Petri Salutem, et fidele in omnibus obsequium. Præcepistis nobis quod faceremus habere priori de Spalding

Norwich, Roger Earl of Clare, Robert fitz Walter, Geoffrey of Buckland, William de Warenne and many others, who all, without exception, agreed. Nevertheless on that day the judgment was not publicly announced because Geoffrey fitz Peter, then chief justiciar of all England was not there, and it seemed to all that inasmuch as the King's letters touching this business were directed to this G. as chief justiciar, so the judgment should be pronounced before him. And so the Abbot and Prior were summoned and a day in eight days was given them.

On that day the aforesaid G. fitz Peter was present and the other justices with him. And when that suit between the Abbot and Prior was recited before him, he contended against them all, wishing to overthrow and annul the judgment which the justices and the barons of the exchequer had made. And they all replied with one voice that they would not, nor ought to make any other judgment, because it seemed to them that they had made a right judgment. And when they had argued much and for a long time upon this, G. fitz Peter, seeing that he could not alone get his way against them all, put off the suit until the next day.

And so in the morning he commanded that all the justices should come before him so that they might discuss the matter. And since they still argued over this, Geoffrey fitz Peter replied that it seemed to him just that, since a difference of opinion had arisen between them on this matter, the process of the whole business from the beginning until that day should be sent to the King in Normandy, and the lord King would do what seemed right to him. This he said because he favoured the party of the Prior of Spalding. At length all the justices agreed in this way, that the Abbot of Croyland and the Prior of Spalding should have letters under the same form and should send their messengers to the lord King and that they should carry to him the letters of the justices touching this business, and what the lord King should write back to them the justices would willingly carry out. The form of the letters was this:-

To their revered lord John by the grace of God the illustrious King of England etc. G. fitz Peter, Greeting and faithful obedience in all things. You have commanded us that we should cause the Prior of Spalding to have his record and judgment touching the suit which is between him and the Abbot of Croy-

recordum et judicium suum de loquela quæ fuit inter ipsum et abbatem de Croyland, de marisco inter Spalding et Croyland: quod tale est, scilicet quod prior de Spalding tempore Regis Richardi fratris vestri, in curia sua clamavit versus prædictum abbatem antedictum mariscum. Idem vero abbas fecit quoddam essonum infra summonitionem, de malo lecti, quo detinebatur apud Croyland. Et cum per judicium curiæ quatuor milites venirent ad videndum ipsum abbatem et infirmitatem ejus apud Croyland, eum ibi non invenerunt, et ita per defectum ejus recuperavit sæpedictus prior saisinam marisci per judicium curiæ. Postea sæpedictus abbas accessit ad Regem Richardum fratrem vestrum, et dedit ei intelligere, quod ipse occasione fratris sui fugati ab Anglia, et quorundam fratrum suorum captorum, non ausus est comparere, sed aufugerit; et impetravit ab eo, quod ipse defectum illum ei warantizavit; et ita resaisitus fuit memoratus abbas de prædicto marisco. Nos igitur considerantes warentiam illam, licet non videatur curiæ vestræ Angliæ, quin dominus Rex frater vester satis licite potuisset warentiam talem facere, et quod vos habetis similem potestatem, noluimus judicium expressum inde facere, antequam vos certificati essetis super prædicto recordo, et antequam voluntatem vestram expressius inde præciperetis. Valeat dominus noster diu in domino.

Cumque scriptæ essent literæ et sigillatæ, utrique parti traditæ sunt. Abbas autem Croyland recedens a curia, reversus est ad proprium. Prior de Spalding statim misit monachum suum sepedictum ad Regem, ut nuncium abbatis de Croyland præveniret, et negotium suum donis et promissionibus perficeret. Monachus vero de Spalding, cum omni festinatione proxima die Sabbati ante omnes a Londino egressus, iter suum versus mare arripuit, et ad Portesmum velociter pervenit, sperans quantocius transfretare, et ad Regem sub celeritate venire. Sed Deo disponente, cui venti et mare obediunt, aliter contigit; nam ibi moram fecit fere per quadraginta dies, quamvis sæpius tentasset, nun-[p. 470] quam valens transfretare. Interea reversus est abbas de Croyland ad domum suam, ut post laborem tanti itineris aliquantulum requiesceret, cui occurrerunt sui, et cum gaudio eum susceperunt.

Post aliquot autem dies misit dominus abbas nuncium suum ad Regem, videlicet Johannem de Freston, qui etiam antea cum

land about the marsh between Spalding and Croyland: which is such that the Prior of Spalding in the time of King Richard your brother claimed the aforesaid marsh in his court against the aforesaid Abbot. The same Abbot when he was summoned essoined himself as detained in bed at Croyland by sickness. And when by judgment of the court four knights came to view this Abbot and his illness at Croyland, they did not find him there and so by his default, the Prior recovered seisin of the marsh by judgment of the court. Afterwards the aforesaid Abbot went to King Richard your brother and gave him to understand that he, because his brother had been chased from England and others of his brothers taken, did not dare appear, but fled, and he obtained from the King warranty of that default; and thus was the aforesaid abbot reseised of the aforesaid marsh. We therefore, considering that warranty, although it does not seem to your court of England that the lord King your brother could not properly enough make such warranty, and that you have similar power, have refused to make a definite judgment thereon until you have been certified upon the aforesaid record and before you have expressly set out your will thereon. May our lord King long prosper in the Lord.

And when these letters were written and sealed they were handed to each party. The Abbot of Croyland, leaving the court, returned to his own place. The Prior of Spalding immediately sent off his often mentioned monk to the King, so that he should get there before the Abbot of Croyland's messenger and complete his business by gifts and promises. Indeed, the Spalding monk having left London speedily before anyone on the next Saturday on his way to the sea quickly came to Portsmouth, hoping to cross at once and come with all haste to the King. But, God disposing, whom the wind and the waves obey, it happened otherwise, for he stayed there nearly forty days, and although he often tried, he was never able to cross. Meanwhile the Abbot returned to his house at Croyland so that after the labour of such a journey he might rest awhile, and his people met him and received him with joy.

But after a few days the lord Abbot sent his messenger to the King, namely John of Frieston, who had also crossed the sea with him twice before. He, trusting more in the virtue of the Lord than in his own wisdom, commending himself to God and the

eo bis transfretaverat. Ipse autem confidens magis in virtute Dei quam in sapientia sua commendans se Deo et orationibus fratrum, statim versus mare profectus est; cumque venisset ad portum qui vocatur Scorham, invenit ibi de nobilioribus regni volentibus Regem adire, inter quos erat episcopus Coventr. cui se jungens prædictus monachus, rogavit ut in conducto suo eum reciperet, ut in protectionem illius transfratare posset: episcopus vero prædictus eum gratanter suscepit, et quamdiu apud prædictum portum moram fecit, humanissime exhibuit. Illis diebus nemo poterat, nec ad Portesmum nec ad Scorham, propter aeris intemperiem et ventorum rabiem, transfretare; et ideo prædictus Johannes ibi perhendinavit unam septimanam, in magna angustia constitutus, timens ne forte adversarius ejus, qui ad alium portum perrexerat, in ipso itinere anticiparet, et coram Rege ipsum præveniret, et negotium prioris de Spalding, nullo contradicente, ad libitum suum perficeret. Contigit igitur una die ut tempestas illa quiesceret, et mare aliquantulum sedaretur, et facta est lætitia magna in populo qui volebat transfretare. Nullus tamen nobilium, qui ibi aderant, iter illud audebant arripere, propter maris turbationem et ventorum inconstantiam, quæ non plene sedata fuerant. Videns autem prædictus Johannes unam navem paratam esse ad transfretandum, quæ quosdam pauperes et peregrinos in se continebat, posuit se inter alios, et domino ducente, in crastinum in Normanniam evectus est, omnibus nobilibus apud Scorham remanentibus, et etiam monachus de Spalding, qui longe eum præcesserat, et apud Portesmum perhendinaverat.

Cumque applicuisset prædictus Johannes, statim iter suum versus Regem arripuit, et apud Rotomagum ipsum invenit. Veniens itaque in conspectu ejus, protulit literas justitiariorum, illi eas tradidit; et ipse summam totius negotii, quam literæ illæ minus intimaverant, viva voce Regi intimavit. Cumque dominus Rex de hoc negotio cum sapientibus de curia sua qui tunc ibi aderant tractasset, et quid sibi agendum esset, ad eis inquireret; responsum est ab illis, quod sicut ipse vellet warantizationem suam, si alicui faceret, firmam esse et stabilem, sic warantizationem factam a Rege Richardo fratre suo, cujus heres ipse fuit, confirmaret. Hæc audiens dominus Rex, voluit et warantizationem illam a Rege Richardo stare, et pecuniam, scilicet centum marcas, ab abbate Croyland sibi promissam, habere.

prayers of his brethren, immediately set out towards the sea, and when he came to the port called Shoreham he found there some of the more noble men of the kingdom wishing to go to the King, among whom was the Bishop of Coventry, and the monk, attaching himself to him, asked to be taken under his protection for the crossing. The Bishop indeed received him willingly and as long as he stayed at the aforesaid port showed him great kindness. At that time, neither at Portsmouth nor at Shoreham, could anyone cross on account of the bad weather and high wind. Therefore the aforesaid John stayed there a week in great anxiety lest perchance his adversary, who had gone to the other port, should anticipate him in his journey and reach the King before him and finish the Prior of Spalding's business according to his will without opposition. Therefore it chanced one day that that tempest was stilled a little and the sea was a little smoother, and there was great gladness among the people who wished to cross. But none of the nobles who were there dared take that journey, on account of the wild sea and the changeable winds, for they had not fully dropped. But the aforesaid John, seeing one ship ready to cross, which contained poor folk and pilgrims, put himself among them and, the Lord being their leader, he was carried on the morrow into Normandy, all the nobles remaining at Shoreham, and also the monk of Spalding, who had set out a long time before he did and had gone to Portsmouth.

When the aforesaid John had landed he immediately set out to the King and found him at Rouen. Coming before him, he produced the justices' letters and handed them to him, and he set out to the King the point of the whole matter which the letters had expressed less clearly. And when the King had discussed the business with his wise men, he asked them what he ought to do. They replied that as he wished his own warranty if he should warrant anything to be firm and stable so he should confirm the warranty given by his brother, King Richard, whose heir he was. Hearing this, the lord King willed that King Richard's warranty should stand and that he would accept the money, namely a hundred marks, promised him by the Abbot of Croyland.[38] And he instructed the monk of

[38] The record of the payment of this 100 marks is preserved in the *Pipe Roll 4 John (1201-1202)*, p. 238.

Mandavitque supradicto monacho Croyland, quod si vellet facere ut pecunia ista promissa ad terminos competentes redderetur, warantizationem quam Richardus Rex abbati de Croyland fecerat, ipse charta sua confirmaret; et insuper alia negotia si qua in curia haberet, libenter audiret. Cogitans itaque prædictus Johannes, quam sæpe mora trahit ad se periculum, timens etiamne nuncius prioris Spalding ad curiam veniret, et eum de negotio suo donis et promissionibus impediret; voluntati domini Regis, cum consilio domini Cantuariensis et domini Eliensis, quos tunc in curia invenerat, adquievit. Tunc dominus Rex præcepit, ut warantizatio abbati de Croyland a Rege Richardo facta, charta sua corroboraretur; et etiam ille mariscus unde defalta illa evenit, sigillo suo, sicut charta Henrici Regis patris continebat, abbati de Croyland confirmaretur; quod et factum est, prout in sequentibus continetur.

Tum igitur hoc et alia negotia quæ sibi injuncta fuerant, perfecisset prædictus Johannes, licentiatus a Rege, et domino ducente eum, quam-[p. 471] cito potuit reversus est in Angliam ad domum suam de Croyland, unde missus fuerat, nuncio prioris de Spalding apud Portesmum in cismarinis partibus adhuc perhendinante, qui postea transfretavit, et Regem adiit, et magna promisit; sed nihil perficiens, recedens a curia, reversus est ad proprium, juxta illud, Confundantur et revereantur, qui volunt mihi mala. Charta autem Johannis de confirmatione limitum abbatiæ nostræ, de qua paulo superius sit mentio, subjungitur in hac forma:

Croyland that if he was willing to see that the money promised should be paid at suitable terms, he would confirm by his charter the warranty which King Richard had made to the Abbot of Croyland and moreover, he would willingly hear any other business if the monk had any to bring in his court. And so the aforesaid John, thinking that delay often is dangerous, and fearing also that the Prior of Spalding's monk might come to the court and hinder him with his gifts and promises, with the counsel of the lord of Canterbury and the lord of Ely, whom he had found in the court, acquiesced in the king's will. Then the lord King commanded that the warranty made to the Abbot of Croyland by King Richard should be confirmed by his charter, and also that that marsh should be confirmed to the Abbot of Croyland under his seal as is contained in the charter of King Henry the father; which was done as is contained in what follows.

Then the aforesaid John had completed the business enjoined upon him and under the King's licence, the Lord leading him, he returned as quickly as he could into England to his house of Croyland, whence he had been sent; the messenger of the Prior of Spalding still staying on this side the sea at Portsmouth. He afterwards crossed over, went to the King and promised great things, but securing nothing and withdrawing from the court, he returned to his own parts, according to that text "They are confounded and brought unto shame that seek to do us evil." The charter of King John concerning the boundaries of our abbey which is mentioned above is added in this form:

There follows a confirmation by King John of the boundaries set out in the charter of Henry II, the so called "great charter" of the abbey.

VI. WRITS RELATING TO THE EYRE OF AUGUST, 1210

Harl. MS. 1708, f. 4. Egerton MS. 3031, f. 29.

[G] filius Petri comes Essex vicecomiti Berk' et sociis suis just' domini Regis itinerantibus in Berk' salutem. Sciatis quod coram domino P. Winton' episcopo et coram nobis et aliis quamplurimis tam magnatibus quam baronibus de scacario [*sic*] inspecte et lecte fuerunt carte quas abbas et monachi de Rading' habent de domino Rege et de antecessoribus suis et consideratum fuit communi omnium consilio et assensu ex tenore earundem cartarum quod abbas et monachi debent habere curiam suam de forinseco hundredo de Rading' quod dominus Rex eis reddidit sicut ius suum de omnibus assisis et recognitionibus et omnibus placitis corone et omnimodis libertatibus et consuetudinibus. Et ideo uobis mandamus quod predictis abbati et monachis sic omnia predicta in curia sua plene et sine omni contradictione tam de forinseco hundredo quam de aliis terris suis habere permittatis . nec in aliquo eos de predictis libertatibus impediatis . uel impediri permittatis. T. domino P. Winton' episcopo apud Westmonasterium iii die Augusti . anno regni Regis Johannis xii.

W. domini Regis thesaurarius . W. archidiaconus Thanton' . et W. archidiaconus Huntindon' et ceteri barones de scacario karissimis amicis suis justiciariis domini Regis itinerantibus in Bercsir' salutem et dilectionem. Inspeximus cartas domini Regis et antecessorum suorum in quibus continetur . quod abbas et monachi de Rading' debent habere curiam suam de assisis et recognitionibus que per preceptum domini Regis uel iusticiarii eius fieri mandantur de terris et hominibus que sunt in bailliua sua. Unde non dubitamus quin predicti abbas et monachi debeant habere eandem libertatem in forinseco hundredo de Rading' quod dominus Rex eis sicut ius suum reddidit . super quo dubitatis ut dicitur . quia justiciarii itinerantes non fuerunt in partibus illis postquam hundredum illud illis redditum fuit nisi modo. Sed propter hoc dubitare non oportet . sed inde sitis certi sicut et nos quod predictas libertates habere debent in forinseco hundredo . sicut in aliis terris suis. Unde consulimus

VI. WRITS RELATING TO THE EYRE OF AUGUST, 1210

Harl. MS. 1708 f. 4. Egerton MS. 3031, f. 29.

1. Geoffrey fitz Peter Earl of Essex to the Sheriff of Berkshire and his fellow justices of the lord King itinerant in Berkshire, Greeting. Know that before the lord Peter Bishop of Winchester and before us and very many others, as well magnates as barons of the exchequer, the charters which the Abbot and monks of Reading have from the lord King and his ancestors were inspected and read, and from the tenor of the same charters it was judged by the common counsel and consent of all that the Abbot and monks ought to have their court of the forinsec hundred of Reading which the lord King has restored to them as their right, in regard to all assizes and recognitions and all pleas of the crown and all manner of liberties and customs. And therefore we command you that you permit the aforesaid abbot and monks to have all the aforesaid matters in their court, fully and without any hindrance, as well in regard to their forinsec hundred as in regard to all their other lands, nor in anything touching the aforesaid liberties do you obstruct them or allow them to be obstructed. Witness, the lord Peter Bishop of Winchester at Westminster on the third day of August in the twelfth year of King John.

2. William the treasurer of the lord King, William Archdeacon of Taunton and William Archdeacon of Huntingdon and the other barons of the exchequer to their dearest friends the justices of the lord King itinerant in Berkshire, Greeting and affection. We have inspected the charters of the lord King and his ancestors in which it is contained that the Abbot and monks of Reading ought to have their court touching assizes and recognitions which are made by command of the lord King or his justiciar in regard to the lands and men in their bailliwick. Wherefore we have no doubt that the aforesaid Abbot and monks ought to have the same liberty in the forinsec hundred of Reading which the lord King has restored to them as their right, upon which you were in doubt, as it is said, because until now itinerant justices have not been in those parts since that hundred was restored to them. But on this account there is no

quod teneatis abbatiam in predictis libertatibus tam in forinseco hundredo suo . quam in aliis terris et bailliuis suis . ita quod in nullo libertates predictas minuatis . ledatis . siue impediatis . uel impediri permittatis. Ualete.

need for doubt and you may be assured, as we are, that they ought to have the aforesaid liberties in the forinsec hundred as in their other lands. Wherefore we advise you that you maintain the abbey in the aforesaid liberties as well in their forinsec hundred as in their other lands and bailliwicks, so that in nothing do you diminish, harm or obstruct the aforesaid liberties or allow them to be obstructed in anything. Farewell.

BIBLIOGRAPHY

Sources Quoted in Footnotes Under Abbreviated Titles

Abingdon Chron. Chronicon Monasterii de Abingdon, ed. The Rev. Joseph Stevenson (Rolls Series, London, 1858).

B.M.: British Museum.

Bigelow, *Placita.* Melville Madison Bigelow, *Placita Anglo-Normannica* (London, 1879).

Bigelow, *Procedure.* Melville Madison Bigelow, *History of Procedure in England* (London, 1880).

Book of Seals. Sir Christopher Hatton's Book of Seals presented to F. M. Stenton, ed. L. C. Loyd and D. M. Stenton (Oxford, 1950).

Bracton's Note-Book. Bracton's Note-Book, ed. F. W. Maitland (Cambridge, 1887).

Brevia Placitata. Brevia Placitata ed. G. J. Turner and completed by T. F. T. Plucknett, Selden Society, **66** (London, 1951).

C.U.L.: Cambridge University Library.

Colchester Cart. *Cartularium monasterii Sancti Johannis Baptiste de Colecestria,* ed. Stuart A. Moore (London, 1897).

Complete Peerage. The Complete Peerage (2nd ed. London, 1910-1959).

C.R.R. Curia Regis Rolls, ed. C. T. Flower (London, 1922-1935) **1-7**.

Delisle, *Recueil. Recueil des Actes de Henri II,* ed. L. Delisle (Paris, 1909-1927).

Earliest Lincolnshire Assize Rolls. The Earliest Lincolnshire Assize Rolls, ed. D. M. Stenton (Lincoln Record Society, 1926) **22**.

E.H.R. English Historical Review.

Eyton, *Itin.* R. W. Eyton, *The Court, Household and Itinerary of King Henry II,* (London, 1878).

Gallia Christiana. Gallia Christiana **11** (2nd ed. Paris, 1874).

Gesetze. Die Gesetze der Angelsachsen, ed. F. Liebermann (Halle, 1903-1916).

Gesta Stephani. Gesta Stephani ed. K. R. Potter (Nelson's Medieval Texts, 1955).

Glanvill. *Glanvill, De Legibus et Consuetudinibus regni Angliæ,* ed. George E. Woodbine (New Haven, 1932).

Hist. of Eng. Law. Sir Frederick Pollock and Frederic William Maitland, *The History of English Law* (2nd ed. Cambridge, 1898).

Howden. Chronica magistri Rogeri de Houeden, ed. W. Stubbs (Rolls Series, 1868-1871).

Landon, *Itin.* L. Landon, *The Itinerary of King Richard I,* Pipe Roll Society (n. s. **13**, 1935).

Liber Eliensis. Liber Eliensis, ed. E. O. Blake (Camden Third Series **92**, Royal Historical Society, London, 1962).

Mon. Ang. W. Dugdale, *Monasticon Anglicanum,* ed. J. Caley, H. Ellis and B. Bandinel (London, 6 v. in 8, 1817-1830).

Orderic. Orderici Vitalis . . . Historiæ Ecclesiastici Libri Tredecim, ed. A. le Prevost (Paris, 1838-1855).

Pipe Rolls are quoted by the year of the king's reign. They are published by the Pipe Roll Society, first series, 1883-1925 and new series 1925 continuing; except for the Rolls for 31 Henry I, (1833) 2, 3, and 4 Henry II and 1 Richard I (1844) published by the Record Commission.

Placitorum Abbreviatio. Record Commission (1811).

Pleas before the King . . . Pleas before the King or his Justices **1** ed. D. M. Stenton, Selden Society, **67** (1953).

P.R.O. Public Record Office.

Ramsey Cart. Cartularium Monasterii de Rameseia, ed. W. H. Hart and P. A. Lyons (Rolls Series, London, 1884).

Ramsey Chron. Chronicon Abbatiæ Ramesiensis, ed. W. D. Macray (Rolls Series, London, 1886).

Red Book. The Red Book of the Exchequer **2**, ed. Hubert Hall (Rolls Series, 1896).

Regesta. Regesta Regum Anglo-Normannorum **1**, ed. H. W. C. Davis (Oxford, 1913).

Regesta Regum Anglo-Normannorum **2**, ed. Charles Johnson and H. A. Cronne (Oxford, 1956).

Registrum Antiquissimum. The Registrum Antiquissimum of the Cathedral Church of Lincoln **1**, ed. C. W. Foster, Lincoln Record Society, **27**, 1931.

Rot. Chart. Rotuli Chartarum **1**, part i, ed. T. D. Hardy (Record Commission, 1837).

Rot. Claus. Rotuli Litterarum Clausarum, ed. T. D. Hardy (Record Commission, 1833).

Rot. de . . . . Præstitis. Rot. de Liberate ac de Missis et Præstitis ed. T. D. Hardy (Record Commission, 1844).

Rotulus Misae. See Cole, Henry.

Stubbs, *Charters. Select Charters and other illustrations of English Constitutional History, ed.* H. W. C. Davis (9th ed., Oxford, 1913).

Writs. R. C. van Caenegem, *Royal Writs in England from the Conquest to Glanvill,* Selden Society, **77** (London, 1959).

Other Works Quoted in Footnotes

Adams, G. B. 1912. *Origin of the English Constitution* (Yale University Press).

Brunner, H. 1871. *Die Entstehung der Schwurgerichte* (Berlin).

Clark, Cecily. 1958. *The Peterborough Chronicle 1070-1154* (Oxford).

Clay, Sir Charles. 1911. *Yorkshire Assize Rolls,* Yorkshire Archaeological Society, Record Series **44**.

—— 1935-1955ff. *Early Yorkshire Charters, Index* to **1-3** (*see* under Farrer, W.) and vols. **4-10**, Yorkshire Archeological Society, Extra Series.

—— 1959-62. "Yorkshire Final Concords of the Reign of Henry II" *Yorkshire Archaeological Journal* **40**, pp. 78-89.

—— 1961. *"Master Aristotle," English Hist. Rev.* **76**.

Cole, Henry. 1844. *Documents Illustrative of English History in the Thirteenth and Fourteenth Centuries (Rotulus Misae)* (Record Commission).

Cronne, H. A. 1957. *"The Office of Local Justiciar under the Norman Kings," University of Birmingham Historical Journal* **6**.

Darlington, R. R. 1963. *The Norman Conquest* (Creighton Lecture 1962) (London, The Athlone Press).

Dodwell, Barbara. 1952. *Feet of Fines for the County of Norfolk 1198-1202,* Pipe Roll Society, n.s., **27**.

—— 1958. *Feet of Fines for the County of Norfolk 1201-1215 and the County of Suffolk 1199-1214,* Pipe Roll Society, n.s., **32**.

Elmore Jones, F. 1958. "Stephen Type vii," British Numismatic Journal **28**.

Farrer, W. 1902. Lancashire Pipe Rolls and Early Charters (Liverpool).

—— 1914-1916. *Early Yorkshire Charters* **1-3** (privately printed).

—— 1923-1925. *Honors and Knights' Fees* **1-3** (London and Manchester).

Fauroux, Marie. 1962. *Recueil des Actes des Ducs de Normandie,* Mémoires de la Société des Antiquaires de Normandie **36** (Caen).

FLOWER, SIR CYRIL. 1943. *Introduction to the Curia Regis Rolls*, Selden Society **72**.
FOSTER, C. W. 1920. *Final Concords of the County of Lincoln* **2**, Lincoln Record Society **17**. See also Walker, M. S.
FOWLER, G. HERBERT. 1913. *The Publication of the Bedfordshire Historical Record Society* **1**, "Roll of the Justices in Eyre at Bedford, 1202."
[FULMAN, W.] 1684. *Rerum Anglicarum Scriptorum Veterum* **1** (Oxford).
GALBRAITH, V. H. 1920. "Royal Charters to Winchester," *English Hist. Rev.* **35**.
—— 1948. *Studies in the Public Records* (Nelson).
HARMER, FLORENCE E. 1914. *Select Historical Documents of the Ninth and Tenth centuries* (Cambridge).
—— 1952. *Anglo-Saxon Writs* (Manchester).
HEARNE, T. 1720. *Textus Roffensis* (Oxford). Facsimile edition, ed. Peter Sawyer (Copenhagen, 1957, 1962).
——, 1769. *The Itinerary of John Leland* 3rd ed. (Oxford).
HILL, SIR GEORGE. 1936. *Treasure Trove in Law and Practice* (Oxford).
HOLT, J. C. 1955. "The Barons and the Great Charter," *English Hist. Rev.* **70**.
HUNTER, JOSEPH. 1835, 1844. *Fines siue Pedes Finium* **1**, **2** (Record Commission).
HURNARD, N. D. 1941. "The Jury of Presentment and the Assize of Clarendon," *English Hist. Rev.* **56**.
—— 1948. "Magna Carta, Clause 34," *Studies in Medieval History presented to Frederick Maurice Powicke* (Oxford).
JOHNSON, CHARLES. 1933. "Some Charters of Henry I," *Essays presented to James Tait* (Manchester).
—— 1950. *Dialogus de Scaccario*, Nelson's Medieval Texts.
JOÜON DES LONGRAIS, F. 1936. "La Portée politique des réformes d'Henry II en matière de saisine," *Revue historique de droit français et étranger*, 4 sér.
KER, N. R. 1960. *English Manuscripts in the Century after the Norman Conquest* (Oxford).
MAITLAND, F. W. See *Hist. of Eng. Law*.
—— 1884. *Pleas of the Crown for the county of Gloucester, A.D. 1221* (London).
—— 1888. *Select Pleas in Manorial Courts*, Selden Society **2**.
—— 1911. *Collected Papers* **1**, "The Beatitude of Seisin." Reprinted from *The Law Quarterly Review*, January, 1888.
MICHEL, F. 1840. *Histoire des Ducs de Normandie et des Rois d'Angleterre* (Paris).
NORTHAMPTON. *Leges Ville Norht*, ed. Councillor Frank Lee, mayor, 1951.
PAINTER, SIDNEY. 1949. *The Reign of King John* (Baltimore).
PALGRAVE, SIR FRANCIS. 1835. *Rotuli Curiæ Regis* **1**, **2**. (Record Commission).
—— *The Collected Works of* **7**.
PARIS, MATTHEW. 1874, 1876. *Matthaei Parisiensis Chronica Majora*, ed. H. R. Luard, **2**, **3** Rolls Series.
PLUCKNETT, T. F. T. See *Brevia Placitata*.
—— 1949. *Legislation of Edward I* (Oxford).
—— 1956. *A Concise History of the Common Law* (5th ed., London).
POOLE, R. L. 1912. *The Exchequer in the Twelfth Century* (Oxford).
POWELL, W. R. 1956. "The Administration of the Navy and the Stannaries, 1189-1216," *English Hist. Rev.* **71**.
POWICKE, F. M. 1928. *Stephen Langton* (Oxford).
RICHARDSON, H. G. 1928. "Richard fitz Neal and the Dialogus de Scaccario." E. H. R. **43**.
—— 1932. "William of Ely, The King's Treasurer, *Transactions of the Royal Historical Society*, 4th Series, **15**.
ROBERTSON, A. J. 1939. *Anglo-Saxon Charters* (Cambridge).

ROUND, J. H. 1888. *Ancient Charters* **1**, Pipe Roll Society **10**.
—— 1892. *Geoffrey de Mandeville* (London).
—— 1899. *The Commune of London* (London).
—— 1911. *The King's Serjeants and Officers of State* (London).
—— 1916. "The Date of the Grand Assize," *English Hist. Rev.* **31**.
SALTMAN, AVROM. 1956. *Theobald archbishop of Canterbury* (London).
Sheriffs, List of 1898. P.R.O. Lists and Indexes, IX.
SLADE, C. F. 1956. *The Leicestershire Survey c. A.D. 1130* (Leicester).
STEENSTRUP, JOHANNES C. H. R. 1876-1882. *Normannerne* (Copenhagen).
STENTON, D. M. 1924. "Roger of Salisbury, Regni Angliæ Procurator," E. H. R. **39**.
—— 1926. "England, Henry II," *Cambridge Medieval History* **5**.
—— 1930. *The Earliest Northamptonshire Assize Rolls,* Northamptonshire Record Society **5**.
—— 1934. *Rolls of the Justices in eyre for Lincolnshire 1218-19 and Worcestershire,* 1221, Selden Society **53**.
—— 1937. *Rolls of the Justices in eyre for Yorkshire 1218-19,* Selden Society **56**.
—— 1940. *Rolls of the Justices in eyre for Gloucestershire, Warwickshire and Staffordshire (recte, Shropshire) 1221, 1222,* Selden Society **59**.
—— 1953. "Roger of Howden and Benedict," *English Hist. Rev.* **68**.
STENTON, F. M. 1913. *The Early History of the Abbey of Abingdon* (Reading).
—— 1920. *Documents Illustrative of the Social and Economic History of the Danelaw* (British Academy).
—— 1922. *Transcripts of Charters relating to Gilbertine Houses,* Lincoln Record Society **18**.
—— 1927. "The Danes in England," *Proc. British Academy* **13**.
—— 1930. *Facsimiles of early charters from Northamptonshire collections,* Northamptonshire Record Society **4**.
—— 1932, 1961. *The First Century of English Feudalism* (Oxford).
—— 1944. "English Families and the Norman Conquest," *Trans. Royal Hist. Soc.,* 4th ser. **26**.
—— 1955. *The Latin Charters of The Anglo-Saxon Period* (Oxford).
TAIT, J. 1920. *Chartulary or Register of the Abbey of St. Werburgh Chester* Chetham Society n.s. **79**.
VINOGRADOFF, P. 1908. *English Society in the Eleventh Century* (Oxford).
WALKER, M. S. 1954. *Feet of Fines, Lincolnshire, 1199-1216,* Pipe Roll Society, n.s., **29**.
WEBB, C. C. J. 1909. *Ioannis Saresberiensis episcopi Carnotensis Policratici . . . Libri VIII* (Oxford).
WEINBAUM, M. 1933. *London unter Eduard I und II* (Stuttgart).
WHITELOCK, DOROTHY. 1930. *Anglo-Saxon Wills* (Cambridge).
—— 1959. "Recent Work on Asser's Life of Alfred," in *Asser's Life of King Alfred,* ed. W. H. Stevenson (Oxford). 2nd ed.
WOODBINE, GEORGE. *See* Glanvill.
—— 1930. "Cases in the New Curia Regis Rolls affecting old rules of English legal history," *Yale Law Jour.* **39**.

Manuscript Sources Quoted or Printed in Appendices

B. M. Reading Cartularies Harl. MS. 1708. Egerton MS. 3031. Stixwould Cartulary Add. MS. 46701.
C.U.L. The Red Book of Thorney Add. MS. 3020, 3021.
Lincolnshire Archives Committee, The Castle, Lincoln, Cragg MS. 3/14a and b.
P.R.O. Cartulary of the Duchy of Lancaster Misc. Bk 5. Ancient Deeds Duchy of Lancaster. Feet of Fines C P 25 (1). Curia Regis Rolls of the Reign of John, KB (26) 55, 57.

INDEX

For Product Safety Concerns and Information please contact our EU representative GPSR@taylorandfrancis.com
Taylor & Francis Verlag GmbH, Kaufingerstraße 24, 80331 München, Germany

www.ingramcontent.com/pod-product-compliance
Ingram Content Group UK Ltd.
Pitfield, Milton Keynes, MK11 3LW, UK
UKHW022156190926
475702UK00003B/51
* 9 7 8 0 3 6 7 1 8 0 0 3 4 *